17·95

ASPECTS OF WAR IN AMERICAN HISTORY

Aspects of War in American History

Edited by David K. Adams and Cornelis A. van Minnen

SERIES EDITOR: DAVID K. ADAMS

KEELEUNIVERSITY**PRESS**

First published in 1997
by Keele University Press
Keele, Staffordshire, England

Composed by Keele University Press

Printed by The Cromwell Press,
Melksham, Wilts

ISBN 1 85331 177 4

Cover photograph: *The American
Second World War Cemetery at
Colleville-Saint-Laurent, Normandy*
(© Christopher J. Tinker, 1995)

Contents

Notes on Contributors

David K. Adams is professor of American studies and Chairman of the David Bruce Centre for American Studies at Keele University, Staffordshire, United Kingdom. Recent publications include volumes 16–25 of his edition, *British Documents on Foreign Affairs: Reports and Papers from the Foreign Office Confidential Print*, Part II, Series C, *North America 1919–1939* (1995).

Manfred Berg received his Ph.D. in modern history from the University of Heidelberg in 1988. From 1989 until 1992 he taught history at the John F. Kennedy Institute for North American Studies of the Free University of Berlin. Since 1992 he has been a research fellow at the German Historical Institute, Washington, DC. He is the author of numerous publications on German and US history.

Oliviero Bergamini is lecturer of American history at the University of Genoa and at the University of Bergamo, Italy. He has published several articles on US military and political history, concerning in particular the Civil War, the Progressive Era and Populism. He is the author of *'A New Army for America': Elihu Root and the Birth of the Modern Military Establishment of the United States* (1996).

Claude Fohlen is professor emeritus at The Sorbonne, Paris, where he has taught American and Canadian history for more than twenty years. His research has included the Civil War and the New Deal, as well as the American Revolution. He has published many books, including *Les Pères de la révolution américaine* (1989), *Thomas Jefferson* (1992), and *De Washington à Roosevelt* (1992).

Daria Frezza is a member of the history department of the University of Siena, Italy. She has edited a selection of Franklin D. Roosevelt's public speeches and has published articles on such subjects as the impact of the mass media on American society and the debate on propaganda in the 1920s and 1930s. She is working on a book on 'The Leader and the Crowd in American Social Sciences, 1900–1945'.

Stanley I. Kutler is the E. Gordon Fox Professor of American Institutions and Law at the University of Wisconsin, Madison. He is the author of numerous publications in American legal and constitutional history. His major books include *The American Inquisition: Justice and Injustice in the Cold War* (1983), and *The Wars of Watergate: The Last Crisis of Richard Nixon* (1990).

Zbigniew Mazur is associate professor at the Institute of English Studies, Maria Curie-Sklodowska University, Lublin, Poland, where he lectures on British and American history and culture. His research concentrates on American colonial history, popular culture and the theory of cultural studies. He is the author of *Settlers and Indians: Transformations of English Culture in Colonial Virginia* (1995).

Cornelis A. van Minnen is Executive Director of the Roosevelt Study Center in Middelburg, The Netherlands. His publications include *FDR and His Contemporaries: Foreign Perceptions of an American President* (edited with John F. Sears; 1992) and *American Diplomats in the Netherlands, 1815–1850* (1993). With David K. Adams he edited *Reflections on American Exceptionalism* (1994).

Peter J. Parish is currently visiting professor of American studies at Middlesex University, United Kingdom. After teaching American history for many years at the Universities of Glasgow and Dundee, he was Director of the Institute of United States Studies, University of London (1983–92). His many publications include *The American Civil War* (1975) and *Slavery: History and Historians* (1989).

Marie-Jeanne Rossignol is associate professor (Maître de Conférences) at the Institut Charles V, Université Paris 7-Denis Diderot, Paris, France. She studied at the Ecole Normale Supérieure and is the author of *Le Ferment nationaliste: aux origines de la politique extérieure des Etats-Unis 1789–1812* (1994).

Axel R. Schaefer studied history at the universities of Heidelberg, Frankfurt, Oregon and Washington. His fields of specialization are American intellectual history, the history of social thought, and comparative social history. He has taught at the University of Washington, and P.J. Safarik University (Presov, Slovakia), and is currently teaching German and American history at J.E. Purkyne University, Usti nad Labem, Czech Republic.

Brooks D. Simpson is a member of the department of history, Arizona State University, and was a Fulbright scholar in the American studies program at Leiden University in spring 1995. His books include *Let Us Have Peace: Ulysses S. Grant and the Politics of War and Reconstruction, 1861–1868* (1991), *The Political Education of Henry Adams* (1996) and *America's Civil War* (1996). At present he is working on a biography of Ulysses S. Grant.

Michael Simpson is senior lecturer in the department of history, University of Wales at Swansea, United Kingdom. His recent publications include *Anglo-American Naval Relations, 1917–1919* (1991) and *Somerville Papers* (1995). At present he is working on a biography of Admiral of the Fleet Viscount Cunningham and his long-term research projects include a book on 'FDR's Navy, 1913–1945'.

Jenel Virden is lecturer in American history in the American studies department at the University of Hull, United Kingdom. She graduated with a Ph.D. from the University of Washington in the United States in 1992. She recently published *Goodbye, Piccadilly: British War Brides in America* (1996) and is currently researching and writing on oral history as well as the impact of war on American society in the twentieth century.

Foreword

In April 1995 some fifty scholars from twelve European countries and the United States met in the Netherlands for the Second Middelburg Conference of European historians of the USA. Two years earlier Middelburg 1 had been enthusiastically welcomed by historians throughout Europe, who found a new collegiality and wider acquaintance in meeting together at a professionally dedicated conference. It was there decided to establish a pattern of biennial meetings. Middelburg 1 also resulted in the launch by Keele University Press of a new series, 'European Papers in American History', initiated by the 1993 conference volume *Reflections on American Exceptionalism* (Keele, 1994), edited by the organizers of Middelburg 1, David K. Adams of Keele University and Cornelis A. van Minnen, Executive Director of the Roosevelt Study Center, Middelburg, home of the conference.

The theme of Middelburg 2 was 'The Phenomenon of War in US History: Foreign and Domestic Implications'. Following a keynote address by Claude Fohlen, professor emeritus at the Sorbonne, sixteen papers were presented in plenary sessions. Space was also provided for a special workshop on 'European reactions to the Spanish–American War of 1898' to initiate a cooperative international research project that had germinated at Middelburg 1. The present volume, *Aspects of War in American History*, is a selection of the Middelburg 2 papers, organized in a form that we hope reflects the chronological and thematic range of the conference. In the planning stage it was surprising to us that we did not receive proposals relating to a number of wars critical to the evolution and development of the United States, but it was always clear that universality of coverage would have been quite impossible.

The Second Middelburg Conference was generously sponsored by the Roosevelt Study Center, the David Bruce Centre for American Studies at Keele University, the Franklin and Eleanor Roosevelt Institute at Hyde Park, New York, USIS, The Hague, and USIA in Washington, DC. We gratefully thank these sponsors. We also acknowledge permission of the University of Illinois Press and of Jenel Virden to print her conference paper, 'The Other Side of War: Overseas Marriages between British Women and American GIs in World War

II', which has recently been published as chapter three in her book *Goodbye, Piccadilly: British War Brides in America* (1996). Last but not least we want to thank Leontien Joosse of the Roosevelt Study Center for her assistance in the organization of the conference and for her technical skills, which have helped to put the several papers into their present form.

David K. Adams and *Cornelis A. van Minnen*
David Bruce Centre, Keele/Roosevelt Study Center, Middelburg
December 1995

1

Aftermaths of War

Claude Fohlen

Any historian of the United States is struck by the frequency and impact of war, and by the changes occurring in the years after the cessation of hostilities. A preliminary task is to make a choice between all these wars, because it is not possible to include them all in this short address. Should we, for example, speak of the War of Independence, which was both a colonial war and a civil war, in so far as it opposed the insurgents to the loyalists? Perhaps it would be better to exclude it. Should we include the War of 1812, which is rather difficult to characterize? Should we include the Mexican War, which helped to shape the country's borders? Others in this volume will discuss the Civil War, the most bloody conflict in American history and which had such far-reaching consequences, still vivid today; the aftermath of the Civil War alone would require several papers. And what about the most recent conflicts, in Korea, Vietnam, the Gulf, all fought far from the home country, but all of which made a tremendous impact on the American people, partly through the increasing presence of the media?

I have deliberately limited my choice to an exploration of parallelism between the aftermaths of the two world wars, which have so many similarities and which authorize an inter-temporal approach. Because of the silence of their Allies on war aims, it fell to the two American Presidents, Woodrow Wilson and Franklin Roosevelt, to define the aims of the coalition, the first in his Fourteen Points of 8 January 1918, the second in the Atlantic Charter of 1941, the latter with the participation of the British Prime Minister, Winston Churchill. The two documents have much in common, even if their approach is different. Wilson specified precise objectives: evacuation and restoration of Belgium and all occupied territory of France, including Alsace and Lorraine, and independence for the various peoples of the Austro-Hungarian and German empires. The Atlantic Charter remained much more general, mentioning only opposition to territorial changes contrary to the wishes of their peoples. Both envisioned a new kind of international relations, but here also lies the main difference. For Wilson it was the League of Nations, founded on the principle of collective security as specified in the covenant: 'for the purpose of affording mutual guarantees of political independence and territorial integrity to great and small states alike'. Roosevelt envisioned a permanent peace structure, the United Nations Organization, relying on 'the four policemen': the Soviet Union, Great Britain, China and the United States, with the later addition of a fifth one, France.

If the League of Nations failed, it was partly because Americans were not yet ready to take up their responsibilities on the international scene. When the Treaty of Versailles was rejected by the Senate, it was not because of its territorial clauses, but because it implied an international involvement which was unacceptable to the Americans. Wilson was disavowed and defeated in the general election of 1920, and so was the Wilsonian dream of collective security and American participation in the League of Nations. With the return to power of the Republicans for more than a decade, all expectations of international cooperation vanished, except as far as the supremacy of their navy and the security of their investments overseas were concerned. Even so, the experience was not entirely fruitless. One of the great achievements of this first aftermath was an attempt to restore economic prosperity and political stability in Europe, with the Dawes and Young Plans, which in some ways foreshadowed the Marshall Plan. But these plans included such drastic conditions for Germany – for instance, payment of reparations over more than half a century – that they were doomed to fail even before they were carried out. One can trace a relationship between these plans, the rise of Nazism in Germany and the outset of the Great Depression.

The outlook in international relations after World War II was entirely different, as the Americans had realized the consequences of their isolationism after World War I. Even the sudden death of Roosevelt in 1945 and the total ignorance in foreign policy of his successor, Harry Truman, did not interrupt the process which had been prepared by a series of conferences starting even before the beginning of the war for the United States in 1941, and culminating in 1943 with the Tehran Conference and in 1945 with Yalta and Potsdam. The Bretton Woods Conference had prepared the financial and economic side of the aftermath, while in Dumbarton Oaks were laid the foundations of the new international political order. Despite Democratic electoral reverses in 1946, there was considerable political continuity, confirmed by the unexpected re-election of Truman in 1948. This time there was a consensus among Americans to accept their responsibilities in the new international order. This time, also, they had little to fear, because they had a monopoly of the atomic bomb, which provided them with a feeling of security that they had not had in the aftermath of World War I, when they were confronted with the Soviet Revolution and the threat of the expansion of the communist ideology. Of course, in the mid-1940s communism expanded in Europe as well as in Asia, culminating with the overthrow of the Kuomintang in 1949 and the victory of the People's Republic of China, and the feeling of security was short-lived. The beginning of the cold war goes back to 1947, the end of the monopoly of the atomic bomb occurred in 1949, and the Korean War started in 1950. But at least the Americans were prepared to accept the challenge with adequate military means.

What is more important is that from the beginning the Americans were eager to draw lessons from their failure in the aftermath of World War I and to restore prosperity in Europe. General Marshall, by then Secretary of State, announced his plan in June 1947 at the Harvard Commencement, less than two years after the end of the hostilities. It was clear for all Americans that the durability of peace rested not only on the possession of the atomic bomb, but on a return to normal conditions of life. All European countries were invited to the conference held in Paris, and if the communist countries declined, the onus fell entirely on them for refusing to be associated with the economic rebuilding of the continent. The Marshall Plan was a major American innovation with long-lasting effects. The United States had shown readiness to take their share in the burden of rebuilding the world.

The American domestic scene after World Wars I and II witnessed many similarities, as well as striking differences. At the start one finds the same basic issue: the return to civil life of millions of citizens who had been serving overseas and who were eager to come back as soon as possible. During World War I, about 5 million Americans were enlisted, 2 million of whom were present in France at the end of the war, half of them fighting on the front line. About 50,000 men had been killed in combat. The figures for World War II are even more impressive: almost 15 million people were enlisted, of whom 10 million were in the army and the rest were in the navy and the air force. Most of them were scattered in overseas theaters, partly in Europe, partly in the Pacific, which made it more complicated to repatriate them than it had been in 1919.

At the end of World War I, 600,000 men were immediately discharged in the United States, and nothing had been provided to bring back the doughboys, who were very impatient. General John J. Pershing tried to keep the divisions busy with various futile exercises, drills and other occupations. But morale and discipline were very low in the American camps in France. There were mutinies, revolts and incidents of violence between the American Expeditionary Force (AEF) and local populations. Americans expected to be able to go back home for Christmas, which proved not to be feasible. Instead of 'Lafayette, here we are', they shouted 'Lafayette, we are still here'. Captain Harry Truman, who was then serving in a field artillery regiment, wrote to a

cousin that he was 'very anxious that Woodie [General Wood][1] cease
his gallivantin around and send us home at once and quickly'.[2] This
was only a dream, because repatriation needed the means of transportation, which, although it existed, did not fit military requirements.
At the end of 1918, the average monthly shipments of soldiers back to
America numbered around 30,000, a figure that gradually rose to
360,000 six months later, and by the summer of 1919 only 40,000 US
troops remained in Europe. Sixteen months after the end of the war in
Europe, the army had returned to a flat 280,000 men. In the meantime
frustrations had accumulated, so that when the veterans landed they
found a country in economic turmoil.

Things were not so different at the end of World War II, except that
they were on a much greater scale. The first order of business was once
again to demobilize the armed forces, but this time the process went at
such a pace that military and civilian leaders warned of a collapse of
preparedness. President Truman and the military urged the maintenance of substantial forces in Europe as well as in the Pacific, but
pressure to repatriate the boys was such that this advice was little
heard, so that by the spring of 1946 about 7 million men had been
released from the American forces overseas. From an organizational
point of view it was a tremendous achievement, but it left the US army
relatively weak for America's new inherited responsibilities on the
international level. It is true, however, that monopoly of the atomic
bomb provided the United States with a feeling of security.

There were other similarities between the periods in consideration,
such as social unrest. With a few exceptions, the war years had been
characterized by social restraint from workers, although prices had
risen, especially during World War I when controls were less efficient.
Samuel Gompers, the president of the American Federation of Labor,
had been a strong advocate of the war effort. This favored membership
of the unions, which rose from 2.5 million in 1914 to 5 million by
1920. The same trend developed during World War II: from 10
million in 1940 to almost 15 million in 1945, representing 36 per cent
of the non-agricultural labor force, against 11.5 per cent in 1933. It is
fair to add that one of the consequences of the war effort was the
achievement of full employment, especially during World War II after
the long anguish of the Depression. The major issue in the aftermath
of World War I was the so-called HCL – high cost of living – with its
counterpart, claims for higher wages. Prices had almost doubled, while
there had been no comparable increase of wages. The same trend was
less true after 1945 because price controls had been more effective,
with consequently less pressure on wages. But in both aftermaths the
country was rapidly confronted by strikes unprecedented in American
history. In 1919 4 million workers went on strike, starting with the

steelworkers and followed by the coalminers. Their argument was that, as companies had accumulated huge profits during the war, it would be unfair to reserve them only for shareholders. A special kind of strike was the one in Seattle in February 1919, which started in the shipyards and then extended to other sectors. It was presented as a revolutionary action in which the Industrial Workers of the World were involved. Such was also the case with the strike of the Boston police, which won Calvin Coolidge, then governor of Massachusetts, a reputation that later paved his way to the White House.

Things were not so different after World War II, but the wave developed more slowly. On 1 April 1946, 400,000 coalminers went on strike, under the leadership of their popular union leader, John L. Lewis. While the government acted as a mediator, the operatives refused to accept the new contract. A new strike was called by John Lewis later in the same year. When opposed by a government injunction at the beginning of December he ordered his miners back to work. Another challenge was the strike of railroad workers in May 1946. President Truman decided to seize the railroads, which prompted a majority of workers to reach a compromise, although a minority decided to continue their strike. This led Truman to ask Congress for special legislation to prevent paralysis of the country by strikes in basic industries. However the Taft–Hartley Act, passed over the veto of President Truman, went further than any previous legislation in requiring, among other provisions, a sixty-day notice before the beginning of a strike.

Another main area of deep trouble after both wars was an outburst of nativism. The hostilities had encouraged a feeling in Americans that they had been pushed into the conflicts by interests that were not directly theirs, and that they had to return to their true values. Anarchists, socialists, foreigners – all came to be seen as deviant people who had become dangerous and were to be controlled more strictly. This feeling was fuelled after World War I by the threat of the Bolshevik Revolution and after 1945 by fear of the expansion of communism in Europe and Asia. Stalin and Mao were both perceived as dangers not only for the international order, but also for the domestic stability of the country.

Similar feelings, developed long before World War I, were reinforced by experience abroad. One issue going back to the nineteenth century was Prohibition. In a country still partly dominated by puritanism – although one of its prestigious products was Bourbon – drinking, even modestly, was considered a European import and almost a sin. It is true, however, that the beer industry was mainly German and the wine industry Italian and Hungarian, both ethnic areas which had provided tens of thousands of immigrants. Without entering into the detail of Prohibition, suffice it to say that the Eighteenth Amendment, prohibiting 'the manufacture, sale or transportation of intoxicating liquors', was adopted at the beginning of,1919, and the Volstead Act, which strengthened the penalties for drinking, at the end of the same year in the wake of the nativist wave. Against all odds, the United States became a *dry* country.

Other signs were even more troubling, such as the Red Scare. Bolsheviks and anarchists were suspected everywhere, particularly among the socialists. One of their leaders, Victor Berger, elected to the House of Representatives in November 1919, was refused his seat and could assume it only four years later. Eugene V. Debs, the founder of the American Socialist Party, served a ten-year sentence in a penitentiary in Atlanta, from which he conducted the presidential campaign in 1919 which won him a little more than 900,000 votes. Public order was disturbed by a series of explosions at the same time in eight different cities, including Washington, DC, near the house of the Attorney-General, A. Mitchell Palmer. One year later, a huge bomb exploded in front of J.P. Morgan's office in New York, killing 38 people. None of these bombings could be attributed to specific groups, but responsibility for them fell on the anarchists. As a result, hundreds were arrested and 840 were put on a boat and sent back to their home country, including the 'Red king' Alexander Berkman, who had been involved in the Homestead strike of 1892, a quarter of a century earlier, and the 'Red queen', Emma Goldman. The scare culminated with the arrest in May 1920 of two Italian anarchists, Sacco and Vanzetti, accused of having robbed and murdered the cashier of a shoe company in South Braintree, Massachusetts. They became a *cause célèbre* during the seven years of their trial, before being executed in the Charlestown State Prison in August 1927. This outburst of nativism and fear of subversion by middle-class mainstream America left a permanent footprint on the new legislation on immigration. This issue was not a new one in American politics, but previously only specific categories had been excluded, for instance, Chinese and Japanese, or people with specific illnesses; and presidents had always been careful to veto bills restricting immigration of white stock. This time, the fruit was ripe: in 1921 a first law restricted immigration to an annual quota of 357,000, while a subsequent law of 1924 lowered it to 150,000. Once and for all, the United States was closed to the free flow of immigration.

After World War II nativist reactions were less immediately visible, but nonetheless they played an important part in domestic politics. Very soon after the end of the war, suspicions were raised about underground activities by communists or former communists. Matters were taken up by the House Un-American Activities Committee (HUAC), created before the war to investigate Nazi, fascist and communist organizations. In 1946 its main target became communism. Among the first to be summoned by HUAC were two former communists, Elizabeth Bentley and Whittaker Chambers, the latter an editor of *Time* magazine. He gave the name of a former official of the State Department, Alger Hiss, who was accused of having passed classified documents to the Soviets before the war. Although the case was never proved, Alger Hiss, by then the president of the Carnegie Endowment for Peace, was sent to prison for five year on conviction of perjury.

The aftermath of World War II had another *cause célèbre* with the Rosenbergs, the equivalent of Sacco and Vanzetti a quarter of a century earlier. Julius and Ethel Rosenberg were implicated in the transmission of top secret documents on the atomic bomb to the Soviets after the revelations of Klaus Fuchs, a German-born scientist working in the atomic laboratory at Los Alamos who had been arrested by the British. In the context of the announcement in 1949 that the Soviet Union had exploded its first atomic bomb a hysteria struck the United States, spies were seen everywhere and the Rosenbergs were its designated victims. Their case appealed to world opinion in 1953, as the Sacco–Vanzetti case had earlier, with the same fate: execution in the electric chair. The hysteria which developed around this and other cases paved the way for McCarthyism, another expression of American nativism generated by the tensions of the aftermaths of wars. As for immigration in 1921 and 1924, McCarthyism also left its mark on American legislation, with the imposition of loyalty tests for all public servants. An executive order by Truman, no. 9835, in 1947, required a thorough investigation of them all. Out of more than 4 million checks, charges were brought against about 9,000 persons, among whom 379 were dismissed and many others resigned. On the other hand, after having opened the gates of the country to thousands of displaced persons after the war, Congress reinforced controls on immigration with the McCarran–Walter Act of 1952, which retained the provisions of the 1924 act on quotas, while removing the total ban against immigration of Asian and Pacific peoples.

Both wars had far-reaching effects on American society, in so far as they resulted in a restriction on immigration; they threw suspicion on left-oriented individuals and fostered a return to nativism. But if there were many similarities, there were also significant differences. The first was economic: the end of World War I was followed in 1919 by a steep recession, characterized by a slump of the stock market and the growth of unemployment. Tens of thousands of doughboys coming back from Europe did not find jobs before 1920, when the economy started its recovery. One of the reasons for the recession was the decision of the administration to get rid of all controls without making any provisions for a fair transition from the war economy to a normal one (the slogan was 'return to normalcy'). Overnight, as soon as the armistice was signed, all controls were removed, starting with the powerful War Industries Board, which Bernard Baruch found no longer useful because it had lost public support. The Food Administration, the Fuel Administration, the Railroad Administration and the War Trade Board were instantly dissolved, engendering economic chaos.

When the GIs returned home in 1945 the fear of unemployment was such that, this time, every possible provision had been made to prevent it. As early as 1943, an orderly transition to peacetime production had been in the making. In October 1944, the Office of War Mobilization had been turned into the Office of Mobilization and Reconversion, the significant change in name underlying its mission to start the reconversion of the economy before the end of the war. The main issue was to maintain or to drop the controls in existence according to circumstances, against the pressure of organized interests to suppress all governmental restraints. The administration hesitated between the demands of the GIs to get jobs and those of the businessmen and farmers for a total liberation of prices. Reconciliation of competing demands represented a major challenge for Washington. The fight centered on maintaining or dropping the Office of Price Administration (OPA), created in 1941 and managed from 1943 by Chester Bowles. Its main purpose was to fight inflation by controlling prices through rationing. It could claim good results, as consumer prices had risen only 31 per cent by VJ Day, compared to 62 per cent on Armistice Day in 1918. The OPA was to last until July 1946, and the administration wished it to be continued for another year, but Chester Bowles, discouraged by its meager results and general criticism, resigned in February 1946. A fight in Congress over maintaining or dissolving the OPA resulted in confusion; it was maintained, but with such reduced powers that it could no longer control inflation. After the November 1946 elections, which gave Republicans a majority in both Houses of Congress for the first time since 1930, Truman decided to end all controls except those on rents, sugar and rice. By then the specter of inflation had vanished.

Anticipating the return of the GIs, Congress had already prepared legislation to facilitate their reinsertion into civilian life. The main act was the GI Bill of Rights, or Servicemen's Readjustment Act, approved in June 1944, which provided payments for tuition fees, books and living expenses for up to four years of education for World War II veterans. It opened to them even the most prestigious private universities, and provided opportunities for higher education previously out of reach for many. It also strengthened universities by diversifying their recruitment and bringing in people who had already an experience in living. And it was a landmark in the social history of the country, so much so that similar bills were adopted after the Korean and Vietnam Wars.

Another entirely new program was the one launched as early as 1945 by the freshman senator from Arkansas, J. William Fulbright. In 1946 he sponsored an amendment to the Surplus Property Act of 1944, establishing an international educational exchange program funded by the sale of American war surpluses. It passed through the Senate without debate, and its first participants went overseas in 1946. 'The exchange program', Senator Fulbright once remarked, 'is the thing that reconciles me to all the difficulties of life. It's the only activity that gives me some hope that the human race won't commit suicide.' He thought it the best means for people and nations to think globally if the world were to avoid self-destruction. The Fulbright program has been a tremendous success: so far, more than 120,000 foreign nationals have visited the United States to study, teach, or research, and 90,000 Americans have travelled overseas. What is amazing is that it is still working fifty years after its launching, although it is presently threatened by the new Republican majority in Congress.

In another sector of social life, race relations, the aftermath of World War II differed from the previous one. The end of World War I had witnessed a revival of racial violence, with riots, the rebirth of the Ku Klux Klan and the creation of Marcus Garvey's Universal Negro Improvement Association which advocated the return of blacks to Africa. Racial tensions and riots also occurred during World War II, for instance in Mobile, Detroit, and Harlem in 1943. But, on the whole, a new trend had been started – albeit under pressure – with President Roosevelt's executive order 8802 in 1941 forbidding discrimination in employment in government and defense industries. Although segregation was still the rule in all military units during World War II, the liberal conscience of Americans was put to shame by fighting Nazi racism abroad and practising racism at home. Truman accepted the challenge of fighting segregation, although his own party was sharply divided on this issue. In 1946 an executive order created a presidential committee on civil rights, which issued a report the following year urging the creation of a civil rights section in the Department of Justice. In 1948, executive order 9981 barred segregation in the armed forces. Although General Omar Bradley proclaimed that the time was not ripe for the army to start social reforms, and opposition was even more vigorous in the navy, which stuck to its 'lily-white' tradition, changes were in the making. Despite all fears, there were no troubles when, for the first time in American history, integrated units fought in the Korean War. The fight for civil rights had entered into history in the wake of the overseas experience of the armed forces and the aftermath of World War II. This is certainly no small accomplishment.

Concluding this sketchy overview of the aftermaths of the two world wars, I shall turn to what the great strategist Carl von Clausewitz has taught us about the role of war and peace in politics. War, he tells us, is only the continuation of peace by other means. We can reverse his saying and consider peace as a pacific form of war, with its appropriate means. This is especially true of the periods under consideration here: both world wars engendered a chain of change which could not be stopped. The basic changes have been the accession of the United States to the rank of a great power and, indeed, to that of a superpower; together with the rise of the middle classes and the emergence of mino-rities. Each American war has had its deep-lasting effects on the domestic as well as on the international scene, from the War of Independence to the Civil War and to the Vietnam War. The only difference is that the two world wars involved more people than any other and therefore modified more permanently the course of American history.

Notes

This paper is based on various readings, above all of memoirs and diaries – for instance those of Dwight D. Eisenhower, Harry S. Truman, J. William Fulbright, George F. Kennan, and many others that I cannot mention extensively here.

For the aftermath of World War I, by far the best approach is Robert H. Ferrell, *Woodrow Wilson and World War I, 1917–1921* (New York: 1985). I also found useful William E. Leuchtenburg, *The Perils of Prosperity, 1914–1932* (Chicago, Ill.: 1958), and Andrew A. Sinclair, *Era of Excess: A Social History of the Prohibition Movement* (New York: 1964). For the aftermath of World War II, in the absence of a book like Robert Ferrell's *Woodrow Wilson and World War I*, one may consult William H. Chafe, *The Unfinished Journey: America since World War II* (New York: 1986), and Dewey W. Grantham, *Recent America: The United States since 1945* (Arlington Heights, Ill.: 1987).

On Woodrow Wilson, the monumental contribution of Arthur S. Link is outstanding, including *Woodrow Wilson and a Revolutionary World, 1913–1921* (Chapel Hill, NC: 1982), and his sixty-nine edited volumes of *The Papers of Woodrow Wilson* (Princeton, NJ: 1966–94).

There is a voluminous bibliography on Sacco–Vanzetti and the Rosenbergs, which can be found in the aforementioned books. On the domestic reaction to communism, see Allen Weinstein, *Perjury: The Hiss–Chambers Case* (New York: 1978); David Caute, *The Great Fear: The Anti-Communist Purge under Truman and Eisenhower* (New York: 1978); and Stanley I. Kutler, *The American Inquisition: Justice and Injustice in the Cold War* (New York: 1983).

For demobilization after World War I, see Burl Noggle, *Into the Twenties: The United States from Armistice to Normalcy* (Urbana, Ill.: 1974). For World War II there are, for example, the various books by Richard Polenberg, *War and Society: The United States, 1941–1945* (Philadelphia, Pa.: 1972), and *One Nation Divisible: Class, Race, and Ethnicity in the United States since 1938* (New York: 1980).

On foreign policy, Jean-Baptiste Duroselle, *De Wilson à Roosevelt: politique extérieure des Etats-Unis, 1913–1945* (Paris: 1960; also translated into English) remains a classic, and for the more recent period Stephen E. Ambrose, *Rise to*

Globalism: American Foreign Policy since 1938 (New York: 1985) is a standard text. There is a huge literature on the Marshall Plan, but the most useful book is still Harry B. Price, *The Marshall Plan and Its Meaning* (Ithaca, NY: 1955).

1. Leonard Wood (1860–1927) had been Chief of Staff of the US army (1910–14) and was still very influential in all military matters, although he had very tense relations with President Wilson. He had been considered as the commander of the AEF, but Pershing superseded him.

2. Letter to Ethel Noland, 20 January 1919, quoted by Robert H. Ferrell, *Woodrow Wilson and World War I, 1917–1921* (New York: 1985), p.180. To the same, 18 December 1918: 'I want to follow a mule down a corn row all the rest of my days or be a Congressman or something where I can cuss Colonels and Generals to my heart's content', ibid., p.284.

2

The Colonial Militia in Anglo-Indian Wars: Virginia, 1622–1677

Zbigniew Mazur

The early history of British colonies in America was punctuated by prolonged periods of war. Seventeenth-century competition among European powers often resulted in military conflicts in the colonies; most frequently, however, the colonists fought against the original inhabitants of the land they had settled.[1] War had a clearly detrimental impact on the development of early American culture, bringing about the demise of the native American societies of the Atlantic coast, causing the loss of thousands of lives and wide devastation of property, and engaging the energies of the settlers in destruction rather than in production of wealth. However, war was also a powerful culture-creative force. The fact that colonial society was caught up in war on a scale unprecedented in England, while the military apparatus of English culture could not be transported to America in its entirety, contributed to wide transformations in socially established practices and in the values regulating them. The colonial communities which emerged in America at the end of the seventeenth century were very much a product of the social, political, and economic processes induced by military confrontations with native American peoples.

One of the institutions whose origins may be traced back to the context of early Anglo-Indian competition is the colonial militia. The present paper examines the origins of the militia in the first British colony in America, Virginia, tentatively assuming that the pattern adopted there was characteristic of the organization of local military forces in early British America. Investigation into the formation, the internal structure, the economic foundation, military technology, tactics, and morale of the colonists' militia provides us with telling insights into the cultural significance of war in colonial America. This paper deals with the problems of mobilization of the colonial population during Anglo-Indian conflicts in the seventeenth century: the war following the so-called 'Indian massacre' of 1622, the Indian uprising of 1644, and Bacon's Rebellion in 1676–7. Identifying the most significant factors contributing to the creation of the colonial militia involves reconstructing the processes by which the English model of national defense was carried over to America and modified by the colonial experience, producing a novel form of military organization and a new set of cultural values associated with the notions of war.

The transfer of English culture to the colonies entailed considerable institutional transformations. The metropolis was unable, or unwilling, to move even the most important institutions of the state to America, so their equivalents or substitutes had to be created by the colonists. One of the most significant features of colonial life in the seventeenth century was the absence of a standing army. The provision of military services, as well as the creation of forces of law and order, was almost entirely left to the settlers themselves. While in the mother country the process of building a national, professional army was well under way throughout the seventeenth century, the socio-economic context of the settlements in America produced a different solution to the problems of defense: the development and reconstruction of the English model of the militia.

In 1607 Virginia was founded as a military garrison, with a disproportionately large number of the first settlers being professional soldiers and adventurers. This arrangement failed to work, as the settlement could not provide for its own professional army. There was not enough food to go round for people whose only job would be to fight in defense of the colony. The military regime did not bring about the expected economic success, primarily because the motivation of individual settlers for communal work tended to be low. Moreover, the presence of a number of people with a strong military background easily antagonized relations with indigenous peoples, for the colony's soldiers hastily gave vent to aggression whenever disagreements appeared. After the 1614 reforms introduced individual ownership of land in Virginia, the enterprising zest of the colonists was rekindled, and the discovery of tobacco as the staple crop showed them in which direction to search for material success. The settlers became totally engrossed in the production of tobacco as long as demand in England continued and the trade was profitable. As, concurrently, a peace was made with the natives of the Powhatan Confederacy, the idea of keeping a permanent, professional military force in the colony was abandoned. After the first decade the colony developed into a cluster of semi-independent settlements, which catered both for the material welfare and the security of their inhabitants. The settlers worked as tobacco-growing farmers, who occasionally became soldiers when they made forays into Indian territories to gain new land which they needed for tobacco cultivation.

The events of 22 March 1622, when the allied forces of the Powhatan Confederacy, in an attempt to halt English expansion and revitalize their own culture, made a surprise attack on English settlements, destroying most of them and killing more than three hundred people, may be considered a turning point in Virginia's history. The massacre enforced a drastic change in the organization of the colony. The question of the settlers' defense became the issue of primary importance for the survivors and the authorities in London. Amidst grave embarrassment, mutual criticism, and reproach following the tragedy, the colony prepared itself for war. Virginia was resettled and the leaders of individual settlements assumed the functions of militia commanders with almost dictatorial powers. Plantations retained their military character as long as the war with the Indians continued.[2] The endorsed strategy required the destruction of the 'Powhatan Empire', or at least the expulsion of the Indians from the English sphere of interest. The natives came to be identified as enemies, as the feeling grew that 'Sauages and Pagans are aboue all other for matter of Iustice euer to be suspected.'[3] A belief that only the unquestioned English political and military domination over the Indians could bring about the colony's success became dogma. The English authorities proclaimed a steady policy of unlimited warfare. What happened in 1622 and in the following years finally convinced the colonists that most of the time they should rely on their own resources and not count on swift assistance from the mother country when they were in danger. In 1624 the Virginia Company was dissolved as the result of an investigation following the massacre, and Virginia became a royal colony, but the crown, although it contemplated dispatching soldiers to Virginia, failed to execute the plans and only occasionally relieved the colonists with supplies.[4]

This is not to say that the Virginia settlers were at any time left entirely to their own devices. The control of the colonists' relations with the local inhabitants was one of the most jealously guarded privileges of the colonial authorities: the principal policy was drawn in London and the immediate decisions in the colony were to be taken by the governor and his council. The Privy Council in London regularly deliberated upon Virginia's affairs and kept sending detailed recommendations to the governor in Jamestown. The English knowledge of Virginia's reality was so inaccurate that many orders sent to the colony could never be put into practice. Arbitrary decisions made in England hardly satisfied the colonists and did not offer them a sense of security. Moreover, communication was too slow for any immediate control by the London authorities over the changing scene of Anglo-Indian relations to be effective. The Indian attack demonstrated that the question of ethnic relations in the colony could be adequately solved only if the solutions chosen by the authorities were accepted by the community of settlers, as the colonists were the only personnel who could put them into practice. Consequently, the 1622 massacre resulted in greater mobilization of the colony, further development of the militia structures, and in the tightening of the Jamestown government's control over Virginia's defense. The Indian threat increased the cohesion of the

white community and temporarily alleviated social tensions, although
it bolstered up the authority of the colonial élite, which was granted
new and sweeping powers for the conduct of the war.

In 1622 the colony conscripted practically all adult males for service
in its militia units.[5] Aware of their vulnerability and of the limited
resources at their disposal, the English did not respond to the massacre
with an all-out counter-attack, but sent several expeditions, whose first
goal was not only to avenge the carnage of 22 March, but also to get
corn from the Indians, as the colony, besieged by the enemy tribes,
faced starvation. Although technologically superior to the natives, the
colonists fought an irregular war, whose course was shaped by the current balance of power. The first pre-planned campaign was launched
in June 1622. Colonial troops set 'uppon the Indyans in all places' at
the same time, killed many, burnt their towns, destroyed their weirs
and the corn that the English were unable to carry away with them. In
the autumn the settlers set on another concerted assault against the
enemy Indians, reaching Pamunkey, the heart of Opechancanough's
kingdom, where dozens of natives were killed and much booty gathered.[6]
Hostilities lasted until 1632, and, although the English eventually
emerged as victors, the war proved a heavy burden for the growing
colony. Throughout this period the colonists tried to deploy their
scant resources efficiently in order to deliver devastating blows to their
Indian enemies. In 1629 the Virginia Assembly drafted a permanent
plan for the rest of the war: regular campaigns were scheduled for
every November, March, and July, at the times when the colonists
could leave their fields and the Indians were most vulnerable. The
colony was arranged into four 'divisions' with assigned areas of military responsibility.[7]

The militia was also perfecting its tactics. The colonial strategists
gradually abandoned their plans for open field battles with major
Indian forces, as the natives avoided such confrontations. It was soon
realized that small-scale expeditions directed against designated Indian
settlements were more effective, in the course of which Indian property was destroyed and the inhabitants killed or at least made to flee.
The colonists knew that the Indians 'are an enemy nott suddenlie to be
destroyde wth sworde by reason of theire swiftnesse of foote, and
advantages of the woodes, to which vppon all ou[r] assault they retyre
but by the way of starvinge and all other meanes y[t] we can possibly
devise we will constantlie pursue their extirpatione'.[8] The settlers tried
to cut the enemy forces off from their bases of subsistence, starve them
into submission, and subjugate them through the use of terror. The
war was extreme in its brutality: in one episode about two hundred
Pamunkeys were apparently poisoned, while on other occasions the
colonists assaulted tribes which had been friendly allies and willing

trade partners, such as the Potomacks. These incidents brought protests from some observers who judged that 'this was contrarie to the equity of God and natures lawes'.[9] Voices like these were rare exceptions; an overwhelming majority of the settlers believed that there should not be any restrictions on the forms of warfare practised against the Indians, who were regarded as treacherous, bestial, pagan enemies, and whose crimes had to be avenged with utmost ruthlessness. European constraints on the limits of war did not apply to the conflict with the Indians.[10] If the colonists did not want to go to the war, it was because it was time-consuming and dangerous and they had their fields to till. The militia commanders had great difficulty in recruiting soldiers for expeditions. The authorities complained of the 'unwillinge people' who 'Crye out of the loss of Tyme, against their Comanders, in a warre where nothinge is to be gained'; the colonialists argued that they had their families to clothe and feed, and that 'the Chief tyme of doeinge the enymie most spoile' was when they had their own fieldwork to do. As early as 1623 the governor of Virginia condemned some people who 'having done & suffered much here thinke themselves Emeritos miltes and free from publique dutyes'.[11]

The tactics chosen for the conduct of the war, however controversial they might be for outside observers, undoubtedly proved successful. Although the Indians put up fierce resistance, the English were not only able to ensure the safety of their settlements, but they pushed the natives away and thus made further development of the colony possible. The fighting prowess and maturity of the colonial militia was perhaps best demonstrated in the reaction of the colony to the second Indian uprising in 1644. At first the assault by the natives was surprisingly effective: although the strength of the confederated tribes was much smaller than in 1622, they managed to inflict even higher casualties (about five hundred colonists were reportedly killed, while others were taken prisoner).[12] A contemporaneous author attributed the natives' desperate assault to the news that the aged Indian leader, Opechancanough, had received of the Civil War in England and his hope that all assisstance to the colony would be cut off by the mother country.[13] The Indians were, however, over optimistic; the colony was able to defend itself even without aid from England. The war that ensued lasted for two years and the natives were beaten by the colonial militia commanded by the new governor, Sir William Berkeley. The English victory proved easier and more decisive than that which followed the uprising of 1622.[14]

Mobilization of the colonial population for the war effort was clearly based on the ancient English model of the militia as the military arm of local government. The national militia in England comprised all male residents aged between fifteen and sixty, and was organized according

to the Statute of Westminster of 1285, slightly reconstituted in the
mid-sixteenth century. A senior peer residing in the county served as
lord lieutenant, assisted by three or four resident gentry or minor peers
as deputy lieutenants. The main element of the militia were the so
called 'trained bands', usually consisting of more respectable house-
holders or their sons, commanded by officers drawn from the local
gentry. The gentlemen were reluctant to put arms in the hands of the
'meaner sort'. Problems with raising money and arms for the militia
resulted from the fact that it was dependent on royal prerogative, not
on parliamentary decision.[15] In Virginia the English model of the militia
was tested in the context of ethnic warfare, adapted to local conditions
and thus greatly modified, producing a new variant which was in turn
to influence the social and political development of the colony.

Revision and modification of the old model of the militia helped the
Virginia colonists to develop efficacious methods of defending the
colony and bringing the natives to subjection. The 'Indian march', a
peculiar colonial creation, was already a familiar feature in Virginia in
1622, and by 1644 it had become a standard, institutionalized form of
English warfare, as best illustrated by the detailed set of the assembly
orders for the 1644 campaign.[16] The 'Indian march' was a punitive or
preventive expedition of the colonial militia, called whenever there was
a 'problem' with the Indians: for instance, an intensification of local
conflicts, resettlement of a tribe, or a dispute over land rights. The
march originated as a method of waging war against the Indians, but
later it acquired more functions. Marches could be called to 'demand
and receive satisfaction' from the natives, to assign lands to them, to
prevent an 'Indian invasion', to 'discover and prevent a threatened
danger', 'to remoove the ... new come Indians without makeing warr
if it may be', 'to parly with them', or to 'assist ... and defend' friendly
Indians.[17]

The power to order a march belonged to the Virginia Assembly, the
governor and the council, and, if the matter was of local importance, to
a county court or an assembly of the county militia. First, a commission
would be issued to the commander, a person of high social standing in
one of the counties, who thus received far-reaching military and legal
prerogatives. He had the authority to press a number of men and provisions from an assigned area; he held judicial powers over his troops
and could punish them even for such misdemeanors as the use of
'improper language'. The commander was given much leeway in the
execution of the march, often allowed to do what he 'thought best' for
the welfare of the colony. In the raids following the 1622 massacre it
was up to him 'either to make peace or war'. Orders in the form of a
commission or a proclamation identified the Indian enemies for particular expeditions, and set forth exact dates, meeting places, and areas

of operation. The authorities could only muster troops who could not be employed all the year long, as they had their families and fields to think about. War was a communal effort, with soldiers being levied from all settlements and equipped by the communities they lived in. Impressment notwithstanding, volunteers were also allowed and even encouraged (as a cost-saving arrangement) to participate in the marches. The number of colonists ready to enter the colony's service against the Indians increased in the second half of the century.[18]

The timing of expeditions against the Indians was regulated by the region's farming calendar. The English authorities attempted to defeat the natives through the destruction of their fields and stores. Governor Wyatt wrote that there was 'no meanes so probable to worke the ruin and destruction of oͬ Salvage and treacherous enemies, as cutting downe their Corne in the fitt season, seeing they haue so many lurkeing places to escape the execution of the Sword by flight'.[19] Accordingly, the colonists went to war when the Indians' corn was ripe, or already collected. That was the surest time to surprise the natives at their settlements, capture or destroy their crops, and make them perish through famine. Expeditions were directed against the whole native population, women and children included. The heritage of the first forty years of Anglo-Indian contact was that *any* Indian was considered a foe. The objective of the colonial militia during a punitive march could be summed up as to 'doe what other hurt or damage to the Indians that they may', or to 'doe all manner of spoile and offence to the Indians that may possibly be effected'.[20]

English military art triumphed only after the colonists had adjusted it to the requirements of their new environment; the Indian march came into being as a result of an adoption of Indian methods of forest warfare, and was based on the model of the Indian war party.[21] In Virginia, as open field battles were rare and there were almost no sieges comparable to those of seventeenth-century European warfare, the colonists found traditional patterns of defense or attack ineffective. In forest warfare the long pikes had to be abandoned as useless, and heavy suits of armor proved impractical, as they slowed down the progress of mobile militia units. The advantage of English firearms was obvious, but the rules of their use had to be modified: volleys were replaced by more effective, single, well-marked shots from hiding-places. The march, an amalgamation of English and Indian military techniques, a short expedition by a mobile, well-armed, though not best-skilled force, with a clearly stated objective, turned out to be the most effective.[22]

The economic aspects of colonial warfare were also regulated by statutes. The charges of a campaign were normally borne by the whole colony. The assembly voted special taxes, and those who stayed at home had to contribute to the charge of sending out the army. Militia officers received salaries, and soldiers were reimbursed for their loss of time. Counties had to cover the costs of their own soldiers and bear their labor while they were away. Occasionally, even those counties which had not taken part in a campaign were expected to contribute to its cost by paying an additional tax. People whose 'civilian' services or property were used for a public purpose were entitled to compensation. Thus, the march had a clear commercial aspect, which affected both recruitment and the manner of execution.[23]

Militia expeditions were at the same time military and trading ventures, often financed by private investors. The practice was that some colonists – frequently the commanders themselves – partly covered the costs of a raid, and then got reimbursement in tobacco or labor for the provisions they had supplied, for shot and powder, the use of boats, or small utensils like pots, hooks, and nails. Surviving lists of 'charges and disbursements' prove that soon after 1622 economic motives far exceeded emotional impulses in the organization of Indian wars. In the 1620s the absence of any valuable property in Indian hands served as an argument to account for the settlers' indifference to the war, but the significance of Indian plunder was increasing. In 1666 the Rappahanock county militia undertook to 'destroy and eradicate' hostile Indians 'without Further encouragement then the spoyles of oʳ Enymies', and the governor declared war on the northern Indians, ordering that 'their women and children be disposed of' according to his own instructions. Spoils became a motive of primary importance for Nathaniel Bacon and his rebels in 1676.[24] The possibility of exploiting the natives would always contribute to the growth of sharper social divisions within the settlers' community. Even during the 1644–6 war, when the colony was displaying an unusual unity in pursuing the destruction of the attackers, it was the colony's power-brokers who were able to obtain the most personal advantages from the victory. Characteristically, the first to receive a grant of land taken away from Indians was William Clairbone, the most famous 'Indian trader' and the commander of the first march against the Indians after their April assault.

The popular sense of danger from the Indians was institutionalized in the official policy of vigilance. For a colonist, at any moment, a war with Indians was either just being fought, or about to break out. The need for vigilance was symbolized by annual celebrations of 22 March and then 18 April as holy days, 'in commemoration of our deliverance from the Indians at the bloody massacres'. Sufficient supplies of arms, powder, and shot had to be stored. The colonists had to be frequently reminded 'not to spend powder at meetings, drinkings, marriages and entertainments'. The fate of the colony, its leaders thought, depended on the settlers' discipline. During the frequent periods of tension Englishmen were required to restrict their movements outside the settlements, never go out unarmed, and restrain from contact with natives.[25] Another element of the vigilance policy was the steady, though futile, promotion of an organized settlement pattern in Virginia which would provide adequate defense. The authorities reiterated their criticism of the sparse manner of settling the colony, which endangered the lives of the greedy planters, not able to defend the land they attempted to occupy. There were constant orders from England to palisade the plantations and keep a constant guard.[26]

The Indian attack in 1622 had helped to establish a pattern of organization in Virginia which increased the power of its social leaders through their administrative and military functions and which persisted with only small changes until 1676. A general Indian policy was formulated by the colonial élite which reflected its political and economic interests. In the 1640s the élite centered around William Berkeley, who headed a small group within the second generation of immigrants, composed mostly of ambitious younger sons of wealthy English middle-class families. These people assumed the position of a ruling landed gentry in Virginia in the 1640s.[27] The assignment of many public offices (councillors, justices of the peace, surveyors, sheriffs, tax-collectors, etc.) became practically the prerogative of the élite, which led to the formation of an inner circle of power, bound by ties of kinship and patronage.[28] The Indian policy of this élite can be reconstructed fairly precisely from the legislation of the Virginia Assembly. It was based on the assumption that contact between individual Englishmen and Indians should be restricted and strictly supervised by the oligarchy. The colonial leadership assumed also that the tributary tribes, which had acknowledged their subordination to the English and had been granted title to their land and approval of their leaders, would perform important military and economic roles for the colony and should, therefore, receive legal protection. The colonial authorities would go as far as to punish those Englishmen who had broken these principles, especially for unauthorized actions against the friendly Indians.[29] The governor customarily reserved for himself the right to 'determine of peace and war' with the natives. Sir William wanted to make the tributary Indians incapable of doing harm to the English and to prevent the English from hurting the natives. He clung to the policy of keeping Indians as tributaries rather than enemies. The friendly natives were useful as frontier guards, scouts, and informants. This way of defending the colony seemed much cheaper than any plan involving colonists on active duty. Thus, the militia was to be aided by loyal Indians assisting the colony against 'strange' tribes.[30]

Apart from their military function, the tributary Indians were assigned the role of intermediaries in the fur trade between the English and the northern tribes. Indian trade was a state monopoly, and the bulk of the profits went to a narrow group within the élite. The business of trading with Indians involved an ethical question, as the natives wanted to receive guns, which could very possibly be turned against the English. Public pressure led to the imposition of bans on trade in firearms. But the people involved in the fur business argued that there was nothing wrong with selling guns to the Indians, as the natives could not be prevented from obtaining them from other sources and the lucrative commerce would be controlled by Dutch or Maryland traders. Secondly, equipping the tributaries with arms would actually make them better defenders of the colony in accordance with the general Indian policy.[31] Berkeley's vision of the political order in Virginia was close to a feudal concept of a single community, including tributary Indians, subject to the law and justice of the king. The governor believed in the necessity of maintaining strict central control over the development of the colony. Within this concept the militia was certainly necessary as a protective force in the colony, but it was also to serve as an embodiment of the social hierarchy, an institution within which, through their superior functions, the colonial élite could demonstrate their supreme power in society. A staunch royalist, Berkeley distrusted the poor, undisciplined whites as much as the Indians. His aim was to regulate the behavior of both groups and establish exact limits within which they would be allowed to move.[32] The stability of the colony was in danger when these limits were crossed:

> the mutuall discontents, complaints, jealousies and fears of English and Indians proceed chiefly from the violent intrusions of diverse English made into their land forcing the Indians by way of revenge to kill the cattle and hogs of the English, and by that meanes injuries being done on both sides, reports and rumours are spread of the hostile intentions of the each to the other, tending infinetely to the disturbance of peace of his majesty's country.[33]

As it turned out in the 1670s, the élite failed to implement its Indian policy chiefly because the poorer stratum of Virginia's society was intensely opposed to any form of control over the exploitation of Indians. Characteristically, the official policy tried to distinguish between particular Indian tribes and prescribed separate courses of action in relations with them. The distinctions between the friendly and the enemy Indians were ignored by individual colonists, motivated by prejudice, hatred, or personalized material interests. Such views found their greatest expression in the most severe social conflict in which the Virginian militia was involved in the seventeenth century: Bacon's Rebellion, 'an abortive revolt in Virginia against royal authority resulting from a failure of Indian policy'.[34] The immediate reason for this conflict between Governor William Berkeley and members of the militia was the latters' unauthorized campaign against the Indians accused of perpetrating attacks against the frontier settlements. In the main, the opponents in the rebellion consisted of the poor and the oppressed on the one side, and the rich and the privileged on the other. Virginia small planters, violent, aggressive, competitive, and materialistic, made up the bulk of the colonial militia and were the most numerous group in Bacon's army. They derived mostly from newly freed, discontented, male indentured servants, who had tried to make a start on their own in the frontier areas, away from the big masters. For them, the Indians were rivals in the relentless quest for survival.[35]

In the 1670s the average colonist came to regard the preservation of existing Indian communities as useless and dangerous. As Nathaniel Bacon put it: 'there was an absolute necessity of destroying the Indians for the prisarvation of the English'. For the people excluded from office and privilege, even the tributary Indians played no positive role; on the contrary, they were a threat and a constant source of fear. The Indians could not be taken for trade partners, as the governor's monopoly prevented most people from entering into this kind of relations, even with their closest Indian neighbors.[36] According to Bacon's 'Manifesto', the natives had been 'for these many years enemies to the King and Country, Robbers and Theeves and Invaders of His Majesty's Right and our Interest and Estates', but had 'by persons in Authority bin defended and protected even against His Majesty's loyall Subjects'. The natives stood in the way of free expansion of the colony, and since they were all believed to be essentially the same in appearance and character, the colonists found it extremely difficult, and at the same time purposeless, to tell the difference between 'friendly' and 'strange' Indians, to 'distinguish this fatall undistinguishable distinction of the Governor'. Due to King Philip's War in New England, the belief in a general Indian 'Combination' was spreading.[37]

In 1676 the colonists were outraged by violent incidents involving Indians and frontiersmen. The natives were blamed for several murders and described as 'Wolves, tigers and bears, which daly destroyd our harmless and innosscent Lambs', 'ill discerning, brutish heathen', 'brutish and inhumane brutes', 'the barbarous and common enemy'.[38] Berkeley, the colonists thought, was not doing enough to protect them. The marches he organized proved costly and ineffective. Defensive measures, like the construction of new forts, did not provide English settlements with appropriate security, but only increased taxes, to the advantage of the 'Grandees'.[39] To Bacon's militiamen, total physical elimination of the Indians in and around Virginia appeared the best possible solution to all their existential problems. On 21 June 1676 the popularly elected burgesses declared war against all those Indians who abandoned their usual places without permission; who refused to deliver all hostages, arms, and ammunition; who received enemy Indians in their villages; and who refused to give account of their names and numbers.[40] The rebels' leader, riding on the wave of popular support for the Indian war, demonstrated the strength of his militia when he forced the governor to grant him a commission to go against the natives. Although the combat proved heavy and arduous, the inhabitants of the colony offered enthusiastic backing for the militia's effort, especially when Bacon put his Indian prisoners and plunder on display. When Berkeley attempted to gather his own troops to regain power in the colony, his soldiers abandoned him, realizing they were expected to fight the celebrated hero Bacon, and not the Indians. Towards the end of the insurrection, the surrendering rebels frequently asked to be retained in arms to fight the Indian enemy.[41] The existence of ethnic prejudice was not enough to inspire the rebels to embark on a campaign of Indian destruction. No doubt in the 1670s there also existed some prejudice against blacks. Still, blacks were admitted to fight in the rebellion side by side with the English, and Bacon even promised freedom to black slaves who would join his army.[42]

Ethnic prejudice was accompanied by other strong psychological stimuli. The rebels – people who had fallen victim to the economic crisis – looked for scapegoats to blame for their hard life. In 1676 they genuinely considered their Indian neighbors to be responsible for most of the troubles that the colony had suffered; a mechanism of psychological projection was at work. Even the bad weather in the summer of 1676 was said to be caused by 'Pawawings, i.e. the Sorceries of the Indians'.[43] The Indians were 'ideal' scapegoats: the whites' frustration could be naturally dispelled in a war against them. They were traditional enemies, the history of Anglo-Indian relations made fighting a common and absolutely acceptable procedure, and there were plenty of reasons to feel entitled to take revenge. Of the many causes of social crisis, the Indians constituted the only one that the poor colonists could reach and do something about. The structure of the militia provided a ready-made mechanism for expression of the settlers' dissatisfaction. The decades of conflict with Indians demonstrated how important the role of common settlers organized in 'trained bands' was for the survival of the colony. In 1676 the rebelling frontiersmen claimed the right to decide about the course of Indian affairs in Virginia. This was also an indirect way of protesting against injustice, challenging the colony's leadership, or something that Edmund Morgan calls 'an instinctive attempt to subdue class conflict by racism'.[44]

Bacon's rebels had a clear economic interest in 'destroying' the Indians; Indian prisoners and plunder were an unquestionable motive for most of them. Within the structures of the militia such motives were perfectly understandable and even encouraged. The so-called Bacon's Assembly of 21 June 1676 legalized the enslavement for life of all Indian captives. The rebellion's leader was reputed to have assaulted the Occaneechees first of all in order to get their large store of beaver furs. The frequent requisitions of property belonging to English opponents prove that material gain, however obtained, was a stimulus for many people to join the fighting. In the long term, the rebels thought that after defeating the Indians they would get rid of a barrier to land acquisition: an act of 'Bacon's Assembly' declared that Indian land should be 'vested in the country' and disposed of to defray the charges of the war.[45] The rebels believed that all Englishmen were entitled to use or abuse Indians to their own benefit. It was hoped that the destruction of the Indians would improve the situation of the poor, underprivileged settlers. In contrast to the rebels, the colonial élite attempted to control the exploitation of the Indians with their own long-term advantage in mind. Incidentally, Berkeley's political regulations only served to separate the poor whites and Indians and added to the frontiersmen's belief that Indians were useless and dangerous.

The suppression of the rebellion, and especially the fall of the popular idol, Bacon, made the public antipathy to the Indians even more intense, adding new elements to the collection of traditional Indian sins and vices. The natives themselves had suffered such great losses that, in the long run, they could not serve any important function for the colony whatsoever. In a few years they were deprived of their most valuable land and lost their privileged status. The provision for Indian enslavement, though repealed in 1677, was re-enacted in 1679. In 1682, for the first time in Virginia, an assembly act introduced segregation along racial lines, lumping blacks and Indians together.[46] In many respects, Bacon's rebels achieved their aims: the Indians were practically 'destroyed' and ceased to matter at all in Virginia's politics. The Virginian militia achieved the purpose for which it had been created, finally and completely defeating its traditional enemy in the Tidewater region.

But Bacon's Rebellion altered power relationships in the colony. The English crown was forced to send troops to America for the first time, and some military tasks were taken over by the standing army. The colonial militia was viewed with distrust in England. Moreover, the events of 1676–7 were one of the factors which inclined the crown to seek new ways of supervising their overseas affairs, as can be seen by the creation of new colonial administrative mechanisms in the 1680s and 1690s. Nevertheless, the importance of volunteers in the defense of the colonies could not be undermined. The Indian danger was reduced, but international competition was to bring new conflicts closer to America. In addition, with the increasing numbers of black slaves in the colonies, the militia was indispensable, as fears of black uprisings persisted. The white inhabitants were drawn together by the novel convergence of interests: the great planters needed the poor whites to keep a tight rein on the slave population.

In conclusion, it should be noted that in the seventeenth century the impact of the development of the colonial militia as an institution was reflected in the continuing participation of individual settlers in local politics to an extent that was unknown in the mother country. The necessity of responding to the problems created by the active Indian presence increased the need for self-responsibility and self-sufficiency in the small colonial communities. Because the survival of plantations was at stake, it was a 'domestic' issue, affecting and involving practically all members of society. Because Virginia's authorities had limited resources and England was not ready to help its colony, the settlers became certain that the management of Indian affairs was almost entirely up to them. This brought about not only changes in cultural values and institutional transformations, but also the growth of a 'gun culture' in Virginia. There emerged a novel phenomenon, unknown in England, when a large number of people, belonging to different social groups, owned firearms. Guns became common items in Virginian households, vividly marking the colonists' new sense of self-reliance.[47]

Compared to its equivalent in the mother country, the colonial militia was a much more common service, uniting settlers of all social ranks. In times of peace, militia musters functioned as important occasions for social meetings and entertainment. Service in the militia was no mere formality, as the presence of the ethnic enemy necessitated frequent participation in military actions. The development of military technology, strategy and tactics evolved differently from those in Europe, amalgamating Indian patterns of forest warfare. The increasing use of violence in dealing with the Indians was another characteristic consequence of the wars fought in the seventeenth century; the colonists resorted more and more readily to brutality. Force was both an official legal method prescribed by the government, and commonplace behavior. The extreme was a rule of terror which, even by seventeenth-century standards, appeared as indiscriminate cruelty. There were occasions when the colonists aimed at the total extermination of Indian tribes – which shows that cultural norms which applied to white enemies in European wars did not extend to American natives. For the British, the systematic genocide of Indians was a new invention; the natives could be killed because they did not possess any legal protection within colonial culture. In 1622–32, 1644–6, and 1676–7 the English conducted fierce campaigns in which the official objective was a complete physical destruction of the Indians, by such means as proved effective.

On the one hand, the Indian issue split colonial society and helped the creation of sharp social divisions. The organization of the militia was not based on any democratic principles. It was supposed to reflect and endorse social inequalities and not to eradicate them. The higher positions were occupied by members of the colonial élite, who used this opportunity to increase their power over the poorer settlers and to enrich themselves by exploiting the possibilities offered by warfare. This arrangement was unsuccessfully questioned by those members of the militia who rebelled against the colonial government in 1676, not in order to start a social revolution, but to demand the right to safeguard their own security, a privilege they thought they deserved as soldiers of the colony. The growth of colonial military forces, parallel to the growth of legislative and judicial bodies, was greatly shaped by ethnic conflict too. The development of those institutions was from the very beginning tainted with the exclusion of a large group of the colonial population – the Indians – from participation in them; furthermore, the colonial militia was founded with the purpose of keeping ethnic minorities away from contact with the whites.

On the other hand, the Indian threat increased social cohesion and united the settlers in a belief in their own ethnic superiority, and in a sense of outside danger. The campaigns against the Indians were those rare occasions when Virginian society had to cooperate around a common goal and when they had to subject themselves to discipline. The threat of the Indian danger, real or imagined, pushed the colonists into greater consolidation and cooperation, and the militia assumed the shape of an institution whose primary function was to defend the colony against the Indians as a military and – even more importantly – cultural menace.[48] The Indians, and, as it was to turn out later, blacks as well, were situated beyond the bounds of white society and were thought to be a threat to its integrity. The colonial militia was built upon the heritage of ethnic antagonism, with exclusionism deeply imbedded in its structure. It was founded to combat the enemy within, and the ideology of cultural rejection was one of the organizing principles which governed the mobilization of colonial society for military effort. The early history of the colonial militia engendered strong bias which was to affect the development of American institutions of self-government and defense in the following decades.

Notes

1. In the early years of English settlement in North America there was a danger of Spanish invasion; in the middle of the century the colonists went on the alert when England waged wars with Holland. However, the Indians were the only enemy with whom the settlers actually fought and

it was this confrontation that had the decisive impact on the organization of the colonial military and the shaping of popular attitudes towards this public service.

2. Susan M. Kingsbury (ed.), *The Records of the Virginia Company of London* (Washington, DC: 1906–35), vol. 4, pp. 105, 188, 190, 209 (henceforth cited as *RVC*); John Smith, 'A Trve Relation', in Edward Arber and A. G. Bradley (eds), *Travels and Works of Captain John Smith*, 2 vols (Edinburgh: 1910), vol. 2, pp. 884–6; *Virginia Magazine of History and Biography* (henceforth cited as *VMHB*) 13 (1905), pp. 336–7; Karen O. Kupperman, *Settling with the Indians: The Meeting of English and Indian Culture in America, 1580–1640* (Totowa, NJ: 1980), pp. 138–9; Edmund S. Morgan, *American Slavery. American Freedom. The Ordeal of Colonial Virginia* (New York: 1975), p. 100; Richard Beale Davis, *George Sandys, Poet Adventurer: A Study in Anglo-American Culture in the Seventeenth Century* (London: 1955), pp. 134–5.

3. *RVC*, vol. 3, pp. 559, 671–3; Warren M. Billings, John E. Selby, Thad W. Tate, *Colonial Virginia: A History* (White Plains, NY: 1986), p. 44; Nicholas P. Canny, 'Dominant Minorities: English Settlers in Ireland and Virginia, 1550–1650', in A. C. Hepburn (ed.), *Minorities in History*, vol. 12 of Historical Studies Series (New York: 1979), p. 54; Wilcomb E. Washburn, *The Indian in America* (New York: 1975), p. 158.

4. See for instance *RVC*, vol. 3, p. 709; ibid., vol. 4, p. 434; *VMHB* 23 (1915), p. 238; W. L. Grant and J. Munro (eds), *Acts of the Privy Council of England*, Colonial Series, 6 vols (London: 1908–12), vol. 1, pp. 92–5.

5. In 1626 only new settlers were exempted from service in the war for one year. All others aged between seventeen and sixty had to serve. *Acts of the Privy Council*, vol. 1, pp. 99–101.

6. *RVC*, vol. 3, pp. 622, 654–5; ibid., vol. 2, pp. 9, 450; J. Frederick Fausz, 'Present at the "Creation": The Chesapeake Land that Greeted the Maryland Colonists', *Maryland Historical Magazine* 79 (1984), pp. 9–10; J. Frederick Fausz, 'Profits, Pelts and Power: English Culture in the Early Chesapeake, 1620–1652', *Maryland Historian* 14 (1983), pp. 17–18.

7. *Acts of the Privy Council*, vol. 1, p. 484; H. R. McIlwaine (ed.), *Journals of the House of Burgesses of Virginia*, 13 vols (Richmond, Va.: 1905–15), vol. 1, pp. 52–3; H. R. McIlwaine (ed.), *Minutes of the Council and the General Court of Colonial Virginia, 1622–1632, 1670–1676* (Richmond, Va.: 1924), pp. 480–4; *VMHB* 13 (1905), pp. 390, 401, see also ibid. 1 (1893), p. 417; Carl Bridenbaugh, *Early Americans* (New York: 1981), pp. 20–2; Wilcomb E. Washburn, 'Moral and Legal Justifications for Dispossessing the Indians', in James H. Smith (ed.), *Seventeenth-Century America: Essays in Colonial History* (New York: 1972), pp. 20–2; Alden T. Vaughan, '"Expulsion of the Salvages": English Policy and the Virginia Massacre of 1622', *William and Mary Quarterly* (henceforth cited as *WMQ*), 3rd ser., 35 (1978), pp. 76–9; Kupperman, *Settling with the Indians*, pp. 179–181.

8. *RVC*, vol. 4, pp. 9–10.

9. *RVC*, vol. 3, pp. 622, 654–5, 696–8; ibid., vol. 4, pp. 221–2, 277; William S. Powell, 'Aftermath of the Massacre: The First Indian War, 1622–1632', *VMHB* 66 (1958), pp. 44–75.

10. 'Victorie of them may be gained many waies: by force, by surprize, by famine, in burninge their Boats, Canoes, and Houses, by breaking their fishing Weares, by assailing them in their hunting ... by pursuing and chasing them with our Horses, and blood-Hounds to draw after them, and Mastiues to teare them, which take these naked, tawned, deformed Sauages, for no other then wild beasts ... by driuing them (when they flye) vpon their enemies against them, may their ruine or subiection be soone effected', *RVC*, vol. 3, pp. 557–8.

11. *RVC*, vol. 4, pp. 237, 451, 474; Davis, *George Sandys*, p. 133; *Minutes*, p. 135; Canny, 'Dominant Minorities', p. 63; Powell, 'Aftermath of the Massacre', pp. 63–4; Edmund S. Morgan, 'The First American Boom: Virginia 1618 to 1630', *WMQ* 28 (1971), p. 181; idem, *American Slavery*, pp. 140–3.

12. Robert Beverley, *The History and the Present State of Virginia* (1705), ed. Louis B. Wright (Charlottesville, Va.: 1968), pp. 60–2; Bridenbaugh, *Early Americans*, pp. 47–8.

13. 'A Perfect Description of Virginia: Being a Full and True Relation of the Present State of the Plantation', in Peter Force (ed.), *Tracts and Other Papers, Relating Principally to the Origin, Settlement, and Progress of the Colonies in North America, from the Discovery of the Country to the Year 1776*, 4 vols (New York, 1837–46), vol. 2, pp. 8, 11.

14. Leo Francis Stock (ed.), *Proceedings and Debates of British Parliaments Respecting North America*, 5 vols (Washington, DC: 1924–41), vol. 1, p. 182; Billings, Selby, Tate, *Colonial Virginia*, pp. 49–50; Washburn, *The Indian in America*, p. 128. In 1644 the population ratio in the colony had already changed to English advantage and Virginia was much more stable economically.

15. J.W. Wijn, 'Military Forces and Warfare, 1610–1648', in J. P. Cooper (ed.), *The New Cambridge Modern History* (Cambridge: 1971), vol. 4, pp. 219–20; Derek Hirst, *Authority and Conflict, England 1603–1658* (Cambridge: 1986), pp. 45–6; M. A. Faraday (ed.), *Herefordshire Militia Assessments of 1663*, Camden Fourth Series (London: Royal Historical Society, 1977), vol. 10, pp. 1–7.

16. *VMHB* 23 (1915), pp. 229–37; K. G. Davies, *The North Atlantic World in the Seventeenth Century* (Minneapolis, Minn.: 1974), p. 283.

17. William W. Henning (ed.), *The Statutes at Large, Being a Collection of All the Laws of Virginia from the First Session of the Legislature in the Year 1619* (New York: 1819–23), vol. 1, pp. 389, 402–3; *WMQ*, 1st ser., 8 (1899/1900), p. 23; *VMHB* 8 (1900), pp. 173–4; ibid., 4 (1896), p. 409; ibid., 13 (1905), p. 390; Beverley Fleet (ed.), *Virginia Colonial Abstracts* (Richmond, Va., 1941), vol. 10, p. 47; *RVC*, vol. 3, pp. 654–5; ibid., vol. 4, p. 115; Francis Jennings, *The Invasion of America: Indians, Colonialism, and the Cant of Conquest* (Chapel Hill, NC: 1975), pp. 146–8.

18. There may have existed some general stores with equipment to be used in emergencies, and since 1622 orders were given to take care of those who would be hurt during an expedition and of the families whose members would be killed. Susie M. Ames (ed.), *County Court Records of Accomack-Northampton, Virginia*, 2 vols (Charlottesville, Va: 1973), vol. 2,

pp. 235, 383; *Statutes*, vol. 1, pp. 126–8, 292–4, 315, 389–90, 402–3;
Minutes, pp. 151, 488–503; *Journals*, vol. 1, pp. 52–3; *RVC*, vol. 4,
pp. 9–10; *Virginia Colonial Abstracts*, vol. 10, p. 47; *VMHB* 4 (1896),
pp. 246–50, 405, 409; ibid. 8 (1900), pp. 70, 173–4; ibid. 13 (1905),
pp. 301, 390, 401; ibid. 14 (1906), p. 263; ibid. 17 (1909), p. 5; ibid. 23
(1915), pp. 229–37; *WMQ*, 1st ser., 8 (1899/1900), pp. 23, 25; ibid., 2nd
ser., 7 (1927), pp. 44–5.

19. *RVC*, vol. 4, pp. 9–10, 98–9, 102; see also ibid., vol. 3, pp. 487, 482, 486.
See J. Frederick Fausz, 'Anglo-Indian Aggression and Accommodation
along the Mid-Atlantic Coast, 1584–1634', in William W. Fitzhugh
(ed.), *Cultures in Contact: The Impact of European Contacts on Native
American Cultural Institutions, A.D. 1000–1800* (Washington, DC: 1985),
pp. 246–7.

20. *VMHB* 4 (1896), pp. 246–50; *Journals*, vol. 1, pp. 52–3.

21. War parties were organized by previously successful warriors who held
authority over their voluntary participants. Scouts were widely employed
by war parties to guard against surprise attacks and keep a constant
lookout for possible foes. War parties aimed to make surprise attacks
and get away before the enemy had a chance to organize resistance or
pursuit. Wendell S. Hadlock, 'War among the Northeastern Woodland
Indians', *American Anthropologist* 49 (1947), pp. 204–21; Marian W.
Smith, 'American Indian Warfare', *Transactions of the New York Academy
of Sciences*, 2nd ser., 13 (1951), pp. 355–7.

22. Powell, 'Aftermath of the Massacre', p. 53; *RVC*, vol. 4, pp. 67, 507–8;
Jennings, *Invasion*, p. 153; Nancy O. Lurie, 'Indian Cultural Adjustment
to European Civilization', in *Seventeenth-Century America*, p. 41. Ships
and boats were frequently used for transportation of English troops,
WMQ, 1st ser., 8 (1899/1900), p. 75; *Minutes*, p. 231.

23. *Statutes*, vol. 1, pp. 294, 315, 337–8; *VMHB* 23 (1915), p. 234; *Minutes*,
pp. 18, 24–5; *WMQ*, 1st ser., 6 (1897/1898), p. 118; ibid. 7 (1898/1899),
pp. 179–81; ibid. 8 (1899/1900), pp. 25–6.

24. See for example the commissions to George Yeardley, Ralph Hamor or
William Tucker, *WMQ*, 1st ser., 2 (1893/1894), p. 177; ibid. 8 (1899/
1900), pp. 24–7; ibid. 21 (1912/1913), pp. 101–2; ibid. 22 (1913/1914),
p. 242; ibid., 2nd ser., 6 (1926), p. 591; ibid. 7 (1927), pp. 44–5, 204–7;
VMHB 23 (1915), pp. 249, 240; *Minutes*, pp. 488–9, 500–3; *Statutes*, vol.
1, pp. 287–8, 292–4, 337–8, 315, 300–1, 287; ibid., vol. 2, pp. 346, 351–2,
404, 440; *Journals*, vol. 2, p. 90.

25. *Statutes*, vol. 1, pp. 290, 459–60; *County Court Records of Accomack-
Northampton*, vol. 1, pp. 105, 265, 268; *VMHB* 13 (1905), p. 399; *WMQ*,
2nd ser., 7 (1927), pp. 248–9.

26. *VMHB* 23 (1915), pp. 249–50; ibid. 26 (1918), p. 240; *Minutes*, p. 147;
Karen O. Kupperman, 'Apathy and Death in Early Jamestown', *Journal
of American History* 66 (1979), pp. 24–40.

27. Bernard Bailyn, 'Politics and Social Structure in Virginia', in *Seventeenth-
Century America*, pp. 98–102; John C. Rainbolt, 'The Alteration in the
Relationship between Leadership and Constituents in Virginia, 1660–
1720', *WMQ*, 3rd ser., 27 (1970), pp. 413–16; Morgan, *American Slavery*,

pp.143, 225; Timothy H. Breen, Stephen Innes, *'Myne Owne Ground':* *Race and Freedom on Virginia's Eastern Shore, 1640–1676* (New York: 1980), pp.48–9.

28. 'Charles City County Grievances', *VMHB* 3 (1895), pp.132–6.
29. W. Stitt Robinson, jun., 'The Legal Status of the Indian in Colonial Virginia', *VMHB* 51 (1953), pp.247–9, 254–6; 'Tributary Indians in Colonial Virginia', *VMHB* 67 (1959), pp.49–64; *Statutes*, vol. 1, pp.322–6, 382, 389–91, 393–7, 402–3, 410, 415–16, 422–3, 453, 467–8, 470, 476, 518; ibid., vol. 2, pp.39, 149–55, 185, 215; *Minutes*, pp.238, 260, 361, 518.
30. *Statutes*, vol. 1, pp.322–6, 389–90, 402–3, 415–16, 422–3, 453; ibid., vol. 2, pp.142–3, 219, 237–8; Wilcomb E. Washburn, *The Governor and the Rebel: A History of Bacon's Rebellion in Virginia* (Chapel Hill, NC: 1957), p.26; Morgan, *American Slavery*, p.231; Jennings, *Invasion of America*, p.124; *VMHB* 1 (1893), p.434; (Thomas Mathews), 'The Beginning, Progress, and Conclusion of Bacon's Rebellion in Virginia (1705)', in *Tracts and Other Papers*, vol. 1, p.8.
31. Thomas Glover, 'An Account of Virginia', *The Philosophical Transactions of the Royal Society*, 20 June 1676, unpaginated; *Statutes*, vol. 1, pp.382, 391, 470, 518; ibid., vol. 2, pp.39, 215; 'Charles City County Grievances', p.137; 'Gloster County Grievances', *VMHB* 2 (1894), p.170; 'A True Narrative of the Late Rebellion in Virginia by the Royal Commissioners, 1677', in Charles M. Andrews (ed.), *Narratives of the Insurrections, 1675–1690* (New York: 1952), p.121; A. J. Morrison, 'The Virginia Indian Trade to 1673', *WMQ*, 2nd ser., 1 (1921), pp.217–36.
32. Warren M. Billings, 'The Causes of Bacon's Rebellion: Some Suggestions', *VMHB* 78 (1970), pp.410–17.
33. *Statutes*, vol. 2, pp.138–9.
34. Wilbur J. Jacobs, *Dispossessing the American Indian: Indians and Whites on the Colonial Frontier* (New York: 1972), p.13.
35. Gary B. Nash, 'Social Structure and the Interpretation of Colonial American History', in *Class and Society in Early America* (Englewood Cliffs, NJ: 1970), p.15; Bernard Bailyn, *The Peopling of British North America: An Introduction* (New York: 1986), pp.99–101.
36. 'Charles City County Grievances', p.138; 'Governor Berkeley to Secretary Williamson', *VMHB* 20 (1912), pp.244–5; 'Governor Berkeley to Thomas Ludwell', *VMHB* 20 (1912), p.247; Morgan, *American Slavery*, p.138; 'A True Narrative', p.126.
37. An. Cotton, 'An Account of our Late Troubles in Virginia', in *Tracts and Other Papers*, vol. 1, p.5; 'A Narrative of the Indian and Civil Wars in Virginia', in *Tracts and Other Papers*, vol. 1, pp.9, 14; 'Nathaniel Bacon's Esq'r his Manifesto Concerning the Present Troubles in Virginia', *VMHB* 1 (1893), pp.57–8; see also 'Charles City Grievances', pp.137–40.
38. Cotton, 'An Account'; 'A Narrative of the Indian and Civil Wars'.
39. 'A True Narrative', pp.120–1; 'Charles City County Grievances', pp. 136–40; Timothy H. Breen, 'Looking Out for Number One: The Cultural Limits on Public Policy in Early Virginia', in *Puritans and Adventurers: Change and Persistence in Early America* (New York: 1980), p.124; Billings, 'Causes of Bacon's Rebellion', pp.429, 435.

40. *Statutes*, vol. 2, pp. 341–2, 348–9. Compare the 1674 declaration of war, ibid., vol. 2, pp. 326–7.

41. 'A True Narrative', pp. 134, 142–4, 146, 148; 'Bacon's Speech at Green Spring', *WMQ*, 1st ser., 3 (1894/1895), p. 121; 'A Narrative of the Indian and Civil Wars in Virginia', in *Tracts and Other Papers*, vol. 1, pp. 9, 33, 45; 'Gloster County Grievances', p. 168.

42. Breen, 'A Changing Labour Force', p. 138; Morgan, *American Slavery*, pp. 233, 328; Breen, Innes, *'Myne Owne Ground'*, pp. 26–7.

43. Billings, 'Causes of Bacon's Rebellion', p. 423; (Thomas Mathews), 'The Beginning, Progress, and Conclusion of Bacon's Rebellion in Virginia (1705)', in *Tracts and Other Papers*, vol. 1, p. 8; Washburn, *Governor and Rebel*, p. 31.

44. 'A True Narrative', pp. 124, 139; Morgan, *American Slavery*, p. 328.

45. *Statutes*, vol. 2, pp. 346, 351–2, 404, 440; 'Narrative of Bacon's Rebellion', *VMHB* 2 (1894), p. 173; *Journals*, vol. 2, p. 90; 'A True Narrative', pp. 140, 152; 'Surry County Grievances', *WMQ*, 1st ser., 2 (1893/1894), p. 172; 'Philip Ludwell's Account', pp. 180–2.

46. *VMHB* 5 (1897), p. 51; Washburn, *The Indian in America*, p. 129; *Governor and Rebel*, pp. 117–18, 136; Billings, Selby, Tate, *Colonial America*, p. 95; *Statutes*, vol. 2, pp. 346, 380, 440, 490–2; Morgan, *American Slavery*, p. 329.

47. As early as 1628, under the threat of punishment, the Privy Council instructed every settler in Virginia to provide himself with both defensive and offensive weapons within a year: *Acts of the Privy Council*, vol. 1, pp. 128–9.

48. Breen, 'Looking Out for Number One', pp. 108–9, 126.

3

Indians, Settlers, and Soldiers:
The War of 1812 and Southern Expansionism

Marie-Jeanne Rossignol

> ... a man who fled here and hid, concealed himself behind respectability, behind that hundred miles of land which he took from a tribe of ignorant Indians, nobody knows how.
>
> William Faulkner, *Absalom! Absalom!*

The War of 1812: A Forgotten Conflict?

A survey of the Humanities Index from 1986 to the present reveals limited recent publication on the War of 1812. In his 1991 assessment of the historiography of this war Reginald Horsman acknowledged that:

> in spite of the efforts of popularizers, the War of 1812 is probably more a blank to the general American public than most other aspects of the American past, and even among those with a general interest in history this war has never attracted the faithful buffs that have studied and restudied aspects of bloodier American wars.[1]

Assuming that 'the study of early American foreign relations has been in the doldrums for a generation', as William Earl Weeks wrote in a recent review article, the War of 1812 stands out as a particularly 'enigmatic conflict' whose most recent analyst, Donald R. Hickey, entitled his book *The War of 1812: A Forgotten Conflict*.[2] Why would this war be so unattractive to the American public and to professional historians? One reason may be that it had been covered too well by previous historians. William Earl Weeks emphasizes that Henry Adams and Samuel Flagg Bemis and their successors, such as Dexter Perkins and Bradford Perkins, had written extensively on the diplomacy of the early republic, including the War of 1812.[3] Another reason may be that most of the recent historical literature published on the War of 1812 is concerned with fields such as military history and with methods such as the search for causation that do not currently arouse great popular interest.

That new approaches and new methods might arouse fresh interest
in the War of 1812 is best exemplified by the success of Steven Watts's
*The Republic Reborn: War and the Making of Liberal America, 1790–
1820*.[4] Horsman's summary of the book highlights Watts's specific
approach:

> Although Watts writes of reasons for war in 1812, he is not really
> concerned with America's diplomatic problems or shifting historio-
> graphical explanations of the war. He is more interested in the ways
> in which the United States in the early nineteenth century was in
> the process of abandoning its eighteenth-century republican values
> and becoming a nation dedicated to individual, liberal capitalism.
> He argues that the War of 1812 played a key role in helping the
> liberalizing impulses.[5]

By linking up the War of 1812 to the larger and more topical
historiographical debates centering around the ideologies of republicanism and liberalism, Watts showed that it could be discussed outside
the confines of traditional diplomatic and military history. Although
The Republic Reborn relies mainly on the methods of cultural history, its
influence spread rapidly to other fields. By contrast, Hickey's narrative
of the War of 1812 largely duplicates, albeit with a number of
differences, earlier narratives such as those by Henry Adams and J.C.A.
Stagg. His work is crucified by Horsman as 'the Sisyphean labor of
constantly reappraising and rearranging the causes, or reexamining
the often less-than-dramatic military encounters'.[6] The traditional
approaches chosen by Hickey in *A Forgotten Conflict* are unlikely to
arouse new interest in the War of 1812.

However, it need no longer be a 'forgotten' conflict, the best histories
of which have already been written and can hardly be improved upon.
In the wake of Steven Watts's innovative efforts, the contention of this
paper is that the conflict does matter within the context of recent
historiographical preoccupations. In the words of Emily S. Rosenberg,
it can be seen as a 'power system' which requires to be examined from
'perspectives situated on the periphery'.[7] Indeed, the War of 1812 was
the last international conflict involving the United States and native
Americans as formal enemies. Native Americans, North and South,
took part in the war as autonomous entities, some openly siding with
the British in the Northwest, the Muskogees going it mainly alone in
the South. The Treaty of Ghent, which ended the war, was likewise
very special, in that native Americans were mentioned, and their title
to the land defined and protected. In fact, the native participation in
the Northwest was deemed so important by the British diplomats that
their main insistence during the peace negotiations was the creation of
an Indian border state.

Seen from the native Americans' 'periphery perspective', the War of 1812 is a turning-point in both the international and domestic history of the United States. Native Americans used the war as an attempt to challenge US power towards them and to reaffirm their identity in the face of local popular expansionism. This was particularly true in the South, where local armies defeated the Redsticks with the clear intention of appropriating their land and that of the neighboring Spaniards. The territorial gains made in the South over the Indians and the Spanish were also the only territorial gains which the USA retained at the end of the war. These territorial gains, and the military actions which led to them, were indicative of two long-term trends which should be seen as totally related: expansionism and slavery.

Land Policies and Expansion: Origins of Native American Involvement in the War

Anger had mounted among the Indian nations of the Northwest in the early 1800s as Governor William Henry Harrison wrought land cessions from them. Like the Iroquois who at about the same time underwent moral and religious regeneration, many Northwest Indians first found spiritual solace in the teachings of a religious leader known as the Prophet. Indian frustration with Harrison's actions and methods was also channeled by Tecumseh, the Prophet's brother and a Shawnee war leader, who declared void the treaties signed by individual chiefs with Harrison and called for attacks against settlers.[8] In the fall of 1811, Tecumseh departed for the South in search of more followers. Harrison used his absence as an opportunity to attack the Prophet's town, where Tecumseh's supporters from the Northwest had gathered. The battle, which took place on 7 November 1811, is sometimes described by historians as the start of the War of 1812, but it was 'hardly a resounding success' for the American troops.[9]

Tecumseh's message of resistance to land cessions found a very receptive audience in the South, where the Muskogees had recently ceded lands and were in danger of losing even more. The 1805 treaty between them and the American Republic 'had allowed the United States to construct and use a "horse path" across the heart of the nation', in fact a road which bolstered settlement in the region.[10] In September 1811, at the time of Tecumseh's visit, Benjamin Hawkins had informed the Creek National Council of the construction of yet another road in the area, thus overriding the Council's known opposition to the project.[11] Tecumseh's visit to Muskogee was followed by a series of earthquakes, which gave a cosmic dimension to the pan-Indian message he had tried to convey there.[12]

The Peculiar Case of Muskogee and of the South

In the early decades of the nineteenth century, southern settlers proved
all the more willing to dispossess native Americans as more lands were
now urgently needed in the South for cotton growing. The cotton-gin,
which was invented in 1791, had turned slaves into valuable capital
again, as the crop required numerous laborers. In order to reap full
profits from their investment in slaves, owners had to move westward,
away from the depleted soils of the Old South.[13] Settlers were thus
putting pressure on the Muskogees, and other southern Indian nations,
to cede their lands, which were the main obstacle to large-scale
migration into the Old Southwest. The land cessions which took place
at the end of the war (1814: Treaty of Fort Jackson; 1816: Cherokee/
Chickasaw/Choctaw land cessions, etc.) opened the floodgates of such
dense immigration in the area that Alabama and Mississippi both rose
to statehood as early as 1819 and 1817 respectively.[14]

Unlike the Northwest Indians, who rightly saw the acquisitive land
policies of Harrison as entirely antagonistic, the Muskogees must have
considered the pressures put on them to sell their lands as perplexing
and even paradoxical. Indeed, a number of them had proved willing to
embrace the white man's civilization as it was presented to them by the
Indian agent, Benjamin Hawkins. Hawkins's efforts had concentrated
on introducing Euro-American methods of agriculture and a more
centralized form of government in Muskogee.[15] In the furthering of
these aims, he was considerably helped by élite Muskogees, often Métis
leaders such as Alexander McGillivray, who had gradually moved to
European conceptions of family relations and property in the late
eighteenth century. 'In short', Joel Martin writes, 'they were pioneering
well before most Anglo-American pioneers arrived', and, we might
add, even before Benjamin Hawkins.[16] A federalist paper, the *Boston
Columbian Centinel*, eulogized their march towards progress in 1813,
opposing it to the supposed backwardness of land-hungry southern
pioneers:

> The lands of the Creeks are so pleasant and fertile that their neigh-
> bors, who are a shade or two less tawny in color, but who on the
> score of real civilization, have little to boast of, have been induced
> frequently to break the tenth commandment; and they have by one
> means or another treatied the Creeks out of a great part of their
> possessions. The incroachments on even their limits as fixed by our
> treaties of 1790 and 1796 are well-known ... The Indian 'savages'
> have no gazettes to trumpet their story – to point their wrongs, or to
> advocate justice in their behalf – and they must be extirpated and,
> without remorse the land of their fathers will be given to aliens ...

But candid men acquainted with the subject, do not hesitate to say, they are a people, under all their provocations *'more sinned against than sinning'*.[17]

However biased against southerners this text may have been, it underscores the dilemma facing Muskogees in 1811, before the War of 1812 started: they had complied with the federal demand for assimilation, to such an extent that their 1790s leader, Alexander McGillivray, had been buried in the European style.[18] Now, instead of being left in peace as their 'civilizing' efforts might have justified, they were increasingly pressured to sell their land and go. Benjamin Hawkins, who posed as the Creeks' protector, is even alleged to have suggested the removal of the Muskogees across the Mississippi.[19] No wonder this situation caused splits in the Muskogee community, which were best revealed by Tecumseh's visit and following events during the War of 1812.

Tribal Divisions and Civil War

The splits in the Muskogee community were along geographical, economic and cultural lines. Hawkins's supposedly 'civilizing' influence was always felt less in the upper towns along the Coosa and Talapoosa rivers than in the lower towns on the Chattahoochee and Flint rivers. In the upper towns, the Indians were more likely to suffer from the encroaching schemes of the people of Tennessee.[20] The rise to affluence of Americanized Métis planters in the late eighteenth century had also brought about nascent class divisions. These corresponded to an opposition between cultural traditionalists and assimilated mixed-bloods. When it appeared that the good relations between the Métis and the whites were not saving the community as a whole from destruction at the hands of settlers and of the federal government, they and their new values soon lost credibility. This stood out clearly as Tecumseh visited the upper towns of Muskogee in the fall of 1811: he 'reminded Muskogees of "the usurpation of their lands by the whites and painted in glowing colors their spirit of encroachment, and the consequent diminution, and probable extinction, of the race of Indians"', this as Hawkins was imposing the construction of the new road on passive town leaders.

In 1812, a small band of Muskogees chose to join Tecumseh in the Northwest, while a movement of spiritual regeneration and revolt, led by the shamans Josiah Francis (Hillis Hadjo), Cussetaw Haudjo and Paddy Walch, spread in the upper towns.[21] While in the Northwest, they took part in the 21 January 1813 River Raisin Massacre, a military débâcle in which the American army was defeated by the Indians and the English.[22] On their way back, they murdered several Tennessee pioneers, for which offense the Creek National Council was asked by Benjamin Hawkins to have the guilty Indians killed, around the end of March. The implementation of white sentences by the Indian leadership had precedents, and was considered by assimilationist chiefs as a way to retain tribal control over crimes committed by Indians against the white community, but this time the executions started a civil war in the nation.[23]

In the upper towns, the prophets led the killing of 'friendly' chiefs in retaliation, and soon those towns were in a state of insurgency, around 2,000 warriors arming themselves with red-painted war-clubs. As a result, the rebellion, which spread throughout the upper towns starting in May 1813, became known as the 'Redstick' rebellion.[24] By early July, accommodationist chiefs were being besieged by the insurgents at Tookabaubatchee, calling to Hawkins and the Georgia militia for help.[25]

A Civilization War

Most historians describe the Redstick rebellion as a civil war, which just happened to intersect with the events of the War of 1812.[26] This is in fact a highly debatable point. From the beginning the insurgents killed the friendly chiefs and harried them out of the upper towns because they had betrayed the Muskogee traditional values of liberty and sovereignty in exchange for the annuities and false promises offered by the whites. What the rebels were rejecting was not a particular type of leadership, or even the assimilationists as such; what they opposed was the unequal relationship with the federal government that these 'friendly' chiefs accepted and which was best embodied by the control exerted over them by Benjamin Hawkins.

Although they claimed that their real enemies were the 'friendly' chiefs and not the Euro-American settlers, there is evidence that the rebel Indians were now disgusted with everything that the white guests even touched. Being symbolic and spiritual, the rebellion involved many meaningful gestures, such as the rejection of implements of husbandry, the killing of their own livestock and the abandoning of their own fields by the insurgents. To accomplish their work of spiritual regeneration, the shamans had first to get rid of Hawkins's allies, but then they were bound to try and roll back European-Americans from their land, as Tecumseh, their inspirator, had advised all Indians to do. The Shawnee chief is alleged to have said to the Muskogees: 'Let the white race perish! ... They seize your land ... Back whence they came, back upon a trail of blood they must be driven! ... Burn their dwellings –

destroy their wives and children, that the very breed may perish.'[27] While Joel W. Martin maintains that the rebels were not intent on going to war with the United States, he has to admit that: '... a good number of the rebels understood that their actions were linked to a much greater drama that might or might not require them to attack Anglo-Americans. If Tecumseh succeeded in the North, then and only then would the Redsticks go on the offensive.' Actually, the Redsticks continued their fight even after Tecumseh had been defeated.

The opposition between accommodationists and traditionalists thus raised the issue of the future of the Southeast Indians: those who sided with the whites during the war believed in cooperation and assimilation, but the others did not.[28] The fact that the Redstick rebellion was not merely a civil war, but a civilization war, paradoxically explains why the Cherokees massively took part in the military engagements on the white side: at the time, traditionalists and accommodationists had just joined forces against the first attempts at removal and were intent on holding their ground in the region, even if that meant provisionally supporting southerners against other Indians.[29] They still believed in accommodation, if only for strategic reasons. This did not prevent individual Cherokees from harboring Redstick refugees.[30]

Southern Armies Crush Muskogee

This being a civilization war, it is no wonder that the insurgents now turned for material assistance to their other European neighbors, the Spanish, as they had done in previous centuries, always pitting one European power against another in an attempt to preserve their independence. Unlike the British, who were powerful and at war with the United States, the Spanish authorities at Pensacola had neither an incentive nor the means effectively to help the Indians. Therefore, when a band of insurgents visited them in July 1813 to ask for munitions, they gave them very few, maybe simply in order to placate them. As the Indians rode home, they were ambushed by a party of Métis and Americans at Burnt Corn, on 27 July 1813. On 30 August, the Redsticks attacked Fort Mims, killing at least 270 Anglo-Americans and Métis. The fort was not a military building, but a stockade hastily erected by settlers who were squatting illegally in the area. This marked the beginning of the war between the United States – in point of fact the southern states – and the rebel Muskogees. Although one does not have to agree with Martin that 'we can argue that many prominent planters feared that the Redsticks might not attack U.S. settlers', it is well-known that the southern planter élite wanted the lands of Muskogee.[31] The attack on Fort Mims provided the opportunity for this to happen.

By 20 September, Tennessee had mustered 2,500 men for the purpose of invading Muskogee. The state of Tennessee had been worried
about the influence of the Prophet and his followers even before the
civil war had started and before the Washington administration felt
that action was needed. After the attack on Fort Mims, the federal
government asked Tennessee to raise 1,500 men, but the state legislature was so keen on crushing the Muskogees that it suggested that
5,000 men should be sent.[32] The expeditionary force was led by Andrew
Jackson and included Sam Houston and Davy Crockett.[33] In November
it was joined by the Mississippi Territory's force of 2,500 in an invasion
of Muskogee. A Georgia army also took the field. All in all, about 8,000
regulars and militiamen pounced on 16,000 Muskogees (women, children, and elderly people included). The Americans largely outnumbered
the Indian warriors, who were mainly armed with bows and arrows,
clubs, tomahawks, and knives, whose towns were devastated and whose
ranks kept thinning as they met defeat upon defeat at the hands of the
Americans.[34] The final military encounter took place on 27 March
1814, during the battle of the Horseshoe Bend, during which the
Redsticks faced an army of 3,000 men led by Andrew Jackson in which
500 Cherokees and 100 friendly Muskogees were also to be found. At
least 800 Redsticks died.[35] The rebellion was over, but the new bastion
of anticolonial resistance now became Florida, where the surviving
rebels fled and were joined by black runaways.

Unfortunately for the Redsticks, British arms and ammunition only
reached the Gulf coast on 10 May 1814. British troops landed in
August, launching the Indians into several actions which finally caused
Andrew Jackson to destroy Pensacola, the capital of Spanish West
Florida.[36] Aimed at the British and their allies, the destruction of
Pensacola, however, was also a hostile act towards the Spanish, who
had not supported the Redsticks.[37]

The National Settlement

On 9 August 1814, Andrew Jackson forced all the tribal leaders to sign
the Treaty of Fort Jackson. Although the 'friendly' Indians had shown
their support of the Americans by continuously fighting alongside the
militia troops, their loyalty was ignored. One can hardly believe that
they could have promised as much land to the southerners as a reward
for their assistance during the civil war (Hawkins hinted at such a
proposal as early as November 1813).[38] In spite of their protests, the
Muskogees lost over half their territory.[39] The Treaty of Fort Jackson
was the realization of the worst dreams of the Redstick rebels.

John Armstrong, the Secretary of War, had originally appointed
Benjamin Hawkins and General Pinckney as peace commissioners,

with wide latitude as to the terms of the treaty. Southerners, and in particular those from Tennessee, viewed these two men as too lenient and unlikely to punish the Creeks as required. The outcry caused Armstrong, in full agreement with President Madison, to trust Jackson with drafting the peace treaty.[40] Even historians sympathetic to Jackson admit that in this instance the federal government gave over its responsibilities to a southern élite intent on getting rid of the Indians in the Gulf region. It was, after all, Jackson who said after the battle of the Horseshoe Bend:

> Their midnight flambeaux will no more illumine their Council houses, or shine upon the victims of their infernal orgies. They have disappeared from the face of the earth. In this place generations will arise who will know their duties. The weapons of warfare will be exchanged for the utensils of husbandry; and the wilderness which now withers with sterility ... will blossom as a rose, and become the nursery of the arts.[41]

Not only had the federal government given over its powers to the southwestern élite concerning their relationships with the Indians, but Andrew Jackson's treatment of the Muskogees initiated a shift in national policy, from assimilation through civilization to removal. The new policy was made clear by none other than Massachusetts-born John Quincy Adams during the peace negotiations at Ghent:

> [I said to the British commissioners that] the greater part of the Indians cannot be prevailed upon to adopt this mode of life [farming] ... It was impossible for such people ever to be said to have possessions. Their only right upon land was a right to use it as hunting grounds; and when those lands ... became necessary or convenient for the purposes of settlement, the system adopted by the United States was by amicable agreement with them to compensate them ... for removing to remoter regions ... To condemn vast regions of territory to perpetual barrenness and solitude, that a few hundred savages might find wild beasts to hunt upon it, was a species of game law that a nation descended from Britons would never endure ...[42]

The International Settlement

The consequences of the Fort Jackson Treaty might have been less drastic had the US government complied with Article IX of the Ghent Treaty, which ended the War of 1812. This article stated that the country should commit itself to restoring the Indians to the rights, privileges and possessions which had been theirs in 1811.[43] Two

questions must be answered. First, why did the British support their
Indian allies, when they had not done so at the end of the War of Independence, ignoring them in the 1783 peace treaty?[44] Second, why did
the Americans not comply with an article in an international treaty?

At the beginning of the negotiations, the British had asked for an
Indian buffer-state to be created between Canada and the Americans in
the Northwest. This ancient demand, which dated to the 1790s, was
rejected out of hand by John Quincy Adams. The British justified their
interest in the affairs of their former Indian allies by comparing them
with Portugal, a secondary power which Britain was also including in
her peace negotiations with other powers at the time. They insisted
that the Indians 'must be considered as independent nations', for the
US government itself 'made treaties with them and acknowledged
boundaries of their territories'.

In a despatch to Secretary of State James Monroe, John Quincy Adams
made very explicit the view that the US government took of the status
of Indian nations living within its borders: 'With respect to the Indian
allies, I remarked that there was no analogy between them and the case
of Portugal ... It resembled more the case of subjects who in case of
invasion took part with the invader ...'[45] In his answer to the British
commissioners, he gave an ironic twist to his denying even more
clearly any claim of Indian sovereignty the British might support. Had
not the British themselves set the example in the past by granting
Indian lands to British colonists without consulting the natives?

> If the United States had now asserted that the Indians within their
> boundaries ... were their subjects, living only at sufferance on their
> lands, far from being the first in making that assertion they would
> only have followed the example of the principles ... frequently
> avowed in express terms by the British government itself. What was
> the meaning of all the colonial charters granted by the British
> monarchs from that of Virginia ... to that of Georgia, if the Indians
> were the sovereigns and possessors of the lands bestowed by those
> charters? What was the meaning of that article in the Treaty of
> Utrecht, by which the Five Nations were described ... as subject to
> the dominion of G.B ...?[46]

In the same letter, Adams defined the Indians' sovereignty as that of
domestic dependent nations, thus anticipating Justice Marshall's 1831
decision:

> ... the Indians residing within the United States are so far inde-
> pendent that they live under their own customs and not under the
> laws of the United States; that their rights upon the lands ... are

secured to them by boundaries defined in amicable treaties between the United States themselves ... That they are so far dependent as not to have the right to dispose of their lands to any private persons, nor to any power other than the United States, and to be under their protection alone, and not under that of any power.[47]

Although Article IX did get into the final treaty, thus ensuring the Indians one feeble sign of internationally recognized full sovereignty, Adams was confident that it 'will have no important evil consequence ... as the relative strength both of English and Indians compared with the United States must diminish and dwindle to nothing in time of peace ...'[48] After the withdrawal of British troops in the spring of 1815 under the terms of the Treaty of Ghent, Major Edward Nicholls was left in Florida as an American Indian superintendent. At first he tried to impress on Hawkins the necessity of implementing Article IX. When he realized that his efforts were of no avail, he went back to England with Francis the Prophet in order to convince the British authorities that they should act. This was in vain.

Through Article IX, the British probably hoped to nettle the Americans, while clearing their own conscience with regard to their Indian allies. By not respecting the terms of the treaty, the Americans firmly established their sovereignty over Indian lands in the face of the world and removed native rights from international discussions concerning 'their' continent. This example was soon followed by other colonizing powers in other continents in the nineteenth century.

The Redstick War as Part of the Early American Expansionist Drive

Taking over Muskogee was just another stage in the development of early American expansionism. Though the Treaty of Ghent finally insisted on a territorial *status quo* with regard to acquisitions between Great Britain and the United States, Americans were paradoxically successful in gaining territory from the Spanish and the Muskogee during the war. As regards the former, this acquisition concerned Florida. In January and February 1813, the US Congress had debated whether it should authorize President Madison to seize the two Floridas, with the avowed purpose of preventing a British landing there. Finally a bill was passed authorizing the President simply to seize the Mobile area, west of the Perdido River. Northern congressmen opposed the section authorizing the seizure of East Florida, which thwarted Madison's plans, as American troops already occupied Amelia Island off the north-eastern coast of the territory – he had to remove them.[49] General Wilkinson occupied Mobile (West Florida) on 10 April 1813, thus effecting 'the only permanent gain of territory made during the war' over another European power.[50]

Needless to say, the Spanish never received any kind of indemnification for this territory seized from them in time of peace.[51] Mobile was just one more stage in the slow grabbing of the Floridas, which the federal government had been coveting ever since it was returned to Spain in 1783. From 1789 to 1793, Thomas Jefferson had threatened Spanish diplomats with the irresistible onslaught of American pioneers if they did not open the navigation of the Mississippi and sell Florida to the United States.[52] In 1803, France ceded Louisiana to the two American negotiators, whose mission originally was to secure New Orleans and the Floridas.[53] In 1810 a group of Anglo-American residents of West Florida seized Baton Rouge and asked that the territory be annexed to the United States. James Madison complied very willingly.[54]

These territorial conquests are usually given short shrift by specialists of the War of 1812. Expansionism during the war is traditionally associated with the military campaigns against Canada. However, the reason why the conquest of Canada was unsuccessful may have had less to do with territorial aggrandizement than with the effective enforcement of commercial retaliation. The War of 1812 started partly because other measures to influence Britain had failed. Among these other measures were repeated embargoes, which were supposed to prevent British goods from entering the US market and to deprive the British West Indies of their regular source of supply. Contraband between Canada and the United States thwarted this plan, as Canadian products replaced American ones in the West Indies. 'Madison believed', writes Stagg, 'that a Canadian war could compel Britain to respect the shipping rights of neutrals. An American victory in Canada would leave Britain little alternative but to accept American terms for trade if its ministry wished to preserve the remnants of its empire from further damage.'[55] Other reasons for the Canadian campaigns were fears on the part of the western states that the British could arm the Indians against them. The fact remains that the only conquest made during the war was in line with trends in early American expansion.

The final question is: was early American expansionism under the influence of southerners? Until the War of 1812 the direction had been both westward and southward. It had been led by southerners such as Thomas Jefferson and James Madison, with the enthusiastic support of most Americans. During the War of 1812 a North/South division became perceptible, especially concerning the invasion of East Florida, which was not eventually attempted. It was also perceptible in the fears of Madison, who wrote in the wake of the battle of the Horseshoe Bend: '... a part of the Union having a jealous eye on the particular interests they, Western states, take in Indian affairs'.[56] However, the only territorial gains made during the war resulted from military operations engineered by Tennessee, Georgia, and the Mississippi Territory. After 1815 the Southwest was one of the key areas of expansion. Maps showing the density of population in 1840 and 1850 clearly reveal that people moved to the South and West in larger numbers than to the Northwest, where Indian land title had been extinguished earlier.

Conclusion

A study of the events in Muskogee during the War of 1812 highlights a number of phenomena usually neglected in traditional historiography of the War of 1812. The Creek War was a turning point in American policy towards native Americans on the domestic level. It also enabled US officials to make it clear that they would never abide by the terms of an international treaty which defined the rights of 'their' native Americans. However much they might protest, the Muskogees and other so-called 'civilized tribes' were but 'domestic dependent nations' from that moment on. Finally, the war in the South proved mainly beneficial to expansionist southerners: they were able to start occupying the rich Gulf area and to gnaw at the remaining Spanish territories. These victories made southerners very confident. James Oakes reports the words of a proud southern expansionist on the eve of the Civil War: 'While the North has not extended her limits northward a single degree since the birth of the Constitution,' D. R. Hundley wrote in 1860, 'the South has already seized on Florida, Louisiana, and Texas, and her eagle eye is now burning with a desire to make a swoop on Cuba, Central America, and Mexico.'[57]

Notes

1. Reginald Horsman, 'The War of 1812 Revisited', *Diplomatic History* 15, 1 (1991), p.115.
2. William Earl Weeks, 'New Directions in Early American Foreign Relations', *Diplomatic History* 17, 1 (1993), pp.73, 88. However, Horsman notes an abundant Canadian historiography on the subject. Horsman, 'The War of 1812', pp.122–3. Donald R. Hickey, *The War of 1812: A Forgotten Conflict* (Urbana and Chicago, Ill.: 1989).
3. Weeks, 'New Directions', p.75.

4.   Steven Watts, *The Republic Reborn: War and the Making of Liberal America, 1790–1820* (Baltimore, Md.: 1987).

5.   Horsman, 'The War of 1812', p.119.

6.   Ibid., p.121.

7.   Ibid., p.94.

8.   Kevin Burnett, 'Tippecanoe and Taylor Too', *Journal of the West* (July 1992), pp.45–6; Richard White, *The Middle Ground: Indians, Empires, and Republics in the Great Lakes Region, 1650–1815* (Ithaca, NY: 1991), pp.513–15.

9.   Henry Adams, *History of the United States of America during the Administrations of James Madison* (New York: 1986), p.67; Reginald Horsman, *The Causes of the War of 1812* (New York: 1979), pp.186; 202; Burnett, 'Tippecanoe', p.46.

10.   Gregory Evans Dowd, *A Spirited Resistance: The North American Indian Struggle for Unity 1745–1815* (Baltimore, Md.: 1992), p.155.

11.   Ibid., p.156.

12.   I use the term 'Muskogee' instead of 'Creek', thus following Joel Martin's convincing explanation of the need to use 'Muskogee': 'In the seventeenth and eighteenth centuries, no Native Americans of the Southeast identified themselves as "Creeks". Rather, the name "Creeks" was originally applied by English traders to a certain group of native people living near an English post on a large creek … Throughout the eighteenth century the name was applied to more and more native groups … By the mid eighteenth century, "Creeks" had become the name the English applied to most native peoples living in what is now central Georgia or Alabama, an area of roughly ten thousand square miles … In a colonial context, the colonizer's power to make names stick is often linked to the practice of terror and violence. The name "Creeks" was not a neutral term but a colonial signification that concealed and rendered invisible a tremendous diversity of peoples and enabled Georgians to rationalize violence. For these reasons, using the term "Creeks" to denominate southeastern native peoples of the colonial period is problematic, especially in a history aiming to recover their sense of their own history', in Joel W. Martin, *Sacred Revolt: The Muskogees' Struggle for a New World* (Boston, Mass.: 1991), pp.7–8; see also pp.114–15.

13.   James Oakes, *The Ruling Race: A History of American Slaveholders* (New York: 1982). Oakes shows that the economy of slavery was indissociably connected with westward migration: 'Demographic mobility was so much a part of life in the slaveholding South that those who yearned for stability were often frustrated', p.87; 'What united small slaveholders with the sons of planters was the goal of purchasing land and slaves and moving west in pursuit of that goal', p.76.

14.   Thomas D. Clark and John D.W. Guice, *Frontiers in Conflict: The Old Southwest, 1795–1830* (Albuquerque, N. Mex.: 1989), p.162.

15.   J.C.A. Stagg, *Mr. Madison's War: Politics, Diplomacy, and Warfare in the Early American Republic 1783–1830* (Princeton, NJ: 1983), p.349.

16.   Martin, *Sacred Revolt*, p.103.

17.   *Boston Columbian Centinel*, 6 October 1813.

18. Martin, *Sacred Revolt*, p. 107.
19. Dowd, *A Spirited Resistance*, pp. 153–4.
20. Stagg, *Mr. Madison's War*, p. 349.
21. Martin, *Sacred Revolt*, pp. 107–8, 121, 126.
22. The massacre was during the battle and after. 'Nearly a hundred Kentuckians fell almost side by side, and were scalped … That night the Indians, drunk with whiskey and mad with their grievances and losses, returned to Frenchtown and massacred the wounded', in Adams, *History of the United States*, pp. 685–6.
23. Hickey, *The War of 1812*, p. 147.
24. Martin, *Sacred Revolt*, p. 129.
25. Ibid., p. 130.
26. This is the case with Martin, whose contention is that the rebellion might have remained a civil war had not the settlers violently provoked the Indians, ibid., p. 150: 'Frontier settlers in Tennessee, Georgia, and Mississipi, interceding at a critical juncture, violently provoked the Redsticks. They forcibly and perhaps intentionally transformed the civil war between Redsticks and friendly Muskogees into a confrontation between the Redsticks and the United States.' See also Hickey, *The War of 1812*, p. 147. Dowd disagrees, stating positively (Dowd, *A Spirited Resistance*, p. 190) that: 'None of the borderland peoples examined in this work entered the war in a spirit of internal unity, and none of them fought the war in order to settle old debts with traditional enemies. Tribal identity had little to do with the war.'
27. Quoted by Clark and Guice, *Frontiers in Conflict*, p. 124.
28. Martin, *Sacred Revolt*, pp. 134, 142–3, 152. White, *The Middle Ground*, p. 518.
29. *Boston Columbian Centinel*, 18 December 1813: 'Tennessee, Knoxville, November 29, 1813. The Creeks again defeated. We are informed that on the 12th inst. Gen White, with 800 mounted whites and 300 Cherokee Indians, proceeded to attack the Hillabee towns … The Cherokees acted with promptitude and bravery …'; Dowd, *A Spirited Resistance*, p. 164.
30. Dowd, *A Spirited Resistance*, p. 158.
31. Martin, *Sacred Revolt*, p. 153.
32. Stagg, *Mr. Madison's War*, pp. 355, 362.
33. Hickey, *The War of 1812*, p. 148.
34. Martin, *Sacred Revolt*, pp. 159–61; Clark and Guice, *Frontiers in Conflict*, p. 146; Stagg, *Mr. Madison's War*, p. 355.
35. Martin, *Sacred Revolt*, p. 162.
36. Dowd, *A Spirited Resistance*, p. 188.
37. James W. Covington, *The Seminoles of Florida* (Florida, 1993), p. 34.
38. *British Columbian Centinel*, 15 December 1813: 'Colonel Hawkins, the U.S. agent at the Creek nation, writes thus: Cree agency, Nov 17. Gen – with the army of Georgia, is here; they are anxious to go against the Red Clubs, as the hostile Indians are determined … We consider all who have not fled to the Lower Towns to be Red Clubs; but all the Lower chiefs are friendly. They have offered their Alabama lands to pay us for assistance. The subject will be discussed and settled after peace.'

39. Dowd registers the complaints of the Indians: Dowd, *A Spirited Resistance*, p.190.
40. James Madison, *The Writings of James Madison*, ed. Gaillard Hunt , vol. VIII (New York: 1908): to George W. Campbell, Montpelier, 25 May 1814: 'I shall then be able to speak with you also on the subject of Gen. Jackson and the Treaty with the Creeks. It will be a patter of regret, if either the State of Tennessee, or that distinguished officer, should be finally dissatisfied', pp.278–9.
41. Andrew Jackson, 'Proclamation, Fort Williams', 2 April 1814, in John Spencer Bassett (ed.), *The Correspondence of Andrew Jackson* (Washington, DC: 1926–33), p.1; in Clark and Guice, *Frontiers in Conflict*, pp.146, 149.
42. John Quincy Adams, *The Writings of John Quincy Adams*, ed. Worthington Chauncey Ford, vol. V, 1814–16 (New York: 1915): to the Secretary of State, no. 139, Ghent, 5 September 1814, pp.115–16. Similar ideas had been voiced in the past by John Quincy Adams, but they were not yet official policy; see Marie-Jeanne Rossignol, *Le Ferment nationaliste: aux origines de la politique extérieure des Etats-Unis 1789–1812* (Paris: 1994), p.282.
43. Mr de Martens, *Nouveau Recueil des Traités*, Tome IV, 1814–15 (Gottingue: 1818), pp.83–4: Traité de paix et d'amitié entre SMB et les Etats-Unis d'Amérique, signé à Gand, le 24 décembre 1814.
44. Elise Marienstras, 'Les Réprouvés de la révolution: nations indiennes et guerre d'indépendance', in *Les Oubliés de la Révolution américaine* (Nancy: 1990), p.41.
45. John Quincy Adams, *Writings*: to the Secretary of State, no. 139, Ghent, 5 September 1814, pp.112, 114–15.
46. Ibid.: answer to the British Commissioners, 9 September 1814, p.126.
47. Ibid.: answer, p.128. This is the answer Justice Marshall gave in 1831 to the question 'Do the Cherokees constitute a foreign state in the sense of the constitution?': 'Though the Indians are acknowledged to have un unquestionable … right to the lands they occupy … yet it may well be doubted whether those tribes which reside within the acknowledged boundaries of the United States can … be denominated foreign nations. They may, more correctly, perhaps be denominated domestic dependent nations.' *The Cherokee Nation v. The State of Georgia*, 1831, in Nelcya Delanoë and Joëlle Rostkowski, *Les Indiens dans l'histoire américaine* (Nancy: 1991), pp.73–5.
48. John Quincy Adams, *Writings*: to Louisa Catherine Adams, Ghent, 20 January 1815, p.271.
49. Henry Adams, *History of the United States*, pp.765–7.
50. Ibid., p.770.
51. Though the Spanish can hardly be portrayed as victims of American expansion, there were simply too few of them to stir up trouble on the western frontier, as Clark and Guice suggest. Clark and Guice, *Frontiers in Conflict*, p.257.
52. Rossignol, *Le Ferment nationaliste*, pp.153–5.
53. Ibid., p.247.

54. I. J. Cox, in 'The American Intervention in West Florida', *American Historical Review* XVII, no. 2 (1912), pp. 290–311, reveals the close collaboration of the Madison administration with the insurgents.
55. Stagg, *Mr. Madison's War*, p. 47.
56. Madison, *The Writings of James Madison*, pp. 278–9.
57. Oakes, *The Ruling Race*, p. 149.

4

Olive Branch and Sword:
Union War-making in the American Civil War

Brooks D. Simpson

In the last fifteen years the study of the American Civil War has enjoyed a renaissance in American historical scholarly circles. However, this renewed interest has had little to do with new understandings of the broad questions of national policy and strategic thought, especially on the part of Union leadership.[1] Rather, the thesis that the war evolved into a total conflict waged in modern ways has remained largely intact, although subject to debates over semantics and terms. First advanced by American military historians after World War II, most ably in T. Harry Williams's *Lincoln and His Generals* (1952), it soon became the accepted way of viewing the Union war effort. Recently Mark Neely challenged this characterization, arguing that the American Civil War was not a total war because Union commanders did not treat all southern whites as combatants.[2] This argument was more clever than profound. None of the historians Neely targeted employed the term 'total war' as he had defined it; other scholars had already pointed out how Union generals approached the issue of civilian behavior. Thus, there was something of the straw man (and an ahistorical one at that) in Neely's insistence that because Union commanders did not wage war as defined by twentieth-century theorists of total war, the American Civil War was nothing more than a traditional Victorian-era military conflict – a problematic claim in itself.

Moreover, Neely's argument shared with its target an emphasis on *how* the Union fought the war, thus narrowing the scope of scholarly inquiry and discussion. It has been left to those scholars who explore the role of slavery and emancipation, states rights and centralization, or other issues to discuss *why* the war was fought. The result has been the bifurcation of inquiry into the political world of the why and the military world of the how, distorting our understanding of the war by divorcing means from ends – a fundamental error, and one all the more surprising in light of American military historians' fascination with the writings of the Prussian military theorist Carl von Clausewitz. As students of Clausewitz have noted, the Prussian is more often cited than read, let alone understood. Scholars of the American Civil War are quick to cite him as the father of the concept of total war – an incomplete and misleading reading of Clausewitz's masterpiece, *On War*. In their rush to celebrate him as prophet, they pass over one of his primary maxims – that war is the conduct of policy through military means. All conflicts, Clausewitz argued, needed to be assessed according to this axiom. The relationship between why one fights a war and how it is fought offers a way to comprehend how civil and military leaders sought an appropriate method to wage war which took into account both the context in which the war was waged and what they sought to achieve through armed conflict.[3]

Studies of the Union war effort could benefit from reference to the above framework. At present the prevailing interpretation of how the Union went about winning the war features two interrelated transformations: the escalation of the conflict from a limited to a total one, and the adoption of emancipation as a war aim. During the first year of the war, Union civil and military leaders strove to limit the conflict. One way to do this was by repudiating emancipation as a war aim, although it soon became apparent that some slaves would gain their freedom (or at least lose their masters) as a result of the war. Notions of limited conflict began to fade with the bloody battle of Shiloh; the Union's failure to exploit its victory there, together with George McClellan's retreat from the outskirts of Richmond, moved Congress and the Lincoln administration to consider broader measures of emancipation, culminating in the Second Confiscation Act, the Emancipation Proclamation, and the eventual enlistment of blacks. Grant's rise to overall command in March 1864 marked the comprehensive implementation of a total war strategy, featuring Grant's war of attrition against Robert E. Lee in Virginia and William T. Sherman's marches through Georgia and the Carolinas.

This summary is not so much an incorrect representation of Union policy as it is an incomplete one. It rests upon the notion that the defeat of the Confederacy depended upon an all-out war against southern society, resulting in its near destruction. Yet this is not quite what happened, as an examination of Union efforts to bring the Confederacy to a negotiated surrender highlight. Rather, Union policy from beginning to end aimed to destroy both the ability and the will of the Confederacy to persist in a struggle for independence. These were two interrelated but distinct resources: a nation at war must possess both to wage war successfully. What changed over time was the relationship between various means of achieving the ultimate objective of reunion. At times the scope and intensity of the Union war effort escalated; at other times Union leaders, both civil and military, displayed a willingness to extend the olive branch when it would achieve their ends. It is not accurate to portray Union policy as moving in unidirectional fashion, from espousing a limited to a total conflict, from reconstruction of the

Union to the reconstruction of the South. Indeed, Appomattox, while it ended Confederate hopes for independence, did not mark the end of the struggle: the terms for reunion were worked out during the postwar period.

From the outbreak of hostilities in April 1861 Union military planning sought military victory through the erosion of Confederate will. The Anaconda Plan offered by Winfield Scott in 1861 embodied one approach. Scott called for the encirclement of the Confederate heartland through a blockade and the seizure of the Mississippi River. This done, he proposed to wait until Confederate will cracked as loyalty to the Union revived. Contrary to the assertions of later historians, Union grand strategy in the end was not simply the working out of this plan – for Grant and Sherman did not sit and wait for the Confederacy to crack. It was also a rather poor plan for retaining the Union public's enthusiasm for the war, as it called for a prolonged, patient strategy rather than the search for the climactic battle that captured the popular imagination. Indeed, the public in both the Union and the Confederacy continued to measure military fortunes by the rather traditional measures of capturing the enemy's capital or a prominent city and winning 'the big battle' – which explains in part the continuing fascination with Gettysburg.

George McClellan, known as 'the young Napoleon', shared this desire for 'the big battle'. His experience as an observer in the Crimean War did nothing to shake him of that notion, although it undoubtedly reinforced in his mind the human cost of such a clash. Believing as he did that wars were won or lost in such battles, he wanted to make sure that at all events he did not lose – and thus proved too cautious, too concerned, and ultimately too afraid of his foe. But there was more to McClellan's search for the climactic battle than simple vanity or illusions of greatness. It was grounded in a larger approach to waging war, which stressed limiting the conflict to the battlefield proper. 'I regard the civil or political question as inseparable from the military, in this contest', he observed.[4]

Shortly after McClellan became General-in-Chief in the fall of 1861 he outlined his policy to his commanders in the West, Don Carlos Buell and Henry W. Halleck. Kentuckians, he informed Buell, 'may rely upon it that their domestic institutions will in no manner be interfered with, and that they will receive at out hands every Constitutional protection'. It was, after all, a war for reunion, not of revolution. Several days later he added that Buell should instruct his men to 'be careful so to treat the unarmed inhabitants as to contract, not widen, the breach existing between us & the rebels'. There were to be no arrests or other harassment; such behavior would persuade the Kentuckians 'that their property, their comfort, and their personal safety will be

best preserved by adhering to the cause of the Union'. To Halleck went
the reminder 'that we are fighting solely for the integrity of the Union'.[5]

McClellan continued to adhere to the same principles throughout
the conflict, warning Lincoln in July 1862 that to escalate the war and
broaden its objectives beyond reunion was to jeopardize whatever
chance there was for a quick and lasting peace based upon true reconciliation. 'Neither confiscation of property, political execution of persons,
territorial organization of states, or forcible abolition of slavery should
be contemplated for a moment', he declared.[6] McClellan elaborated
on this argument elsewhere, arguing that 'our efforts should be directed
towards crushing the armed masses of the rebels, not against the
people; but that the latter should, as far as military necessities permit,
be protected in their constitutional, civil, and personal rights'. He
deplored 'any policy which tends to render impossible the reconstruction of the Union', adding that escalation would 'make this contest
simply a useless effusion of blood'.[7] Several days later he reminded his
men in a general order 'that we are not engaged in a war of rapine,
revenge, or subjugation; that this is not a contest against populations,
but against armed forces and political organizations'.[8]

In making this argument, McClellan demonstrated an awareness of
the relationship between the conduct of military operations and overall
policy goals. But in the end his vision could not overcome several
considerations. First, the Union commander underestimated the persistence and depth of Confederate will – although he was not alone in this
regard. Second, even had McClellan secured the victory he sought, the
peace that would have followed would have kept slavery – which was
somehow at the root of sectional division – intact. At best, a Union
victory on such terms would have postponed settlement of this issue; at
worst, it would have led to an unstable peace, perhaps another war. As
Ulysses S. Grant later observed: 'it became patent to my mind early in
the rebellion that the North & South could never live at peace with
each other except as one nation, and that without slavery. As anxious as
I am to see peace reestablished I would not therefore be willing to see
any settlement until this question is forever settled.'[9] Finally, in order
for McClellan to secure the peace he sought, he would have to triumph
on the battlefield, winning that climactic victory. This proved beyond
his capability as a commander. Although Little Mac has his defenders,
they have been unable to suggest how their hero would have eventually
overcome his hesitancy and procrastination to achieve victory. For if
ever a Union commander had a chance to wipe Robert E. Lee's army
of northern Virginia off the board, it was McClellan on 16, 17 and 18
September 1862, on the fields and farms surrounding Sharpsburg, Maryland. That he failed to do so suggests that he never could have gained
the military triumph that was essential to keep the war a limited one.[10]

There had been a time when Lincoln would have nodded his head in agreement with McClellan on the need to keep the war a limited one. As he had told one Kentuckian, he wished to suppress the insurrection confronting him 'with the least possible disturbance, or annoyance to well-disposed people anywhere'.[11] He refused to mandate emancipation as a war goal, aware that it might tip the precarious balance in several Union slave states, erode the strength of Unionist sentiment in the Confederacy, and intensify and broaden support for the Confederacy within its borders. Through July 1862 he advocated a policy of gradual, compensated, and voluntary emancipation followed by support for the colonization of freed blacks, while countermanding the proclamations of military commanders that mandated emancipation.[12] In adopting this strategy, Lincoln hoped to woo Confederates back into the Union, cultivate the loyalty of the border states, and revive Unionist sentiment in the South – which he believed was the true sentiment of the majority of white southerners in the Confederate states. But by the summer of 1862 it was becoming apparent that the assumptions that underlay this approach were false ones. Both the Confederate military and Confederate civilians proved more persistent than anticipated: Union gains in West Tennessee, New Orleans, and the Atlantic coast were offset by McClellan's failure to capture Richmond. Southern Unionism proved frail and hesitant where it did appear, and in most cases it did not appear. It was time to reassess how to wage the war, and to reconsider slavery as an appropriate target of the Union war effort. Even as McClellan warned Lincoln of the consequences of escalation and emancipation, the President began to contemplate taking such steps, while Congress debated legislation to confiscate secessionists' property, including slaves.

It is worth remembering that the preliminary Emancipation Proclamation, issued by Lincoln on 22 September 1862, was also a document of reconstruction, giving southern whites 100 days in which to come back in the Union before emancipation took effect. During that period, Lincoln worked hard to organize congressional elections in occupied areas with precisely that aim in mind; where he saw progress or unavoidable delays, as in Tennessee, he proved willing to exempt those areas from the final proclamation, reaffirming its character as a war measure, while refusing to alienate southern Unionists.

Much the same perspective applies to Lincoln's efforts to erect wartime Reconstruction governments. Lost in the continuing debate over what such governments meant for the future of the freedmen in the postwar South was the fact that their mere existence was to serve as a rallying point for disaffected Confederates as well as local Unionists. Lincoln moved on many fronts in his capacity as Commander-in-Chief, seeking various ways to weaken the Confederacy and woo back

southern whites. On 4 March 1865 he delivered his most eloquent
statement of the need for reconciliation in his second inaugural.
Instead of gloating over the triumph of Union forces, Lincoln merely
noted the present situation as he moved on to discuss why the war
came and the best way to end it. 'With malice toward none; with charity
for all', Lincoln called upon Northerners 'to bind up the nation's
wounds' in endeavoring for 'a just, and a lasting peace'.[13]

Indeed, Lincoln had already explored several options for peace. As
1865 began he watched as Francis P. Blair, sen., journeyed to Richmond in pursuit of a peace settlement. Blair's mission proved a failure,
and its notion of an armistice followed by a joint invasion of Mexico
did not comport with the President's ideas about how best to resolve
the conflict. But at least it demonstrated that Lincoln was willing to
maintain open lines of communication with Jefferson Davis. Soon this
connection would be tested. In February 1865, Lincoln and Secretary
of State William H. Seward traveled to Hampton Roads, Virginia, to
meet with three Confederate representatives – Vice-President Alexander
H. Stephens, Robert M. T. Hunter, and John A. Campbell – to talk
over peace terms. The conference proved fruitless; nevertheless, upon
returning, Lincoln for the last time discussed compensated emancipation, only to find his cabinet opposed. He did so in the spirit of his
instructions to military commanders in West Tennessee, when he
reminded them that 'the object of the war' was to 'restore and maintain
the blessings of peace and good government'.[14] It had been the stub-
bornness of the Confederate commissioners on this point that had
doomed the meeting from its inception.

Yet Lincoln continued to make clear his willingness for a lenient
peace. At the end of March he conferred with Grant and Sherman
aboard the *River Queen*, anchored off Grant's headquarters at City
Point, Virginia, and shared his thoughts with them. Even after the fall
of Richmond, the President pondered his options. As Grant pursued
Lee across south central Virginia, Lincoln was still willing to negotiate
the terms of a peaceful settlement based upon the preconditions of
reunion and emancipation – as he told John A. Campbell, who was
trying to discover some way to end Virginia's participation in the Confederacy. He added that he was willing to remit confiscated property
(other than slaves) to owners (unless it had passed into the hands of
a third party) in states which withdrew from the Confederacy.[15] This
effort proved abortive, for Lee's surrender effectually withdrew Virginia
from the war, while Campbell misinterpreted Lincoln's proposal as
recognizing the legitimacy of the present state legislature.

Lincoln was not the only Union leader who had reassessed his
approach to waging a war for reunion in the summer of 1862. Advocates of a harder war cheered a series of orders issued by General John

Pope, which promised a tougher stance toward hostile civilians and guerrillas in Virginia. Other Union generals who had once urged restraint also reconsidered their position in light of circumstances. Among them was Ulysses S. Grant. At the outset of the conflict Grant believed that the war would be of 'short duration' in which the Confederates would abandon the struggle after Union armies gained 'a few decisive victories'.[16] He constantly impressed on his men that it was of the utmost importance that they did not interfere with slavery or harass civilians. To commit any such acts would only intensify and broaden Confederate support by convincing civilians that the Union army was bent on abolition and subjugation. In Missouri he discovered that his insistence upon discipline had paid off. 'When we first came there was a terrible state of fear existing among the people', he told his wife. 'They thought that every horror known in the whole catalogue of disa[sters] following a state of war was going to be their portion at once.' Well-disciplined and well-mannered soldiers created a different impression: civilians 'find that all troops are not the desperate characters they took them for', despite some incidents of misbehavior. As his men returned from an expedition, they passed once more by local residences. This time, however, people came out to greet them. Grant felt vindicated: 'I am fully convinced that if orderly troops could be marched through this country, and none others, it would create a very different state of feeling from what exists now.'[17] Nevertheless, Grant worried that many civilians in Missouri leaned towards the Confederacy. 'You can't convince them but what the ultimate object is to extinguish, by force, slavery', he observed. Grant's efforts to explain otherwise met with little success.[18] 'They are great fools in this section of [the] country and will never rest until they bring upon themselves all the horrors of war in its worst form', he concluded. 'The people are inclined to carry on a guerilla Warfare that must eventuate in retaliation and when it does commence it will be hard to control.'[19] Such a war would complicate the process of reconciliation and the restoration of the Union. What kind of war would be waged depended in large part on whether Confederate civilians blurred the distinction between combatant and non-combatant.

In September 1861, Grant responded to news of the Confederate invasion of Kentucky by moving to seize the strategically located town of Paducah. The operation proved an easy one; pacifying Paducah's residents might prove more of a challenge, especially in light of Kentucky's wavering position between the Union and the Confederacy. Grant met it by issuing a proclamation: 'I have come among you, not as an enemy, but as your friend and fellow-citizen, not to injure or annoy you, but to respect the rights, and to defend and enforce the rights of all loyal citizens', he began. 'I have nothing to do with opinions. I shall

deal only with armed rebellion and its aiders and abetors.' He elaborated
in the instructions that he left to the commander of the occupation
force in the town: 'You are charged to take special care and precaution
that no harm is done to inoffensive citizens ... Exercise the strictest
discipline against any soldier who shall insult citizens, or engage in
plundering private property.'[20]

Grant also complied with directives prohibiting the Union army
from protecting black fugitives who sought refuge from their owners.
He knew that to embrace emancipation at this early date would erode
support for the Union among many residents of the border states,
while it would escalate the intensity of Confederate resistance. He
wanted 'to visit as lightly as possible, the rigors of a state of war upon
noncombatants'. Such reasoning also guided his marching orders for a
January 1862 expedition. Soldiers should not take it upon themselves
to interpret and execute the confiscation legislation passed by Congress,
for the resulting behavior 'makes open and armed enemies of many
who, from opposite treatment would become friends or at worse non-
combatants'.[21] Yet Grant was also willing during these early months of
the war to take sterner measures when appropriate. When Confederate
civilians fired into a troop train, Grant scoured the countryside to find
them. 'The party in pursuit will subsist off of the community through
which they pass', he informed headquarters, although he added that
foraging parties would follow strict rules. Although he opposed
'indiscriminate plundering', he authorized local commanders to hold
secessionist citizens hostage and to take all property used to assist
Confederate forces. Other orders provided for the confiscation of the
printing press and type of a local secessionist newspaper, and the seizure
of bank deposits. 'Give secessionists to understand what to expect if it
becomes necessary to visit them again', he instructed his subordinates.[22]
Grant calibrated the attitude of his command toward civilians in response
to their behavior, especially when they came close to becoming combatants themselves. When Confederate civilians fired on Union soldiers,
Grant moved quickly to quash such behavior, once going so far as to
establish the Civil War equivalent of a free-fire zone.[23]

Although Grant would later remark that it was the battle of Shiloh
that caused him to revise his notions of a short and limited conflict, his
contemporary correspondence reveals that his true change of heart
occurred afterwards, when he encountered the frustration of attempting
to pacify the population of West Tennessee. The refusal of civilians to
respond to his efforts to revive Unionist loyalty led him to adopt
harsher measures. He cracked down on secessionist newspapers and
countered guerrilla activities by levying assessments on the property
of Confederate civilians – arguing that many of these people were
civilians by day and guerrillas by night. Later he ordered the expulsion

of secessionist families from areas of guerrilla activity. He also enforced confiscation legislation and freed (or recognized as already free) black slaves.[24]

These measures reflected new beliefs about waging war. As General-in-Chief Henry Halleck observed in March 1863: 'The character of the war has very much changed within the past year. There is now no possible hope of reconciliation with the rebels ... There can be no peace but that which is enforced by the sword. We must conquer the rebels, or be conquered by them.'[25] Grant struck at slavery with a vengeance, supporting the enrollment of black soldiers. Yet he also looked for other ways to erode support for the Confederacy. One of the reasons he decided to parole the Confederates who had been captured at Vicksburg was to allow them to spread their sense of defeat and disillusion as they made their way home. He encouraged white Mississippians who sought to re-establish a Unionist regime, ordering Sherman to make sure that Union soldiers cultivated that sentiment by their behavior.[26] When the activities of Confederate civilians threatened to get out of hand, however, Grant moved decisively in response, and at times overlooked the very distinctions that elsewhere he drew with much care. The promise of guerrilla warfare proved especially irritating to him, blurring as it did the distinction between combatant and non-combatant. In 1864 Grant revealed his anger in responding to reports about the activities of John Singleton Mosby and his band of partisan rangers. Unwilling to recognize 'Mosby's men' as an official component of the Confederate army, Grant ordered Philip H. Sheridan to send a cavalry division through Loudoun County, Virginia, 'to destroy and carry off the corps, animals, negroes, and all men under fifty years of age capable of bearing arms'. He argued that such people 'can fairly be held as prisoners of war and not as citizen prisoners. If not already soldiers they will be made so the moment the rebel army gets hold of them'. Nor was this all. Grant also authorized Sheridan to seize the families of Mosby's men and hold them 'as hostages for good conduct of Mosby and his men. When any of them are caught with nothing to designate what they are hang them without trial.'[27]

Mark Neely observes that it was Grant who was breaking down distinctions between combatant and non-combatant, but in fact Grant was responding to the behavior of Confederate civilians which eroded such boundaries.[28] Indeed, as Neely himself relates, within days Grant modified his orders when he was informed of the number of white southerners in Loudoun County who were not Confederate sympathizers.[29] The incident revealed that Grant was willing to distinguish between Unionist and Confederate as well as between combatant and non-combatant. He knew that the goal of the war was to reunite the country by destroying the Confederacy, not the South. How to do so depended on circumstances, for there were different ways to take aim at armies, material resources, and morale. The means might differ, but the goal remained the same, and Grant thought carefully about the relationship between means, ends, and circumstances; he was also careful to distinguish between 'the Confederacy' and 'the South', as might well be expected from a man who once himself owned a slave and was married to a slaveholding southerner.

Grant's sense of the interplay between olive branch and sword, however, was most evident in the aftermath of the 1864 presidential contest. Lincoln's re-election virtually assured Union military victory: whether the Confederacy would be able to prolong the conflict by adopting new approaches to waging war – most notably through guerrilla operations – remained unclear. In addressing this problem, Grant revealed his determination to destroy the Confederate will to resist, as well as its ability to do so. Sometimes the two were explicitly linked: Confederate desertion rates skyrocketed, weakening Lee's army while demonstrating that a growing number of soldiers thought their cause was already a lost one. Grant approved Sherman's plan to march through the Confederate interior to encourage desertion as well as to demoralize Confederate civilians; he had already approved plans to encourage desertion by flooding enemy lines with an offer of a safe passage home or employment for deserters. He lent his support to Unionist supporters in Alabama, explored the possibility of securing a separate peace agreement in Texas, and did much to bring about the encounter between Lincoln and a trio of Confederate commissioners at Hampton Roads.[30]

It was in the final campaign against Lee, however, where Grant's understanding of the relationship between military means and political ends was most vividly demonstrated. For months Grant had pinned Lee against Richmond and Petersburg, knowing full well that desertion was a far less bloody way of reducing the strength of his opponent. With the arrival of spring, however, the Union commander feared that Lee would abandon his entrenchments and march westward, either to link up with other armies in North Carolina or to reach the Blue Ridge Mountains, where he could wage a nasty guerrilla war. This time, victory would not elude Grant. Lee's army, as its commander noticed, did not move with 'the boldness and decision' that once characterized it, in large part because of the disillusion of the men and letters from home encouraging them to desert. In contrast, Grant's columns first cut off Lee's line of retreat to North Carolina, then blocked its path to the mountains. Grant called for Lee's surrender; Lee, realizing that his army could no longer serve the cause of Confederate independence, submitted.[31] When the two opposing commanders met in the parlor of Wilmer McLean's farmhouse that Palm Sunday afternoon, Grant demonstrated that he knew how to make peace as well as he knew how to wage war. The terms he offered Lee – no formal surrender of officers' swords, men and officers to keep their animals, and, most importantly, a parole of prisoners that protected them from US authorities so long as they observed the terms of the parole – formed a cornerstone of peace and reunion by avoiding humiliation, lending a helping hand, and cutting short any attempt to try Confederate military leaders, including Lee, from being tried on charges of treason. When Union soldiers celebrated the news, Grant quelled their enthusiasm, remarking: 'The war is over. The Rebels are our countrymen again.'[32]

Grant's actions during the war reveal him to be not a total warrior, but a general who comprehended the nature of the conflict in which he was engaged. He calibrated his conduct of operations according to circumstances: the result reflected the degree to which issues of civil and military policy were intertwined in the Union war effort. As Clausewitz himself put it, at the highest levels 'strategy and policy coalesce: the commander-in-chief is simultaneously a statesman'.[33] Grant was not alone in possessing this understanding of war. If any Civil War military leader is identified with the concept of total war it is William T. Sherman. The general's blunt and frank appraisal of armed conflict – 'War is hell' – provides many historians with a point of departure for describing the Union war efforts in terms of escalation toward totality. Thus, biographers of the fiery redhead describe their subject as a 'merchant of terror' whose methods of waging war foreshadowed what would happen in Vietnam, making free use of Sherman's own extravagant and extreme statements to paint a portrait of a total warrior bent upon destruction. A more dispassionate examination, however, reveals that Sherman's approach to waging war offered variations on the themes sounded by Grant.

Sherman believed that what the Confederacy lacked in terms of military resources it more than made up for in unity, persistence, and a commitment to victory. Moreover, Union military conquests and battlefield triumphs might capture strategic points and erode Confederate military manpower, but in themselves they did not inflict sufficient damage on civilian will and determination. He dismissed southern Unionists as of no account because of their refusal to make themselves felt; he mocked talk of a limited war rooted in a desire to reconcile the foe, although he did not embrace emancipation. 'As to changing the opinions of the People of the South that is impossible, and they must be killed or dispossessed', he told his father-in-law. 'We have finished the first page of this war in vainly seeking a union sentiment in the South, and our Politicians have substantially committed suicide by mistaking the Extent and power of the Southern People & its Government, and are about Entering on a Second period.'[34]

Sherman feared that in this second period 'the war will soon assume a turn to extermination, not of soldiers alone, that is the least part of the trouble, but the People'.[35]

Nor did Sherman care much for Grant's concern about the impact of the behavior of Union soldiers upon civilian loyalties. Whatever the merits of such an approach in theory, he argued, it was too hard to exert sufficient discipline upon volunteer soldiers. Volunteer regiments 'are composed of good men, good farmers & mechanics, but men not accustomed to restraint, who do pretty much as they please', he observed. 'They commit acts of trespass & violence along the Roads and convert Union men into Enemies', failing to pacify the population.[36] During the Vicksburg campaign, Sherman, who would later use Grant's cross-country march as a model for his own advances through Georgia and the Carolinas, expressed shock at what he saw: 'Of course devastation marked the whole path of the army, and I know all the principal officers detest the infamous practice as much as I do', he told his wife, adding: 'this universal burning and wanton destruction of private property is not justifiable in war'.[37] But he accepted it as inevitable, and dismissed notions that one could distinguish between friend and foe in such operations.[38]

If, according to Sherman, it was impossible to implement a policy that discriminated between friend and foe, it was unwise to observe traditional notions that distinguished between combatants and non-combatants, for to do so was to miss the real reason for Confederate persistence: the durability of public support for the war effort. 'The Government of the United States may now safely proceed on the proper Rule that all in the South are Enemies of all in the North', he informed Salmon P. Chase, the secretary of the treasury, in the summer of 1862; 'and not only are they unfriendly, but all who can procure arms now bear them as organized Regiments or as Guerillas'.[39] Union armies had to strike at Confederates by eradicating the distinction that many drew between battle front and home front, soldier and civilian, until the entire enemy 'are not only ruined, exhausted, but humbled in pride and spirit'.[40] He often expressed the thought that the only way to achieve a lasting peace would be to 'repopulate' the South: fighting on their home soil, Confederates 'have an advantage that we cannot overcome without a complete destruction of all the inhabitants'.[41] But the picture of Sherman that emerges from such remarks – a relentless warrior who embraced destructive war as both unavoidable and necessary – requires modification, lest we mistake it for a complete understanding of the man. His assessment of the southern people was grounded in a firm respect for them. While white southerners continued to support the Confederacy he would show them no quarter: but whenever Sherman saw signs of reviving loyalty, he was willing to foster the process. After Vicksburg's surrender he reported that 'subdued' white Mississippians wished to return to the Union: 'I profess to know nothing of politics but I think we have here an admirable wedge which may be encouraged', he told Grant, adding that the news 'will have a powerful effect over the South'.[42]

These themes resurfaced in Sherman's mind in the aftermath of the capture of Atlanta. 'War is cruelty, and you cannot refine it', he told the town's mayor; 'those who brought war into our Country deserve all the curses and maledictions a people can pour out'. However, all that would end once the southern people abandoned the Confederacy:

> Once admit the Union, once more acknowledge the Authority of the National Government, and ... I & this army become at once your protectors & supporters, shielding you from danger let it come from what quarter it may ... I want peace, and believe it can now only be reached through union and war, and I will ever conduct war partly with a view to perfect & early success.[43]

Coming just ten days after the fall of Atlanta, this was an impressive statement. Sherman was willing to go even further. Georgia Unionist Joshua Hill contacted the Union commander about the possibility that Governor Joseph E. Brown might be willing to withdraw his state from the Confederacy in exchange for some considerations. Sherman jumped at the chance to achieve the restoration of the authority of the United States through negotiated means. He promised that, if Brown came to terms, 'I will keep our men to the high roads and commons, and pay for the corn and meat we need and take'. It would be, he believed, 'a magnificent stroke of policy, if I could without wasting a foot of ground or of principle arouse the latent enmity to Jeff Davis, of Georgia'.[44] Grant welcomed the idea, believing that 'it will be the end of rebellion, or so nearly so that the rebelling will be by one portion of the South against the other'.[45] Only when the scheme fell through did Sherman begin planning for what would become known as the March to the Sea. He aimed a blow at the enemy's soul by striking at its heartland, demonstrating that the Confederacy could no longer protect its people. Sherman's purpose, as aide Henry Hitchcock noted, was to 'produce among the people of Georgia a thorough conviction of the personal misery which attends war and of the utter helplessness and inability of their rulers to protect them'. Sherman concurred, noting, 'We are not only fighting armies, but a hostile people, and must make old and young, rich and poor, feel the hard hand of war, as well as their organized armies.'[46] Such a struggle went beyond the battlefield. 'This may not be war, but rather Statesmanship', Sherman explained; in fact, it demonstrated rather clearly the interrelationship between the two.[47]

Sherman's marches accomplished their designer's intentions. The destruction wrought by his soldiers was real enough: it was magnified in the Confederate mind even as it was augmented by the behavior of Confederate cavalrymen, escaped slaves, Union deserters, and others who added to the chaos and destruction. The general reveled in the terror he struck in the heart of white southerners, telling women that 'their sons & brothers had better stay at home to take care of the females instead of running about the country playing soldiers'.[48] Many of the women apparently heeded his advice. 'My march through Georgia and South Carolina, besides its specific fruits actually produced a marked Effect on Lee's Army, because fathers & sons in his Ranks felt a natural Solicitude about children or relations in the regions through which I had passed with such relentless Effect', Sherman remarked on 9 April, unaware that, as he wrote, Grant was accepting Lee's surrender.[49] Nevertheless, Sherman's interest in wooing Confederates back to the Union also increased during the last five months of the war. Although the popular image of the March to the Sea is one of fire, plunder, and destruction, Savannah, the terminal point of that march, was spared the same fate – largely because its residents submitted without much protest. Sherman, detecting 'a decidedly hostile spirit to the Confederate Cause' among the people, reported that 'with a little judicious handling and by a little respect being paid to their prejudices, we can create a schism in Jeff Davis' dominions'.[50]

If Sherman's men treated South Carolina with especial severity, they exercised more restraint when they entered North Carolina, for Sherman wanted to cultivate Unionist sentiment in that state. He also sought to contain the conflict. Petrified by what might happen should Confederate soldiers become guerrillas, he did what he could to prevent such an occurrence during his negotiations with Confederate commander Joseph E. Johnston at Durham's Station in April 1865: 'There is great danger that the Confederate armies will dissolve and fill the land with robbers and assassins', he argued.[51] He told Grant that 'the point to which I attach most importance is that the dispersion and disbandment of these armies is done in such a manner as to prevent their breaking up into guerrilla bands'.[52] In fact, the initial surrender agreement proved so lenient that it was rejected by the authorities at Washington, and Grant travelled down to North Carolina to supervise the signing of a second agreement modeled on the Appomattox terms. Nevertheless, the man most closely identified with the notion of total war sought to limit the nature of the Civil War.[53]

This brief examination of how the Union's President and three of its most prominent generals waged war is meant to be suggestive rather than definitive. Nevertheless, it should raise questions about the validity of traditional assertions that the American Civil War became a total war as well as the more recent claim that it was a traditional Victorian-era military conflict. Both arguments focus on the how rather than the why of waging war, making the mistake of divorcing the two concerns. A better understanding of how the Union waged civil war begins with the reintegration of the whys with the hows in the spirit of Clausewitz. Such a perspective will remind us of the dynamic and fluid nature of making war, as civil and military leaders calibrated and recalibrated their approaches in accordance with circumstances, while keeping in mind the overall objective of the conflict.

At the close of the war, Sherman noted 'how intermingled have become civil matters with the military, and how almost impossible it has become for an officer in authority to act a purely military part'.[54] It would be wise for historians of the Union military effort to keep that in mind. For the Union waged war with olive branch as well as sword always in hand, seeking a more perfect peace. Whether it achieved that aim – and whether other ways of waging war could have improved on the result – remains a subject worthy of future inquiry.

Notes

1.   A few titles must be excepted from this characterization: Herman Hatta-way and Archer Jones, *How the North Won: A Military History of the Civil War* (Urbana, Ill.: 1983); Richard E. Beringer, Herman Hattaway, Archer Jones, and William N. Still, *Why the South Lost the Civil War* (Athens, Ga.: 1986); and Archer Jones, *Civil War Command and Strategy* (New York: 1992).

2.   Mark E. Neely, jun., 'Was the Civil War a Total War?', *Civil War History* 37 (March 1991), pp. 5–28.

3.   Carl von Clausewitz, *On War*, translated and edited by Michael Howard and Peter Paret (Princeton, NJ: 1976), pp. 87–8.

4.   George B. McClellan to Henry W. Halleck, 1 August 1862, in Stephen W. Sears (ed.), *The Civil War Papers of George B. McClellan* (New York: 1989), p. 382.

5.   McClellan to Don Carlos Buell, 7 and 12 November 1861, and McClellan to Henry W. Halleck, 11 November 1861, ibid., pp. 125, 130, 132.

6.   McClellan to Abraham Lincoln, 7 July 1862, ibid., pp. 344–5.

7.   McClellan to Henry W. Halleck, 1 August 1862, ibid., p. 381.

8.   General Orders No. 154, Army of the Potomac, 9 August 1862, *Official Records of the War of the Rebellion* (Washington, DC: 1880–1901), series 1, XI, part 3, pp. 362–4.

9.   Ulysses S. Grant to Elihu B. Washburne, 30 August 1863, in John Y. Simon *et al.* (eds), *The Papers of Ulysses S. Grant* (Carbondale, Ill.: 1967), vol. 9, pp. 217–18.

10.   Three essays that explore the escalation of conflict in 1862 are Brooks D. Simpson, '"The Doom of Slavery": Ulysses S. Grant, War Aims, and

Emancipation', *Civil War History* 36 (March 1990), pp.35–56; Daniel E. Sutherland, 'Abraham Lincoln, John Pope, and the Origin of Total War', *Journal of Military History* 56 (October 1992), pp.567–86; and Mark Grimsley, 'Conciliation and its Failure, 1861–1862', *Civil War History* 39 (December 1993), pp.317–35.

11. Abraham Lincoln to Simon B. Buckner, 10 July 1861, in Don E. Fehrenbacher (ed.), *Abraham Lincoln: Speeches and Writings* (New York: 1989), vol. 2, p.262.
12. Lincoln to John C. Frémont, 2 and 11 September 1861, ibid., vol. 2, pp.266–8; Proclamation of 19 May 1862, ibid., vol. 2, pp.318–19; First Annual Message, 3 December 1861, ibid., vol. 2, p.292.
13. Lincoln, Second Inaugural Address, 4 March 1865, *Speeches and Writings*, vol. 2, pp.686–7.
14. Lincoln to West Tennessee Commanders, 13 February 1865, in Roy A. Basler (ed.), *The Collected Works of Abraham Lincoln* (New Brunswick, NJ: 1953–5), vol. 8, p.294.
15. Lincoln to John A. Campbell, 5 April 1865, ibid., vol. 8, pp.386–7.
16. See Brooks D. Simpson, *Let us Have Peace: Ulysses S. Grant and the Politics of War and Reconstruction, 1861–1861* (Chapel Hill, NC: 1991), pp.10–13.
17. Grant to Julia Dent Grant, 19 July 1861, *Papers of Grant*, vol. 2, pp.72–3.
18. Grant to Jesse Root Grant, 3 August 1861, ibid., vol. 2, pp.80–1.
19. Grant to Julia Dent Grant, 3 August 1861, ibid., vol. 2, p.83. See Michael Fellman, *Inside War: The Guerrilla Conflict in Missouri during the American Civil War* (New York: 1989), for the fulfillment of Grant's prediction.
20. Proclamation to the Citizens of Paducah, 6 September 1861, *Papers of Grant*, vol. 2, p.194; Grant to Eleazer A. Paine, 6 September 1861, ibid., vol. 2, p.195.
21. Grant to Jesse Root Grant, 27 November 1861, ibid., vol. 3, pp.226–7; Grant to CSA MG Leonidas Polk, 5 December 1861, ibid., vol. 3, p.259; General Orders No. 3, District of Cairo, 13 January 1862, ibid., vol. 4, p.45.
22. Grant to CPT Speed Butler, 22 and 23 August 1861, ibid., vol. 2, pp. 128, 135–6; Grant to CPT R. Chitwood, [25 August 1861], ibid., vol. 2, p.136; Grant to COL William H. Worthington, 26 August 1861, ibid., vol. 2, pp.139–40. Mark Neely offers a somewhat different discussion in *The Fate of Liberty: Abraham Lincoln and Civil Liberties* (New York: 1991), pp.33–4.
23. Simpson, *Let us Have Peace*, pp.13–23.
24. Ibid., pp.23–30.
25. Henry W. Halleck to Ulysses S. Grant, 30 March 1863, *Papers of Grant*, vol. 8, pp.93–4.
26. Simpson, *Let us Have Peace*, pp.35–50.
27. Grant to Philip H. Sheridan, 15 August 1864, Ulysses S. Grant Papers, Library of Congress.
28. Neely, *The Fate of Liberty*, p.81.
29. Ibid., pp.82–3.
30. Ibid., pp.68–75; William S. and Mary Drake McFeely (eds), *Ulysses S. Grant: Memoirs and Selected Letters* (New York: 1990), p.1198.

31.   Simpson, *Let us Have Peace*, pp. 75–83.

32.   Ibid., pp. 84–5.

33.   Clausewitz, *On War*, p. 111.

34.   William T. Sherman to Thomas Ewing, sen., 10 August 1862, Files of the William T. Sherman Project, Arizona State University.

35.   Sherman to Ellen Ewing Sherman, 31 July 1862, Sherman Family Papers, University of Notre Dame.

36.   Sherman to John Sherman, 8 January 1862, Sherman Papers, Library of Congress.

37.   Sherman to Ellen Ewing Sherman, 6 May 1863, Sherman Family Papers, University of Notre Dame.

38.   Sherman to Ethan Allan Hitchcock, 25 January 1863, Record Group 94, Adjutant General's Office, Generals' Papers (Sherman), National Archives.

39.   Sherman to Salmon P. Chase, 11 August 1862, Salmon P. Chase Papers, Library of Congress.

40.   Sherman to David Tod, 12 March 1863, Record Group 94, Office of the Adjutant General, Generals' Papers, National Archives.

41.   Sherman to Thomas Ewing, Sen., 24 December 1861, Thomas Ewing and Family Papers, Library of Congress.

42.   Sherman to Ulysses S. Grant, 21 July 1863, *Papers of Grant*, vol. 9, p. 90.

43.   Sherman to James Calhoun *et al.*, 12 September 1864, Miscellaneous Manuscripts, Houghton Library, Harvard University.

44.   Sherman to Abraham Lincoln, 17 September 1864, Robert Todd Lincoln Collection of Abraham Lincoln Papers, Library of Congress.

45.   Grant to Julia Dent Grant, 30 September 1864, *Papers of Grant*, vol. 12, pp. 250–1.

46.   Lloyd Lewis, *Sherman: Fighting Prophet* (New York: 1932), pp. 452, 468.

47.   Sherman to Ulysses S. Grant, 6 November 1864, *Papers of Grant*, vol. 12, pp. 373–5.

48.   Sherman to Ellen Ewing Sherman, 12 March 1865, Sherman Family Papers, University of Notre Dame.

49.   Sherman to Philemon B. Ewing, 9 April 1865, Sherman Files, Arizona State University.

50.   Sherman to Edwin M. Stanton, 19 January 1865, Stanton Papers, Library of Congress; Sherman to Ulysses S. Grant, 29 January 1865, Philadelphia Free Library, Pennsylvania.

51.   Sherman to Joseph D. Webster, 17 April 1865, Huntington Library, San Marino, California.

52.   Sherman to Ulysses S. Grant, 18 April 1865, *Papers of Grant*, vol. 14, pp. 419–20.

53.   Sherman to Ulysses S. Grant, 18 April 1865, Record Group 94, Papers of the Adjutant General's Office, National Archives.

54.   Simpson, *Let us Have Peace*, p. 254.

5

The War for the Union as a Just War

Peter J. Parish

During the late 1970s and early 1980s, discussion of the theory of the just war enjoyed something of a revival – certainly in the United States and Britain – in works by Michael Walzer, James Turner Johnson, Geoffrey Best, and William V. O'Brien, among others.[1] No doubt the moral dilemmas raised by nuclear weapons and the looming threat of nuclear war had much to do with this debate – and so too did the Vietnam War. More recently, the Gulf War inspired a brief revival of the debate, and the Catholic bishops in both Britain and the United States issued statements which questioned the deployment of massive allied forces in that conflict.

The theory of the just war has a long history, all the way from Augustine through Aquinas, right down to our own times. The medieval theologians and canon lawyers drew an important distinction between the *jus ad bellum* (the permissible recourse to war) and the *jus in bello* (the just conduct of war), although the two are intimately and necessarily connected. The scale of a conflict and the methods pursued in waging it obviously have to be seen in relation to the scope and importance of the issues at stake. Aquinas emphasized that the presumption must always be against war; the taking of life was justified only in exceptional circumstances. His basic criteria for the justification of the resort to war may be summarized in a few basic propositions. First, there must be a competent authority to order war for a public purpose. Second, there must be a just cause – normally self-defense, but possibly also protection of rights by offensive war. Third, all peaceable solutions must have been exhausted. Fourth, the means used must be appropriate to the end. Fifth, there must be right intention on the part of the belligerent – that is, to restrain evil and assist good. The belligerent is restricted to pursuit of the avowed good cause, and the ultimate object must always be a just and lasting peace.[2]

Despite the enormous changes in warfare through the ages, and the vastly greater destructiveness of modern war, the legacy of Aquinas lives on. The statement of the Catholic bishops of England and Wales at the time of the Gulf War has much in common with his basic principles. The bishops' statement defines three basic requirements for a just war. First, every opportunity must have been taken to resolve the crisis by economic and diplomatic means. Second, even if the cause were just, and all the alternatives had been tried, resort to war would only be justified if there were a real prospect of achieving the just objectives. Third, the physical and political damage caused by the war must not be out of all proportion to the injustice which such action seeks to correct or prevent.[3]

However, the nature and the destructiveness of modern war have changed the way in which the basic principles are to be applied, even if they have not undermined the principles themselves. Governments and peoples have had to adjust to new circumstances and new techniques of war-making, and to seek some new understanding of the proportionality of means and ends in armed conflict. This is where the American Civil War enters the story, for it surely marked a key stage in the translation of old-established ideas about the just war into the context of modern society and modern warfare. Indeed, James Turner Johnson suggests that, because the characteristics both of modern war and of modern attempts to limit war were already visible in that conflict, 'what we discover here should provide a prism through which to view the wars of the twentieth century'.[4] The pivotal role of the American Civil War manifested itself in a number of ways. First, it raised the question of the applicability of notions of a just war to a revolutionary or civil war situation. Earlier commentators had acknowledged the right of revolution, but there was a reluctance to extend the *jus ad bellum* to a revolutionary struggle. However, it was conceded that an organized revolutionary government, capable of sustaining conflict for a reasonable time, might be regarded as a competent authority to wage war. As this question relates more to the justification of Confederate belligerency, it is not the main concern of the present discussion of the justification of the war to save the Union. It will suffice to say that the Richmond government would seem to have satisfied these criteria. Second, the Civil War introduced the large-scale use of new and more destructive weapons of war and methods of waging war. The rifled musket, the explosive shell, the ironclad warship, all backed by the railroad and by expanding industrial production, escalated the costs and enlarged the scale of war. In the space of four years, the scope and character of warfare were transformed. New questions were raised, or could have been raised, about the proportionality of means to ends in the conduct of war. Third, this was a war of peoples, of mass popular participation and involvement, and requiring mass popular support. In short, this was the first major war waged by, or indeed in, a modern democratic society – 'democratic' at least in the sense of having something like universal manhood suffrage, along with a high degree of literacy, and of political awareness and participation. In the context of the debate over the just war, this is probably the most important and interesting point of all. The need to justify war to a much larger and wider public stimulated changes, probably in the nature of the arguments used and certainly in the method and style of their presentation.

The main contention of this essay is that, in the process of presenting the case for a just war at the bar of this broader public opinion, there was a significant shift of emphasis in the grounds on which engagement in war was justified. That change was from an initial emphasis on the justice of a defensive war embarked upon out of sheer necessity, to the later, more ambitious, interpretation of the conflict as an opportunity for national atonement, purification and regeneration. The transition is from self-defense born out of sheer necessity, to a great crusade born out of God-given opportunity. Because the Civil War was the first major conflict of the era of liberal democracy, where public opinion was crucially important, it may have helped to set a pattern discernible in more recent wars involving the United States in particular, and western democracies in general.

At the moment of entry into a war, and in its early stages, participation is justified, whether in secular or religious terms, on grounds of sheer necessity or inevitability. The people at large have to be persuaded that fundamental interests, perhaps national survival itself, are at stake. However, as a war proceeds, and the casualties and the costs mount, to fight solely in defense of one's interests seems inadequate, unworthy, even sordid. The justification of the war seeks out some higher ground – a moral crusade, a national rebirth, a spiritual revival, a new world order. In short, democracies need to convert wars into crusades. The American Civil War offers an early case study of this process. For example, a young Pennsylvania soldier, writing home in 1863, expressed his apprehension that fighting for mere political unity would appear selfish, and would not be understood by the world at large. The addition of 'the magic word freedom' would raise the cause to an altogether different and higher level.[5]

The Civil War is also a fascinating example of the interaction between the need to cope with the escalation of a war and its rising costs, and the psychological and moral need to transform or transcend what was originally a fight in self-defense. Soaring costs, in terms of bloodshed, suffering and depletion of resources, demand some higher justification for the conflict – and, in turn, that higher justification legitimates or even sanctifies the greater costs. There is a kind of ratchet effect at work, based upon a calculus of suffering and its justification. Raymond Aron suggested that, in the world wars of the twentieth century, exaggerated ends had to be devised in order to justify the far-reaching effects of the means adopted.[6] But, surely, there is a two-way, reciprocal process; more drastic means stimulate more ambitious ends, which in turn justify further escalation of the conflict.

The main substance of this essay is based upon an analysis of the religious arguments deployed at the time in support of the war for the Union as a just war – and on some examination of the parallels between religious and political justifications of the conflict. Such an emphasis on the arguments advanced by Protestant churchmen of various denominations can be justified on a number of counts. It serves as a reminder of the intensely and profoundly Protestant character of mid-nineteenth-century American society. Furthermore, the arguments are normally presented in a clear-cut, undiluted manner, free from some of the self-serving and calculation of political rhetoric. However, it is also true that there are striking similarities between the arguments used by churchmen on the one hand, and by politicians and other secular commentators on the other.

It would be an over-simplification to say that the northern Protestant denominations were in effect the Republican party at prayer – although there were times when they looked and sounded remarkably like it.[7] In other words, this is more than a matter of coincidence or parallel; it is a matter of interconnection and interaction, and also of mutual reinforcement. One may take the remarkable example of Methodist Bishop Matthew Simpson, who became a confidant of Lincoln himself, and who officiated at his burial in 1865. Simpson harbored no doubts about the God-given mission of the United States, and was determined to fit the Civil War somehow into the divine plan. 'If the world is to be raised to its proper place,' he declared, 'I would say it with all reverence, God cannot do without America.' Simpson's wartime fame derived from his 'war speech' – a patriotic address for which he could command a large fee, and which he delivered in most of the larger cities of the North. The speech went through several versions. It included some actual, as well as a good deal of metaphorical flag-waving; its dominant themes were trust in providence, the value of sacrifice, and confident expectation that God would ensure the salvation of the Union because he needed America in order to fulfil his plans for the world. Simpson claimed to be above party, but it is hardly coincidence, for example, that he delivered a supercharged version of his war speech to a huge audience in New York City three days before voting in the presidential election of 1864.[8]

American churchmen were better able to cope with the question of God's role in the historical process because of the millennial framework within which their ideas were cast. The great majority of Protestant churchmen at this time were post-millennialists, rather than pre-millennialists; that is to say, the prevailing belief was that the second coming would happen after a thousand years of progress and preparation

– and not that the second coming would itself usher in the millennium. Post-millennialists also believed that the thousand years of preparation might be heralded by a great catastrophe – and it took no great leap of the imagination to cast the Civil War in that role. Such beliefs left some room for individual choice and the individual will. They offered a vision of an ideal society towards which people might strive, and in the realization of which the war for the Union might have a part. In the apt phrase of James H. Moorhead, 'post-millennialism was the moral government of God stretched out on the frame of time'. Such a view chimed in quite well with the arguments of secular believers in America's mission to the world who, in their own ways, needed to understand and to justify the war in terms of its place in the fulfillment of the national destiny.[9]

The secession crisis and the outbreak of war in the spring of 1861 provoked much debate among both religious and secular commentators about the *jus ad bellum*, the permissible recourse to war (although it was seldom expressed precisely in that language). Certainly, whatever their earlier hesitations and reservations about the use of force against the seceded states, most ministers of religion, like most other northerners, rallied to the flag with great fervor, as soon as the first shots were fired in Charleston harbor. They showed little of that revulsion against the use of force which is expected of clergymen in our own time. Indeed, they often seemed to lead, rather than to follow, the first surge of patriotic support for the war to save the Union. The Revd W. W. Patton, of the First Congregational Church in Chicago, stated in the first days of the war that 'the present struggle is one in which every Christian may rise from his knees and shoulder his rifle'. The Methodist Bishop Ames asserted that, if required to fight himself, he would shoot fast, and he would 'fire into them most benevolently'. The Revd A. L. Stone, of Park Street Congregational Church in Boston, praised a fellow minister who had joined the army and who, after shooting his enemies, intended to address them from afar: 'My poor fellow, God have mercy on your soul.' 'That is the way to fight', cried Stone. 'It is mercy to go strong and strike hard … This is the message of the Law of Love.'[10]

Clearly, Lincoln's determination that, if a first shot was going to be fired, it was going to be fired by the other side, paid a handsome dividend, and smoothed the way for early justifications of the conflict as a defensive struggle. Lincoln's message to Congress on 4 July 1861 consists largely of an elaborate justification of the North's essentially defensive response to what had become an inescapable, and potentially mortal, challenge. (In many respects, it was a masterly work of fiction, but it served its purpose.) The Crittenden–Johnson Resolutions, passed by huge majorities in both houses of Congress later in July, embraced a limited and strictly defensive view of the war for the Union.[11] Phillip

Paludan has argued persuasively that secession and the violent challenge which followed from it aroused such strong reactions in the North because they were widely perceived as a fundamental threat to law and order.[12] Evidence from both secular and religious sources bears this out. In an 1861 essay, James Russell Lowell declared that 'the doctrine of the right of secession ... is simply mob-rule under a plausible name'. And again, 'rebellion smells no sweeter because it is called secession, nor does order lose its divine precedence in human affairs because a knave may nickname it coercion. Secession means chaos, and coercion the exercise of legitimate authority'.[13] In a discussion of the meaning of loyalty, A. L. Peabody, professor of Christian morals at Harvard, began by saying that 'our Constitution claims our allegiance because it is law and order'. In the course of a somewhat ambiguous discussion of the concept of defensive war, he goes on to present an argument which precisely parallels the dominant Republican view of the constitutional basis of the struggle to save the Union:

> But if any over-scrupulous moralists demur at the present conflict as bearing the unChristian title of war, we would reply that, on the part of the United States, while it has the form, it has none of the essential characteristics of a war. It is the self-defence of government against anarchy. It is a grand police movement for the suppression of multi-tudinous crime, and is to be justified on the same principles, and no other, on which our civil authorities employ force in apprehending burglars or murderers, at the risk of their lives if they make violent resistance.[14]

This is a concise statement of a double-barreled justification of the resort to arms in order to save the Union. The war was not really a war, but a police action on a large scale; but, if it was a war after all, it was a struggle purely in self-defense.

Amid all this high excitement, a few churchmen found time to look at the broader grounds upon which a Christian might support a war – and this war in particular. Several commentators challenged the pacifist notion that war was inherently sinful, and took exception to the peace movement's attempt to appropriate the desire for peace as something which was exclusively theirs. An article in the Unitarian journal, *The Christian Examiner*, drew attention to the spread during the nineteenth century of the idea that war 'is not only a moral but an historical archaism, and that the profession of arms can no longer be justified'. Every right-minded man ought to sympathize with the desire for peace, but there were distinctions to be made: 'There is a living, and there is a dead peace; the one obtaining place where justice prevails, the other where it is not even held precious ... the former indicates the highest health of nations, the latter their leprosy and lowest debasement ...' Later, the same author makes his point more starkly:

> Love and terror, these are the two powers which uphold civilization. It avails not to say, 'If love enough abounded, fear could be dispensed with.' It were as wise to say, 'If we dwelt in the moon,' – and thereupon assume that we do dwell in the moon. Terror in the service of love holds the world together; and no sooner are its sharp ministries withdrawn than human society is dissolved, and chaos come.[15]

Various commentators used Old Testament and more recent historical examples to support the argument that, for all its horrors, war had been the instrument of human progress – that it was indeed God's agency for such progress. One Congregational minister, S. W. S. Dutton, dwelt on the moral advantages of a righteous war, despite the fearful strains that it imposed upon society: 'Such a war is not the greatest of evils; it will even bring great benefits, if we keep up this vital moral tone. Yet it heals by wounding – by using the caustic. Its efficacy is like that of the ploughshare to the turf-bound earth; or rather like that of the surgeon's knife to the dissected body.' Only if the body politic was morally sound could the surgery of war do its healing work.[16]

Early in the war, James M. Sturtevant, president of Illinois College, voiced his hope that the fighting would cure America of a 'morbid philanthropy' which taught that even a defensive war was criminal. To seek to extinguish the evils of war by a pledge not to take up arms was, he thought, about as effective as the attempt to banish the vice of drunkenness by persuading individuals to pledge themselves never to take an intoxicating drink. Americans should be, not shocked, but inspired by the belligerence of many of the great figures of the Old Testament. The age of true peace would not come:

> till men shall have so learned in the school of hard and bloody national experience the relations of retributive justice and penalty to all order, to all freedom, and to all government, that they can enjoy long peace and freedom without reproaching as bloodthirsty cutthroats, those ancestors by whose bravery and prowess on the field of battle these blessings were purchased.[17]

A rather more thoughtful and subtle discussion of the justification of war in general, and this war in particular, came not from one of the mainstream Protestant denominations, but in an article in the *Universalist Quarterly* in 1861. The author recalls that, until the war came, he had thought war incompatible with the teachings of the Sermon on the Mount. He had not been active in the non-resistance movement, but had lived with the potential conflict between his disapproval of war and his support of a government which rested ultimately on force, in much the same way as he managed to live from day to day with the doctrine of free will and necessity. Now the war had swept metaphysical discussion to one side, and demanded immediate practical answers. Unless the Christian faith was to fail him in his hour of need, there must be a way of combining loyalty to the government with loyalty to 'the captain of our salvation'. What did it mean to be opposed to war? Surely everyone opposed war for its own sake. When a nation's rights and existence were threatened, there were two fundamental questions: are there alternative means of protection apart from war? and, if not, is it the Christian duty of the nation to sacrifice itself? If the answer to both questions was no, the decision to fight was justified.

Government was ordained by God, the article continued, and all government rested on force. The real question, therefore, was not whether a government could wage war, but whether a people had a right to government. War could be reconciled with the overall spirit of loving one's enemies. In the American crisis, a Christian soldier was a better soldier, and could pray to God that his 'fearful missiles' would find their mark. The justification of war depended on the justice of the cause. Examples from history – the English martyrs, the Revolutionary heroes, Calvary itself – showed that there were interests more precious than life, which justified the sacrifice of life. The example of Christ himself had also established one of the cardinal principles of Christianity – that the innocent must suffer for the guilty. Having made the negative point that war was not forbidden, the author concluded on a strong positive note. Permission to act became in certain circumstances the command to act, and killing one's enemies was not justified as a right or a privilege, but as a duty. America's free institutions were a legacy in trust from God, and the Christian had the duty to defend them on behalf of generations yet to come: 'In such a contingency, we cannot be Christians unless we fight.' In that sense, this was indeed God's war.[18]

Once the general principle of the justice of defensive war had been established, it was not difficult to justify this specific struggle for the Union as a defensive war. Southern hot-headedness during the crisis of 1860–1 proved an invaluable ally to those anxious to make this case, and more than one northern religious paper hinted that its attitude might have been different if the South had pleaded patiently for a peaceful, negotiated separation rather than launched itself into a shooting match.[19] In February 1861, the conservative Presbyterian newspaper, the *Observer*, begged both North and South to heed sober second thoughts, and then, if they really felt that they could no longer live together, to part in peace. For the sake of the Prince of Peace, they should not dabble the banner of their common Christianity and country in fraternal blood. However, as soon as the war came, the *Observer* came out staunchly in support of a defensive war of patriotism and self-preservation. In this, it faithfully reflected a whole mass of hitherto uncertain opinion.

With the *Observer*, as with all those who justified a defensive war, the question inevitably arises: defense of what? The immediate answer, shared by all, was defense of the Union; but, beyond that point, there was a significant division between two schools of thought. The more conservative view, typified by the *Observer*, was that defense of the Union was defense of duly (that is to say, divinely) constituted authority. Government was ordained of God, and submission to it was submission to God. Obedience was a religious duty, except where the sheer scale of political or social evil justified the exercise of the right of revolution. In northern eyes, southern secession had no such justification, and must therefore be suppressed. The *Observer* conceded that the American political and constitutional system might be less than perfect. The framers of the constitution had made serious mistakes, notably because of the 'infusion of French infidelity our politics may have received in that period'. However, stretching the historical evidence to the very limit and beyond, the paper went on to assert that 'no well informed man will deny that this was designed to be a religious Government bound by a written law, and governed by men under the restraints of an oath' – the violation of which would be punished by a just and holy God.[20]

The conservative argument in defense of duly constituted authority did not satisfy those of more progressive or radical outlook. For them, defense of the Union was justified above all by the ideals and principles for which it stood. For some, the sinfulness of slavery was the prime concern, and they wished not merely to defend the Union, but to purge it of the foul blot of slavery. For many others, the issues were much wider still; the Union symbolized and guaranteed a whole set of ideals and beliefs, embracing liberty, republicanism, equality, and opportunity, all generously flavored with evangelical Protestantism. The *Independent*, the leading liberal religious journal of the time, began from a position not far removed from that of the *Observer*. An editorial in May 1861 reminded readers that: 'Our position is on the side of law against violence, and of government against anarchy. Our armies go forth in defence of a long-established Government ...' But, in contrast to the *Observer*, the *Independent* editorial goes on:

> Let it be remembered also that our position is on the side not only of an established Government and an existing civil order, but of republican selfgovernment against the 'architects of ruin.' We are called, in the providence of God, to defend the best civil constitution

ever given to any people against disorders which, if allowed, will
wreck the cause of freedom throughout the world.

As the war went on, the *Independent* increasingly identified the cause of
Christianity with the struggle for national existence. Civil and religious
liberty went together: 'the Altar and the Ballot Box, in America, will
stand or fall together'.[21] In the words of an article in the *Universalist
Quarterly*, the war was not to defend the Union *per se*: 'we are not
idolators of the Union'. Rather, it was to defend the principles for
which the Union stood – order, democratic liberty and popular institutions. The causes of Christianity and progress were the same. A fight
in good faith was sure to succeed; 'To doubt this is atheism.' The list
of causes riding on the defense of the Union could be extended almost
indefinitely. For a writer in the *Christian Review*, the fight to save the
Union was 'the cause of culture against barbarism, of Christianity
against feudalism, of the nineteenth century aganst the tenth'.[22] All this
is a far cry from the cautious, limited justification of a war in defense of
established authority, as propounded by conservative spokesmen, in
the *Observer* and elsewhere.

There were a few more sober voices which uttered words of caution
not only about excessive bellicosity, but also about glib identification of
the cause of the Union with the purposes of the Almighty. Charles
Hodge was a professor in the Princeton Divinity School for more than
fifty years, and boasted that not a single new idea had emerged from
that institution during that half-century. As the leading spokesman for
conservative old school Presbyterianism, he was particularly strict in
his definition of the proper role of the church in the midst of a civil
war. In 1861, he challenged the resolution of the General Assembly,
which urged the church to strengthen, uphold and encourage the
federal government. As a loyal citizen, he agreed with the sentiments
expressed, but he denied the right of the General Assembly to impose
its view upon church members. He personally supported the war
for the Union, but every individual must make his or her own choice.
Everyone, he argued, owed loyalty to the government under which
they lived – but what if there were differences of opinion about the
government to which allegiance was due? Such differences commonly
arose between two countries in Europe – for example, where there
were competing claims to sovereignty over a disputed territory. In the
American context, the argument was between the claims of the federal
and the state government. The correct judgment between the two was
a matter of moral indifference to the church. Every citizen owed a duty
of loyalty to the government, but individual conscience must dictate
where that duty lay. Hodge himself reaffirmed his national loyalty and
his belief that secession was unjustifiable. Supporters of secession were

guilty of a great crime, but they were not amenable to church discipline. Loyalty to the federal government was not a condition of salvation. 'We agree with this decision of the Assembly; we only deny their right to make it.'[23]

Later in the war, Hodge poured cold water on another notion popular with his fellow clergy – namely, that war was God's punishment for national sins. He also argued that it would be morally wrong to make abolition of slavery the object of the war (though it might be a proper means to the achievement of other, legitimate ends). In many ways, Hodge epitomizes the conservative argument in justification of a defensive war to save the Union – but no more than that. Slavery was a great evil, but so were other things like despotism and false religion – and the mere existence of an evil did not justify war against it: 'Nothing can be a legitimate object of a war but something which a nation has not only a right to attain, but which also it is bound to secure.' Such legitimate objectives would include the security of a nation's territory, the safety of its citizens and the preservation of national existence. Such was the evil of war that it was justified only by absolute necessity. Under the constitution, the federal government had neither the right nor the obligation to abolish slavery in the states; therefore, to make abolition the object of war would violate the oath of allegiance to the constitution, as well as the law of God. There was, Hodge claimed, all the difference in the world between abolition as a means of waging war for the Union, and abolition as a war aim: 'The difference ... is as great as the difference between blowing up a man's house as a means of arresting a conflagration, and getting up a conflagration for the sake of blowing up his house.'[24] This is a far cry from the crusading zeal of many of Hodge's fellow clergymen. Whenever those churchmen moved beyond justification of a strictly defensive war, they often strayed into territory which was on the periphery of the established just war tradition, if not indeed well outside it, and they strove to give their case a broader popular appeal. In both their arguments and their mode of expression they were reflecting the character and the attitudes of the open, democratic and intensely Protestant society which they needed to address.

If attention is switched from the *jus ad bellum* to the *jus in bello* – the just conduct of war – the Civil War again raises important questions. Such notions as the proportionality of means to ends, and the distinction between combatants and non-combatants, were placed in a new context – and even called into question – by dramatic changes in the nature of warfare. This was the first large-scale war of the modern industrial age, with all the increased destructive power which that brought in its wake. Interestingly, it was also the war which produced, in the shape of US Army *General Orders No. 100* of 1863, the first modern military manual on the laws of war.[25] (Curiously enough, those orders, which were largely the work of Francis Lieber, seem to have attracted little attention from religious and other commentators on the moral justification of the war.)

Like most modern conflicts, the Civil War began in the confident expectation that it would last for a few weeks, or at most for a few months, and that, after one or two battles, which would be almost ritual confrontations, the struggle would end in a compromise peace. Instead, the war lasted for four years and cost hundreds of thousands of lives. Instead of the limited, almost eighteenth-century, warfare of the War of 1812 or the Mexican War, came the bloodbaths of Shiloh, Antietam, Fredericksburg and Gettysburg, the bitter trench warfare around Richmond and Petersburg, the devastation of the Shenandoah Valley, and Sherman's destructive marches through the deep South.

Did the churches cry out in horrified protest at the soaring escalation in the bloodshed and the suffering? For the most part, the answer seems to have been no. On the whole, northern Christian leaders and spokesmen seem to have accepted with a a surprising degree of equanimity the relentless march of the armies towards a tougher, more ruthless, more destructive kind of warfare. To be fair, there were occasional expressions of concern. Some people – including even a veteran antislavery champion like the respected Presbyterian minister, Albert Barnes – came to the conclusion by 1863 that the war could not be won, that the South could not be forced back into the Union, and that a compromise peace should be sought, perhaps on the optimistic basis of a plan for gradual or delayed emancipation.[26] But this kind of opposition to the continuation of the struggle stemmed more from a military and political calculation of the prospects than from moral objection to the hideous cost of the war. At its root lay political defeatism rather than moral condemnation. Others became increasingly concerned about the threat posed by protracted warfare to individual morality and public virtue. That very proper Bostonian, Robert C. Winthrop, a pillar of the Episcopal church, inveighed against the reckless extravagance, the dishonest contracts, the gambling speculations, the corrupting luxury, the intemperance, profligacy and crime which followed in the trail of the war. 'The secession of the soul from God', he warned, 'was far worse than secession from the Union', and, when the brave soldier boys came home, they should not 'come reeking with the proverbial vices of camp life, but in a condition to resume their places as virtuous and valuable citizens'.[27]

A few clerical voices did express concern about the methods by which the war was being fought, but their motives were somewhat mixed. The editor of the *Observer* addressed himself in 1863 to the question of why the North, with all its superiority in numbers and resources, had not yet managed to win the war. He found his answer in the unrighteous methods by which this righteous war was being conducted, and he found grist to his mill in reports from South Carolina about plunder, looting and wanton destruction by northern troops. The lesson was clear, if unpalatable: 'God will not smile upon a war that is not waged in righteousness, in his fear, and under the guidance of that constitution and law which were made for war and peace alike.'[28] At various times during the war, there was discussion of the morality of fighting on a Sunday. From Bull Run onwards, it was suggested, God had shown his displeasure at those who affronted the Sabbath in this way. The consensus seemed to be that defensive fighting on a Sunday was permissible, but that commanders would do well to avoid initiating a battle on that day.

Charles Hodge was another who took the view that the Union could not be saved by sinful means; proper conduct of the war must include humane treatment of prisoners, respect for the lives of non-combatants, and protection of private property. Echoes of such language can be found, of all places, in General McClellan's Harrison's Landing letter of July 1862. Seeing the conflict escalating far beyond his own traditional ideas of the proper conduct of war, McClellan pleaded that the conflict be kept within recognized limits, and conducted 'upon the highest principles known to Christian civilization'. Private property and the rights of individual civilians should be respected. 'It should not be at all a war upon a population, but against armed forces and political organizations.'[29]

The majority voice among churchmen usually sounded a good deal more bellicose than General McClellan. Those who did express disquiet about the growing destructiveness and ruthlessness of the war must frequently have felt like voices crying in the wilderness. Why, then, did churchmen generally accept with so little protest the unforeseen horrors of the new warfare? Joseph P. Thompson, a prominent New York Congregationalist minister, offered one answer (if not an altogether convincing one) in a thanksgiving sermon for the capture of Atlanta in 1864. At least, he did address the question: 'why should we, a Christian people, rejoice in the bloody triumphs of war?' After painting a gruesome picture of the thousands of dead, and thousands more maimed or enfeebled by disease, he answered his own question rather limply with the assertion that rejoicing was warranted because the cause was just. 'As a Christian people, we cannot delight in war for its own sake ... Yet, though we are a Christian people, and even *because* we are such, we may rejoice in military successes that indicate a righteous cause.' Relying heavily upon examples drawn from the Old Testament, Thompson claimed that 'the Scriptures teach us that the arbitrament of war is a method of referring to Almighty God the righteousness of a cause against the machinations of bloody and deceitful men'.[30]

Perhaps the most common explanation of the war's mounting costs and suffering was simply that God was using the war to punish the United States for its sins – the sin of slavery certainly, but also a whole catalog of national failures to live up to the role assigned to America in the divine plan. The more severe the punishment, in the shape of military defeats and lengthening casualty lists, the clearer the evidence of the enormity of America's sins. This offered a fail-safe explanation of everything that went wrong with the Union war effort, and Gilbert Haven, for example, worked it out in considerable detail to show how, whenever the North failed to come up to the mark, another battlefield chastisement was inflicted upon it. For example, God had sent military setbacks and their attendant casualties to push the North, first into a commitment to the emancipation of the slaves, then into the recruitment of black soldiers.[31]

There is one further explanation of the widespread acceptance of the trend towards all-out war. It took the form of a new application – almost a perversion – of the just war principle that the means employed in a war should be proportional to its ends. At first, when the object of the war in the view of many northerners was simply the restoration of the Union – even restoration of the *status quo ante bellum* – a limited war, within old-established rules, provided the appropriate means. But once the idea took hold that the war would not merely restore but re-model the Union – and in particular that the South would have to be conquered and the slaves freed – a much tougher kind of all-out warfare to achieve total victory seemed both appropriate and justifiable.

Participants in both the moral and political debate relied upon this kind of ratchet effect in their arguments. Rising costs and casualties demanded more radical war aims to justify them; in their turn, more far-reaching objectives justified the agony and the mounting death toll. Indeed, both churchmen and many Republican politicians came to look upon the initial and humiliating defeat at Bull Run as a very special divine blessing. If the North had enjoyed early success in the war, the South might have sued for peace, the old Union would have been restored, and slavery preserved. Instead, initial northern setbacks had not merely ensured a longer, harder, bloodier struggle, but had created the opportunity to establish a more perfect Union – and to eliminate slavery, a goal which even abolitionists had regarded as quite beyond their immediate grasp when the war began.[32] Here indeed was evidence of the working out of the divine plan for America – and here, too, was the ultimate justification of the hideous costs of the struggle not merely for the salvation of the Union, but for its rebirth.

The incremental relationship between means and ends reached its climax, during the latter part of the war, in the growing need – almost a compulsion – to justify the conflict in some more broadly conceived, constructive, ambitious, even grandiose, manner. The defensive war, born out of sheer necessity, was transformed into a crusade for the moral regeneration of America, if not indeed for the salvation of the world. There was a plethora of sermons and articles in the religious press sharing the same basic themes, which might be summed up, in some kind of logical sequence, as: ordeal, chastisement, repentance, purification and regeneration. Of course, many commentators had been determined all along to find positive benefits arising from the war. But, as the prospect of victory came closer, the urge to find some more profound and uplifting meaning in the struggle became stronger than ever.

Faith that the war had some unique historical significance was commonly associated with a sense that the nation was passing through a great ordeal or testing-time, out of which a stronger and better America would emerge. For example, Joseph P. Thompson declared in 1864 that the providence of God had brought the nation to a great test of its virtue. After a three-year trial of its courage, sacrifice and endurance, the nation now had to resist the siren song of those advocating an easy compromise peace – and it had to vote the right way in the coming presidential election. Every man would carry the safety, unity and liberty of the nation wrapped in the paper which he would drop in the ballot box. 'God is putting you to the test, the world awaits the issue.'[33]

Henry Bellows, a leading New York Unitarian and secretary to the United States Sanitary Commission, opened his New Year's Day sermon in 1865 with the theme of national ordeal, and then sought to explain its meaning and purpose. The war had been a test of whether liberty was 'strong and stable, competent to protect and perpetuate the state she adopts', or, 'lovely, noble and gracious as she is', does she also have 'a woman's weakness as well as a woman's beauty'? Only a civil war could have been an adequate test of fundamental principles: 'What other war would not have called out chiefly the vulgar and unwholesome passions of our people, commercial and economic rivalries, hatred of race, pride of blood, and the coarse and degrading sentiments that mark the feeling between Frenchmen and Englishmen, Austrians and Italians?' Survival of the ordeal of civil conflict reinforced the conviction in the American mind that 'God [had] reserved this North American continent for an advanced form of political life, in the interest of the whole human race.' But the threat to that divinely inspired historic role had come not only from slavery, but from the pursuit and accumulation of wealth. 'Without this trial', thought Bellows, 'I am confident the American people would in a generation or two have perished of their own undigested prosperity ... This trial, sharp, long and not yet over, is our probable salvation.' The message which America, Europe and the world should heed was spiritual as well as political:

An era of enlightened, rational, independent faith and worship was born in the despised manger of democratic institutions, and has now burst the tomb, and found resurrection of universal life, after the bloody Calvary of four years of Civil War that threatened religious liberty with final crucifixion and annihilation.[34]

Among both politicians and churchmen there was a division between those who interpreted the war as a national punishment specifically, or even exclusively, for the sin of slavery, and those who saw it as chastisement for a much longer and more varied catalog of national sins and shortcomings. Characteristically perhaps, Abraham Lincoln managed to straddle this divide. His second inaugural is the most famous statement of the idea of the war as punishment for slavery. Having observed that both sides had earlier looked for 'an easier triumph, and a result less fundamental and astounding', he noted that the Almighty had his own purposes:

> If we shall suppose that American slavery is one of those offences which, in the providence of God, must needs come, but which, having continued through his appointed time, He now wills to remove, and that He gives to both North and South this terrible war, as the woe due to those by whom the offence came, shall we discern therein any departure from the divine attributes which the believers in a living God always ascribe to him.

But, almost two years earlier, in his proclamation of 30 March 1863 calling for a national fast day, Lincoln had offered a much broader interpretation of the punishment of national sins through the war. Americans had been made complacent by the long years of peace and prosperity and spectacular growth, and had attributed these bounties to their own superior wisdom and virtue: 'Intoxicated with unbroken success, we have become too self-sufficient to feel the necessity of redeeming and preserving grace, too proud to pray to the God that made us.'[35]

Churchmen deployed their arguments and their rhetoric in support of both the narrower and the broader interpretation of American sinfulness. Among those who concentrated on the single, overriding issue of slavery, none spoke more vehemently or melodramatically than the Baptist preacher George Ide. He believed that 'the hot furnace of civil war' would purify America of the wickedness of slavery. Switching to a new metaphor, he described the hand of God at work in the struggle:

> In the pride of our vain wisdom, we marked out for ourselves the way to political greatness. Across the shaking morasses of Expediency, over the bottomless bog of Compromise, we formed the track, and

laid the rails, and put on the train, and got up the steam, and with rush and roar were sweeping onward in our self-confidence, heedless of the abyss which Slavery had dug in our path, and whose yawning depths lay just before us. But God put his hand to the brakes, and switched us off on a new track, which He laid, and not man. There was surprise, terror, outcry, at first. There are doubts, apprehensions, tremblings still. But the road is firm and straight, the engine sound, the cars stanch, the Conductor all-wise and all-powerful, and the end of our journey – a vindicated Government, a restored Union, a Free Nation – already in sight.

A 'free nation' meant an America free from slavery, and Ide believed that the Emancipation Proclamations had 'allied us with Heaven'.[36]

Many other churchmen were not content with this concentration on slavery as the one great national transgression. They were more in tune with Lincoln's fast-day proclamation, and interpreted the war as divine punishment for a multitude of sins, many of them arising from prosperity and materialism which had deflected America from its true moral purpose. The catalog of national wickedness which they compiled included, at the individual level, neglect of God, intemperance, adultery and Sabbath-breaking, and, at the national level, boastfulness, hypocrisy, prejudice and unfaithfulness to American principles. Most commonly condemned of all were the sins encouraged by American affluence and a long, soft peace – luxury, idleness, selfishness, corruption and materialism. The war would not merely chastise the sinful; it offered the opportunity for atonement and repentance, for the purification of American society, and either its regeneration or the restoration of the virtues with which the Republic had come into the world.

One or two examples from the abundance of sermons and writings on this theme will suffice. The Congregationalist James M. Sturtevant, writing on 'The Lessons of Our National Conflict', described easy prosperity and peace as 'but the delusive daydreams of our national childhood. It is in adversity, in conflict, in the times of national trial and calamity, that a nation's fallow ground is broken up, and the seeds of future greatness are sown, and rooted in the soil.' In order to fulfil its destiny, any great nation had to pass through a 'baptism of suffering'. In particular, Sturtevant saw in the war a trial of the attempt to reconcile prosperity and virtue: 'Long-continued and unusual prosperity has a terrible influence to enervate and unman a people.' Extravagance had played havoc with the moral fiber of the descendants of the Founding Fathers. The nation was now paying the terrible price of having enjoyed 'a kind of millennium of moneymaking'. If the nation accepted its trial and its punishment, it could lay the permanent foundations of the true American character, and create 'a regenerated nation moving on ... to take possession of a continent in the name of freedom, of justice and of God'.[37]

Much the same message was conveyed in a series of editorials in the New York Presbyterian paper, the *Observer*. One editorial, headed 'The Decay of Public Virtue', picked up the reference in Lincoln's fast-day proclamation to pride as the national vice, and lamented the sad departure from 'the simplicity of living which marked the habits of our fathers'. It goes on: 'Our individual prosperity, the increase of riches and the cupidity with which money is now made, have led us to the indulgence of the "pride of life" to a degree utterly inconsistent with the humility that belongs to a virtuous age and people.' Having condemned such excesses as attendance at the theater, the opera and the ballet, or at balls and similar social occasions, the author warns that, because social degeneracy and corruption were so rife, 'God has a controversy with us. He has already summoned this nation to judgment' – and nations, unlike individuals, were judged in this world only. The war would be an 'unspeakable blessing' if it restored the nation to its rightful role.[38]

But what was that role to be? What was envisaged as the end product of this traumatic wartime experience of suffering sacrifice, punishment, purification and regeneration? The general expectation seems to have been that, tempered in the furnace of war, the United States could go on to fulfill its God-given destiny in the world. The Civil War did not inspire any major redefinition of America's world mission, but rather a belief that a reborn America would be both physically able and morally equipped to carry out more effectively its historic mission to promote liberty and free institutions around the world – or, in spiritual terms, to further Christ's kingdom on earth.

In his book *American Apocalypse*, James Moorhead has stressed the extent to which American churchmen saw the war as the gateway to the millennium. But a word of caution may be needed here. It seems quite possible that the widespread use of apocalyptic or millennial terminology was often a convenient and familiar form of words (almost a professional jargon) rather than a literal interpretation of what the war portended.[39] Indeed, as some of the evidence cited earlier has indicated, the direction in which many of the preachers and religious writers looked was backward at least as much as forward. The war was often seen as restorative rather than innovative, let alone revolutionary or apocalyptic. The restoration which was sought was not to the *status quo ante bellum*, but to the republican virtue of the Founding Fathers and the Christian virtue of the Pilgrim Fathers. The war would purge the vices of easy prosperity and the foul blot of slavery, and put America back on its true course. The churches looked at least as much to the recovery of a golden age from the past as to the arrival of the millennium in the future. They were firmly in that American tradition, a blend of a belief in progress with a yearning for the simple virtues of an earlier age, which Richard Hofstadter called 'a forward-looking return to the past'.[40]

In this as in many other ways, the evolving religious justification of the war for the Union was closely in step with political and other secular explanations. Lincoln himself moved from the arguments of his first message to Congress on 4 July 1861, which were based essentially on the right of self-defense, through the dedication of the nation to a new birth of freedom in the Gettysburg Address, on to the agonized reflections on just punishment of national sins and the fulfillment of divine purposes in the second inaugural. Lincoln habitually harked back to the Declaration of Independence, but treated the application of its eternal principles as a continuing process – and a process of universal significance.[41]

Writers such as James Russell Lowell and E. L. Godkin produced what amounted to secular equivalents of many of the arguments advanced by the churchmen, and revealed the same broadening out from justification of a defensive war to a much more elevated and far-reaching interpretation of the conflict. In 1861, Lowell had condemned secession as chaos and supported coercion as the exercise of legitimate authority. By 1864, he was declaring that, underlying loyalty to the Union and the constitution, 'there was an instinctive feeling that the very germinating principle of our nationality was at stake, and that unity of territory was but another name for unity of idea'. The rebels had declared war not just on the constitution, but on the principle of free institutions. Lowell vehemently denied that the war had been turned from its original intention; on the contrary, 'the popular understanding had been gradually enlightened as to the real causes of the war'. This, in turn, had confirmed the people in the view that the only way to finish the war properly was 'by rooting out the evil principle from which it sprang'.[42]

In his famous article on 'Democratic Nationality' in the second issue of *The Nation* in July 1865, E. L. Godkin struck a somewhat similar note: 'The territorial, political and historical oneness of the nation is now ratified by the blood of thousands of her sons cementing the national polity as the only government possible for the American people.' The war had been a test of the possibility of 'a nationality under democratic forms', something which Greece and Rome had never achieved. Quoting the conclusion of the Gettysburg Address, Godkin claimed that the war had determined that it was possible to combine national sovereignty with personal liberty and local self-government. England and France were amazed by the outcome: 'We see the principle of nationality under democratic forms asserting itself with a grandeur of military strength, a unity of political counsel, a dignity of moral power, before which the empires of Caesar, of Charlemagne, and of Napoleon, dwindle into insignificance.'[43] Clearly, it was not only preachers who were sometimes carried away by the force of their own rhetoric.

The Civil War witnessed the first attempt in modern history to justify a major war, which was directed at a mass public of literate, free, enfranchised citizens, whose support was vitally necessary but could not be taken for granted. If some of the arguments have a familiar ring to twentieth-century ears, others do not. These attempts at popular justification of the war testify, however crudely, to the fact that the mid-nineteenth-century United States was an open, democratic society (at least for white males). They also demonstrate that this was an intensely Protestant society, shot through with an evangelical fervor and a crusading spirit which was not afraid to identify the Christian God as a God of battles. There was a strong belief in an interventionist God, manipulating and even instigating bloody conflict for his own stern purposes. However, it still seems reasonable to suggest, or at least to speculate, that this first attempt at justification of a costly war in a modern democracy helped to set a pattern for the participation of the United States – and perhaps other western democracies too – in the world wars of the twentieth century. In particular, the same sequence of arguments found in the Civil War can surely be detected in later conflicts: the initial reliance on the justice of a defensive war waged out of sheer necessity to protect vital national interests; then the constant raising of the stakes during the conflict, as the rising toll of death and suffering demands more far-reaching and ambitious war aims, which in their turn can be used to justify still more ruthless and bloody war-making; and finally the transformation of a defensive war into a great crusade in pursuit of national or universal goals.

War as moral crusade encourages an all-or-nothing approach and requires the destruction of a wicked enemy – just as the Civil War ended in the destruction of the slave society of the old South. More ambitious justifications of war are part of the apparatus of modern total war, and feed the clamor for total victory. The demand for unconditional surrender in World War II may, in some small way, have stemmed from an approach to warfare greatly stimulated, if not actually implanted, by the Civil War eighty years earlier. The twentieth-century American approach to warfare has owed much to both the historical fact of the Civil War and to the way in which it fixed itself in the minds of Americans of both that and later generations. The war for the Union did not sweep away old-established traditions of the *jus ad bellum* and the *jus in bello*. But for modern democracies seeking popular support for engagement in war it showed the need to reformulate old ideas in a new context, and to find new modes of expression for them.

Notes

1. Michael Walzer, *Just and Unjust Wars: A Moral Argument with Historical Illustrations* (New York and London: 1977); Geoffrey Best, *Humanity in Warfare* (New York: 1980); James Turner Johnson, *Just War Tradition and the Restraint of War: A Moral and Historical Enquiry* (Princeton, NJ: 1981); William V. O'Brien, *The Conduct of Just and Limited War* (New York: 1981). See also Barrie Paskins and Michael Dockrill, *The Ethics of War* (London: 1979). A great influence on much of this work was Paul Ramsey, *The Just War* (New York: 1968) and *War and the Christian Conscience* (Durham, NC: 1961).

2. For a good brief discussion of Aquinas and, more generally, of the earlier history of the just war tradition, see O'Brien, *The Conduct of Just and Limited War*, chapters 2 and 3.

3. See the discussion of the bishops' statement in *The Independent* (London), 1 December 1990.

4. Johnson, *Just War Tradition*, pp. xii–xiii, 49–50, 63–4, 281–326. The quotation is on p. 283.

5. Quoted in Earl J. Hess, *Liberty, Virtue and Progress: Northerners and their War for the Union* (New York: 1988), p. 29.

6. Raymond Aron, *The Century of Total War* (Garden City, NY: 1954), pp. 27–8.

7. For a subtle analysis of the complex relationship between the churches and party politics before the Civil War, see Richard J. Carwardine, *Evangelicals and Politics in Antebellum America* (New Haven and London: 1993).

8. George R. Crooks, *The Life of Bishop Matthew Simpson* (New York: 1891), pp. 380–5, 391–5; Robert D. Clark, *The Life of Matthew Simpson* (New York: 1936), pp. 236–44.

9. James H. Moorhead, 'Between Progress and Apocalypse: A Reassessment of Millennialism in American Religious Thought, 1800–1880', *Journal of American History* 71 (1984–5), pp. 524–42. See also Moorhead, *American Apocalypse: Yankee Protestants and the Civil War, 1860–1869* (New Haven and London: 1978), and Ernest L. Tuveson, *Redeemer Nation: The Idea of America's Millennial Role* (Chicago, Ill.: 1968).

10. Patton and Stone are quoted in Chester F. Dunham, *The Attitude of the Northern Clergy toward the South* (Toledo, Ohio: 1942), pp. 136, 111. Ames is quoted in Charles B. Swaney, *Episcopal Methodism and Slavery, with Sidelights on Ecclesiastical Politics* (Boston, Mass.: 1926), p. 300.

11. Abraham Lincoln, *Collected Works*, 8 vols, ed. Roy P. Basler (New Brunswick, NJ: 1953), vol. 4, pp. 423–6. On the Crittenden–Johnson Resolutions, see Phillip S. Paludan, *A People's Contest: The Union and Civil War, 1861–1865* (New York: 1988), pp. 63, 87–8.

12. Phillip S. Paludan, 'The American Civil War Considered as a Crisis of Law and Order', *American Historical Review* 77 (1972), pp. 1013–34. See also Paludan, *A People's Contest*, pp. 10–15.

13. James Russell Lowell, *Writings*, Riverside Edition, 11 vols (Boston, Mass.: 1899), vol. 5, 'Political Essays', pp. 48, 52–3.

14. [A.L. Peabody], 'Loyalty', *North American Review* 92 (1862), p. 158.

15. 'The Sword in Ethics', *Christian Examiner* 72 (January 1862), pp. 15, 17.
16. [S.W.S. Dutton], 'Home Duties during the War', *New Englander* 19 (1861), p. 681.
17. J.M. Sturtevant, 'The Lessons of our National Conflict', *New Englander* 19 (1861), pp. 895–8.
18. 'Christianity and the War', *Universalist Quarterly and General Review* 18 (1861), pp. 373–95.
19. See, for example, 'The War', *Christian Examiner* 71 (1861), pp. 99–102.
20. *Observer* (New York), 7 February, 16 May, 22 August, 7 and 28 November 1861; 2 October 1862.
21. *Independent* (New York), 2 May, 27 June 1861; 18 September 1862.
22. 'Our Civil War', *Universalist Quarterly* 18 (1861), pp. 264–9, 275–6; 'The War', *Christian Examiner* 71 (1861), p. 100.
23. Charles Hodge, 'The General Assembly', *Biblical Repertory and Princeton Review* 33 (1861), pp. 556–67.
24. Idem, 'The War', *Biblical Repertory* 35 (1863), pp. 150–5.
25. On the significance of these orders, and the role of Francis Lieber in drafting them, see Johnson, *Just War Tradition*, pp. 292–322.
26. *Observer*, 22 January 1863.
27. Robert C. Winthrop, *Addresses and Speeches on Various Occasions from 1852 to 1867* (Boston, Mass.: 1867), pp. 576–78.
28. *Observer*, 26 February 1863. The same theme was pursued in a series of later articles in the *Observer*, 9, 23 and 30 April, 7 May 1863, commenting on Lincoln's proclamation of 30 March 1863 calling for a national fast day.
29. Hodge, 'The War', pp. 155–7. On McClellan's Harrison's Landing letter, see Stephen W. Sears, *George B. McClellan: The Young Napoleon* (New York: 1988), pp. 227–9.
30. Joseph P. Thompson, *Peace through Victory: A Thanksgiving Sermon* (New York: 1864), pp. 3–4.
31. Gilbert Haven, *National Sermons: Sermons, Speeches and Letters on Slavery and its War* (Boston, Mass.: 1869), pp. 398–405.
32. For examples, see ibid., pp. 266–8, and *Christian Examiner* 73 (1862), pp. 440–1. George M. Fredrickson, *The Inner Civil War: Northern Intellectuals and the Crisis of the Union* (New York: 1965), pp. 73–6, cites several more examples of commentators who saw long-term benefits in the Bull Run defeat.
33. Thompson, *Peace through Victory*, pp. 13–14.
34. Henry W. Bellows, *The New Man for the New Times: A Sermon Preached in All Souls Church on New Year's Day, 1865* (New York: 1865), pp. 4–8, 11.
35. Lincoln, *Collected Works*, vol. 8, pp. 332–3; vol. 6, pp. 155–6.
36. George B. Ide, *Battle Echoes: or Lessons from the War* (Boston, Mass.: 1866), pp. 153–5.
37. Sturtevant, 'The Lessons of our National Conflict', pp. 894, 899–902.
38. 'Decay of Public Virtue', *Observer*, 16 April 1863.
39. Moorhead's book is a fascinating study of an important subject, but its focus on millennial and apocalyptic themes has the inevitable effect of minimizing other elements in Protestant interpretations of the war.

40.   Richard Hofstadter, *The American Political Tradition and the Men who Made It* (New York: 1948), pp. v–vii.

41.   See Garry Wills, *Lincoln at Gettysburg: The Words that Remade America* (New York: 1992), chapters 3 and 4, for a provocative discussion of Lincoln's conception of the Declaration of Independence as a statement of eternal principles, towards the achievement of which the United States must constantly strive.

42.   Lowell, 'McClellan or Lincoln?' (1864), in *Writings*, Riverside Edition, vol. 5, pp. 167–8, 175.

43.   E. L. Godkin, 'Democratic Nationality', *The Nation* I, 2 (18 July 1865), p. 39.

6

Nation, Organization and the Individual: The Military Thought of Theodore Roosevelt

Oliviero Bergamini

The purpose of this essay is to analyze Theodore Roosevelt's ideas and policies concerning the military establishment of the United States, considered in the broader context of the Progressive Era. Historians have long debated the nature of progressivism, and whether it can be meaningfully used as a category of historical interpretation. But although its richness and diversity has been uncovered, the Progressive Era (roughly extending from the 1890s to World War I) still stands as a crucial phase in American history, characterized by public life-level response to the tremendous impact of full-grown industrial revolution.[1] With Eldon J. Eisenach, I am convinced that we can broadly identify a progressive political culture, with certain distinctive traits, such as the deliberate intention to build a new, organic and integrated nation, the recognition and theorization of the rising importance of professional expertise, the demand for efficient government of an administrative and managerial kind, and the advocacy of an increased role for the state.[2]

State-building, the rise of large-scale organization, and professionalization are historical features of the Progressive Era that in a broad sense were reflected and embodied by the development of the US military system during the first part of the twentieth century. Between 1899 and 1903 several important changes opened up a new era in American military policy. The professional army was enlarged from less than thirty thousand men to a maximum of a hundred thousand and provided with a modern general staff, the system of military professional schools was reorganized and capped by a newly instituted War College, innovations were introduced in officer corps and personnel policies, the National Guard was federalized, and as a whole the military establishment was made more centralized, professionalized and war-oriented. The army's relation to the rest of society was strengthened; gradually it would become more and more relevant as a social institution, a source of technological research, a field for social science applications, and it would begin to formulate its own policy and be influential within the national political context.[3] The main architect of this transformation was Elihu Root, secretary of war from 1899 to 1904, during the

McKinley and Roosevelt administrations. Theodore Roosevelt, however, also was a protagonist of military modernization and expansion. His determination to provide his country with the forces of a first-rate international power was an essential part of his global political attempt to reshape the American nation and promote its rise to world power.

The Idea of War

Theodore Roosevelt placed a high value on war and military spirit. His conception of life was based on a Darwinian survival-of-the-fittest model, and his personal strife to overcome his own physical weakness had rendered him an apostle of the 'strenuous life'. This he projected on the historical and collective level. To him, nations, just like individuals, were engaged in a constant struggle for life which required physical strength, energy, character, high moral temper, and dedication to greatness.[4] As a consequence, even though peace was to be sought and preserved, war could and should not be ruled out; on the contrary, it was a structural component of history, with several positive aspects.

First of all, it was inextricably connected with the laws of physical survival and material progress. Nations were bound to compete to pursue their economic and political interests: military strength and hard fighting could not be done without by any nation, inasmuch as she wanted to hold on to vital resources and increase her share of the world's wealth and power. Second, war had an idealistic side. It was the way through which a nation could develop and assert not only her material interests, but also her spiritual and moral essence. To the United States, military conflict, such as in the Philippines or in Panama, was necessary to enact her national mission of spreading civilization and promoting the world's progress. Under this perspective, war became a matter of 'responsibility', of 'honor', of 'loyalty' to the 'high spirit' of the nation. Peace was to be discarded if it was not 'just' and 'righteous'; it was better to go to war, even at the cost of high and even ruinous material losses, than submit to dishonorable peace. Third, in an American version of end-of-the-century western irrationalism, war had an intrinsic value as a regenerating experience, which tempered individuals and nations, keeping them alive and strong. War, fighting, even the very act of killing (which Roosevelt performed extensively in his much-advertised hunting trips) possessed a value of their own because they kept a man virile, vital, a little barbaric, in a way preventing him from lapsing into a state of weakness and becoming prone to material comfort and security.[5]

Roosevelt's ideas on war were strictly related to his foreign policy creed. He was a leading exponent of the group of navalist-expansionists (such as Albert Beveridge and Henry Cabot Lodge) who since the 1890s had urged the United States to take up a more active and aggressive role on the world scene in order to secure their commercial expansion and rise to world power. Alfred T. Mahan was their military ideologue; subscribing to his idea of command of international sea routes as essential to a nation's strength and welfare, they advocated a strong navy and the acquisition of strategic territories. Although they did not ask for all-out territorial expansion, they did aim at building an American empire based on economic penetration, political hegemony, selected colonial possessions, military strength, and pervaded by a 'white man's burden' creed, heightened by the ideological tradition of American exceptionalism and moral superiority. Theodore Roosevelt was the man who most ardently and effectively embodied the navalist-expansionist drive. He incessantly proclaimed the need to provide the United States with a first-class navy, and largely succeeded. At the end of his second term as President, his goal of building a navy 'second only to Great Britain' was achieved.[6]

The Army

This essay, however, does not focus primarily on the navy, but rather on the army. Not only has the navy build-up already been studied rather extensively, but the army is more significant as an object of progressive reform; in fact, at the end of the nineteenth century it was an organism deeply rooted in the political and social institutions and practices of pre-industrial America. Its transformation was important because it was connected with the rise of America on the international scene, but also because it represented in itself a relevant aspect of the evolution of American political structures.[7]

At the end of the nineteenth century the United States military system was actually composed of three different bodies. First came the regular army; it was a professional army, very small if compared to European armies (numbering less than thirty thousand troops in the 1880s, expanded to less than one hundred thousand after the Spanish–American War). Many of its officers were rather old men, most of whom had fought in the Civil War; promotion was slow; military life largely consisted in wearisome routine spent in small posts scattered throughout the West, and the ranks abounded with foreign-borns and social misfits. The command system was obsolete and awkward. At the head of the army rested a commanding general, constantly struggling for authority with the secretary of war on one side and with the chiefs of the staff bureaux on the other. These were officers who directed the several logistical and administrative bureaux (normally called staff bureaux or staff departments) into which the War Department was divided. With no central authority coordinating their work, they had developed close ties with congressional leaders, on the basis of their authority over supply contracts and assignments. A bitter resentment divided the 'line' officers, who considered themselves the fighting and essential part of the army, and the 'staff' officers, who enjoyed comfortable offices in the main cities and faster chances of promotions, in spite of their having seen little field service and conceiving themselves basically as civil servants.

The second component, the so-called National Guard, consisted of the different state military volunteer organizations. They were amateur citizen soldiers units who trained a few days a year, paraded on the Fourth of July, and were often engaged in the repression of class conflicts. Their military training was poor, and so was their equipment. Guard officers were commissioned by state governors, and the units responded to state authority (except in exceptional circumstances, in which they could be called for federal service). Often characterized along ethnic, social or local-community lines, National Guard units were an integral part of the system of political patronage and social bondage that was typical of the nineteenth-century 'state of parties and courts'. The third component was virtual: it consisted of the federal volunteers who could be called out in case of war. There was no law providing fixed procedures for either mobilizing the National Guard or calling out and organizing the volunteers.[8]

This composite system had dramatically shown its inefficiency in the Spanish–American War. Mobilization had occurred through improvised legislation; raising volunteer forces had been a haphazard business, influenced by political considerations. Volunteers were untrained; some National Guard units had volunteered in mass, but as a rule guardsmen had performed very poorly, partly on account of antiquated and unspecialized equipment. Regular troops, on the contrary, had performed rather well, in spite of poor leadership by the many aged commanders, but the logistical management of the expedition to Cuba had been disastrous, at least in its initial stage. The war had been won essentially by the navy, and some of the most successful actions had been performed by volunteer units which had managed to bypass or overcome inefficiencies in organization and leadership.[9]

Theodore Roosevelt went to Cuba as commander of one of these citizen soldier units, the celebrated Rough Riders, and received firsthand experience of the bad shape of the national armed services. In the rage of criticism that ensued, he was one of the most ardent advocates of a radical reform of the military establishment.[10] When he ascended to the presidency, changes had already begun under the leadership of William Howard Taft's secretary of war, and Roosevelt's personal friend, Elihu Root. From then on, Root and Roosevelt joined efforts. In his annual presidential reports, Roosevelt devoted significant attention to military matters and called incessantly for improvements in the service. He actively supported Root's initiatives, which in the end turned out to be largely successful. In 1901 a 'detail system' was inaugurated, providing for staff positions to be filled through a four-year detail from the line instead of permanent appointment (the system, though, was limited to ranks below colonel, and therefore did not affect the authority of the bureau chiefs in Washington); the reorganization and enlargement of the army-school system and the creation of the War College, plus some pathbreaking decisions concerning promotions and assignments, were accomplished to renew and reinvigorate the officer corps with a more 'warlike' and professional spirit. In 1903 a modern general staff was instituted and a new militia law, replacing the archaic eighteenth-century militia legislation, laid the foundations for the uniformization of equipment, better training, federal financing and growing federal control of the state guards.[11]

Roosevelt boosted Root's reform efforts by his unconditioned political support. Military strength was one of his major concerns. Although his main interest was – by far – the navy, he wanted very much to make the army stronger and more efficient, bring it to a high peak of excellence, and provide it with up-to-date technology and expertise in the 'art' of modern warfare. He wanted to modernize it and integrate it, and render it the effective instrument of a new course in the nation's foreign and military policy. He thought that Americans needed to think afresh military matters, and learn to prepare for war even in times of peace. Preparation meant intensive training, preselection of officers, operational planning, and ample provisions for modern weaponry. It also implied a change of attitude: a new readiness to fight and a new aggressive patriotism, which envisioned war not as an accident, but as a natural element of the nation's life on its way to greatness.[12]

Roosevelt's ideas were not original; since the 1880s a small, but rather determined military reform movement had developed; it was composed of regular army officers and a few politicians, with occasional support from the press. The military 'managerial revolution' brought about by the industrial revolution and epitomized by the German general staff, the changing international role of the United States, and the new developing reform-oriented political culture were behind their desire for a radical reshaping of the American military establishment. To a large extent they were inspired by the ideas of a regular army officer, Emory Upton, one of the major American military thinkers, whose writings developed a stringent criticism of US military policy and offered suggestions for a larger and more modern army, at least partially inspired by European models. The new army envisioned by these 'Uptonian reformers' did away with the localistic and voluntaristic traditions, was internally integrated and externally insulated, led by professionals, authentically national, and pervaded by a new spirit of efficiency and readiness. Their language had much in common with that of progressive reform. As Stephen Skowronek has observed: '[L]ike the leaders of the civil service reform movement, the army's new professionals sought to build national administrative authority so as to play a key role in the high affairs of state, and, like the civil service reformers, their vision called into question the entire mode of government operations.'[13] In its general terms, Roosevelt shared this approach; but on the military he also had ideas of his own.

Professionalization

Theodore Roosevelt's conception of military service and efficiency was mainly individualistic. He believed that the effectiveness of an army depended largely on the individual quality of its enlisted men and, even more, of its officers. They needed to be 'fine natural fighting men', to possess a sort of inborn attitude to war. Roosevelt's ideal soldier much resembled the western frontiersman (and the idealized Rough Rider): daring, self-sufficient, showing initiative, disregardful of manual-style tactics, determined and cruel if necessary.[14] Actually, Roosevelt claimed that modern warfare had grown even more individualistic than before: 'In the circumstances of modern warfare the man must act far more on his own individual responsibility than ever before, and the high efficiency of the unit is of the utmost importance. Formerly this unit was the regiment; it is now not the regiment, not even the troop or company; it is the individual soldier', he declared in 1902.[15] Consequently, he believed in the 'need of giving the widest scope to individual initiative under the present conditions of actual warfare'.[16]

The individual character of modern warfare merged in Roosevelt's mind with American individualism as such. Consistently, he was critical of the spirit and training methods of European armies, and particularly the German army, which at the time was considered the best in the world:

> In various sociological books by authors of Continental Europe there are jeremiads as to the way in which service in the great European armies, with their minute and machine-like efficiency and regularity tends to dwarf the capacity for individual initiative among the officers and the men. There is no such danger in America ... I know no larger or finer field for the display of advanced individualism than that which opened before us as we went from San Antonio to Tampa.[17]

On the basis of these assumptions, Roosevelt thought that the volunteer soldier could easily become as good as the professional, provided he was 'accustomed to the use of fire arms, accustomed to taking care of themselves in the open ... intelligent and self reliant', and possessed 'hardihood and endurance and physical prowess; and above all ... the fighting edge, the cool and resolute fighting temper': all the qualities, in brief, which characterized the Rough Riders.[18] Brief, intensive training was sufficient, once these basic individual qualities and abilities were there. As to the regulars of his time, Roosevelt thought that they did not possess enough of these soldierly qualities and needed to develop them in order to raise their 'efficiency'. The necessity for this kind of improvement is the most persistent theme in his annual reports. For enlisted men and officers alike, he emphasized the need for intensive training in the field. Again and again he called on the army to exercise 'in large bodies', under war conditions. He especially insisted on training soldiers in the basic abilities to shoot, manage themselves in the open, and endure physical effort. Marksmanship and familiarity with shooting were a special concern of his.[19]

Roosevelt also wanted to improve and revitalize the officer corps. His aim was to let the most energetic men rise to the higher grades, introducing meritocracy to the army. He criticized openly the seniority system then in use, denouncing the way in which it brought men to high positions when they were too old and weak and could remain in office for too short a time to exert effective leadership. As a solution, Roosevelt strongly advocated the introduction of selection by elimination, that is compulsory retirement for officers who were judged unfit for further promotion by examination boards; and sheer promotion by merit, that is, the possibility to promote meritorious men 'over the heads' of their seniors. The former device would free the army of the ageing or undedicated officers; the latter would insure internal competition and initiative, allowing the best men to rise where they could exert effective leadership.[20]

Even though promotion by merit enjoyed the support of younger reform-minded officers, a majority of the regular army officers opposed these provisions: most of them were rather old men who did not want to see their routine upset by new methods and were afraid of being overstepped by ambitious, obnoxious youngsters. Many of the congressmen who had been soldiers in the Civil War also opposed this reform as a betrayal of the old army spirit and a concession to a new professionalism which endangered the citizen soldier tradition, bringing about 'militarism'. Besides, they accused Roosevelt of enhancing the careers of his political pets, introducing political favoritism into the service.[21]

This use of progressive-like, anti-patronage arguments against professional reform may appear paradoxical. But Roosevelt's ideas on the

subject were themselves rather contradictory. He recognized the importance of officers being trained and made familiar with some basic
organizational principles (drill, marching formations), but he thought
an industrious individual could learn these things quickly, and that
they were secondary. His idea of good officership was based essentially
on personal character and field-command performance. He indicated
'youth, character, fitness, intelligence and demonstrated ability to
command' as the main considerations in the selection of an officer.[22]
He argued repeatedly that the education given at West Point was too
'scholastic', involving too much mathematics and not enough experience of command in the field. Although he was aware of a developing
professionalism in the military, to him an officer's professional profi-
ciency was not so much connected with long training, fully developed
professional doctrine, or familiarity with the managerial activities typical
of modern warfare as with his being young, energetic, courageous,
aggressive, honorable, inspiring, and endowed with a sort of irrational
thirst for the fight. His desire to rejuvenate the army was almost obses-
sive; on innumerable occasions he attributed shortcomings and failures
to old age and a subsequent lack of vigor on the part of commanding
officers.[23] This attitude was reflected in Roosevelt's actions. While
Root was organizing the new regiments for the 1901 enlargement of
the regular army, Roosevelt kept harassing him with recommendations
of personal acquaintances for commission. His endorsement was
invariably based on the 'war record' of the man, and very often on his
having been with him during the Cuban campaign.[24]

Even more indicative was his promotion policy. Under the current
legislation the President could pay no regard to seniority except when
filling a general's position. Therefore Roosevelt promoted several officers
to the rank of general, over the heads of hundreds of senior officers,
almost always on account of their relative youth, high energy and
impressive fighting record. This was the case of Leonard Wood and of
John Pershing and others, among whom many (including Wood) had
entered the army as volunteers and had never been through West
Point. Even though Roosevelt always claimed that his appointments
were always made in the full and exclusive interest of the service, and
opposed the tradition of distributing appointments on the basis of state
'quotas' in favor of a technical approach not involving politics, his
promotion policy was strongly affected by personal consideration, and
very closely resembled old-style patronage.[25] Although he occasionally
praised Root's work in this field, Roosevelt never seemed to be very
interested in the system of specialized schools through which the army
was developing a modern professional culture (where organization,
logistics, management and methodical planning were growing in importance, as opposed to old-style heroic leadership in the field) and by

which selection based only on apolitical, standardized, internally certified professional expertise was pursued.

The National Guard

Roosevelt's attitudes towards the crucial question of a military reserve are also significant. Apart from the small regular army, the United States had no peacetime military reserve. State guards had been trying to be officially recognized as a national reserve, but until 1903 no law defined precisely their relation to the national military establishment, and the question of federal control and authority over them was very controversial.

Although he had been a member of the New York Guard, Roosevelt knew and admitted that the National Guard was a very ineffective fighting force. In his recollection of the Spanish War he claimed that federal volunteers (and his Rough Riders in particular) had performed much better than guardsmen, and declared that guard service provided only about 5 per cent of a soldier's training. As governor of New York, he had taken up the problem of improving the guard service by sending William Sanger abroad to study foreign militia systems (he personally admired the Swiss citizen soldier army) and by establishing higher standards for guard officers; at the same time he had joined in the calls for new legislation, which would put the National Guard under federal control, define the exact relation between federal and state forces, and improve the quality of the service.[26] When he became President, he openly supported Root's efforts to bring the National Guard under federal control and promote higher standards of efficiency in exchange for federal funds and official recognition, and exposed the need for legislative provisions to predispose an effective and orderly employment of volunteers in time of war. 'Action should be taken in reference to the militia and the raising of volunteer forces', he declared in his 1901 annual report:

> Our militia law is obsolete and worthless. The organization and armament of the National Guard of the several States, which are treated as militia by the appropriations by the Congress, should be made identical with those provided for the regular forces. The obligations and duties of the guard in time of war should be carefully defined, and a system established by law under which the method of procedure of raising volunteer forces should be prescribed in advance ... Provisions should be made for utilizing in the first volunteer organizations called out the training of those citizens who have already had experience under arms, and especially for the selection in advance of the officers of any force which may be raised.[27]

Federalization of the state guards, however, was a compromise and a setback on the road to a truly national, centralized army under exclusive federal authority. It did represent an attack on localism, an extension of the role of central government, and an erosion of the principle of self-sufficient citizen-soldiery; on the other hand, it also legitimized the guard as first military reserve, while preserving a large share of the states' authority over its organization, administration, and employment. Emory Upton and some of the Uptonian reformers had envisioned a more radical solution; they suggested marginalizing the National Guard by confining it to a territorial defense service (or even abolishing it altogether) and creating an authentic national volunteer reserve, trained and officered by regular professionals. Their proposal clearly pointed in the direction of universal military training and conscription, which Upton significantly upheld as 'truly democratic'. Radical Uptonian reformers did not think that the guard could ever become an effective reserve; their contempt for the amateur citizen soldier was a sign of growing professional awareness and self-reliance, and at the same time of a desire to do away with the ethnic, regional, and social differences embodied by guard units in favor of a new, uniform and standardized service.[28] Although such a project was much too radical and militaristic for public opinion and Congress, Root considered it and proposed a watered-down version, which received no support. With the Dick Act of 1903, he accomplished a much-needed reorganization of the guard which laid the foundations for its gradual development as part of a centralized and truly national military system. However, the act was also hailed as a victory by the National Guard Association.[29]

Roosevelt basically shared Root's approach, but he was not so much interested in its institutional aspects as in its effectiveness in cultivating military 'habits' within the American population. In his annual reports after 1903 National Guard issues did not receive much attention, except with regard to practical training 'in the field'. The President praised joint field maneuvers of the National Guard and the regular army, inaugurated in 1903, and stressed the importance of rifle practice among citizens; this was to be encouraged throughout the National Guard, whose main job would be to fight the tendency, typical of 'a great industrial civilization such as ours', 'to do away with, to eliminate those qualities which make a man a good soldier'.[30]

In 1901 Roosevelt did ask for the establishment of a National Naval Reserve, whose main duty would be to man the coastal fortifications, and who should therefore train extensively with their sophisticated artillery, but he did not push the issue, and he appears never to have considered a similar provision for the army. In his mind, the country, in case of war, should rely mainly on volunteer citizen soldiers, the typical military expression of a democracy, rather than on professionalized men. Therefore, he was more concerned with nourishing the fading military and frontier-like spirit of the American people than with setting up a large, permanent, bureaucratically organized, institutional structure.

The General Staff

The nature of Theodore Roosevelt's military policy is best exemplified by his attitude towards the reorganization of the command system of the regular army. In 1903, after a bitter political struggle and much opposition by the 'Old Army' men, including the powerful Commanding General Nelson A. Miles, Root succeeded in having Congress pass an act establishing a general staff corps, led by a chief of staff, which was to replace the commanding general. The new body was intended to be a sort of 'expert commission' supervising not only the regular army, but the entire military establishment, federalized National Guard included. It would be broadly responsible for military efficiency, prepare war plans, and coordinate the work of the staff bureaux.[31] This at least was the theory, based on the German model. Actually, the new agency's powers and functions soon proved to be blurred, controversial and precarious. The bureaux retained much of their independence, and the chief of staff had to struggle for several years in the attempt to establish his authority over the army.

As already noted, Roosevelt had been one of the foremost critics of the management of the American land forces during the Spanish–American War, gaining a reputation as a military man. 'Our army is in need of sweeping reforms', he declared in 1899, and in his correspondence with Henry Cabot Lodge he deplored the fact that the act providing troops to fight the Filipino insurrection had been stripped of some articles introducing organizational reform.[32] Consistent with this belief, as President, he supported Root's proposals for a reorganization of the command system. In 1901 his first report flatly stated: 'A General Staff of the Army should be created'; but the boldness of the statement was not followed up by any stringent argument. Rather, the President moved on in the same paragraph to ask for other provisions.[33]

Although Roosevelt later took some credit for it, the creation of a modern general staff, possibly the most seminal of Elihu Root's reforms, did not involve him very much, and even later on he never seemed fully to appreciate the importance of such a body for a modern military organization.[34] In 1906 he clearly expressed his opinion about the relationship between line and staff officers: 'The line officer, the fighting man, is the pivotal man in the navy, and in the army. He is the man who does the vital work, and the staff officers exist to enable him to do his work.'[35] And in 1908, while discussing the command system of the navy, he remarked that the solution to inefficiencies and blunders did not consist in proper managerial organization, or even in having line officers (the 'fighting men') directly in charge of staff departments, but rather in being able to select 'the right kind' of individuals for command positions – by which he meant young and energetic officers, full of initiative and fighting spirit.[36]

Even when in his autobiography he re-examined retrospectively his experience as a Rough Rider, his criticism of the War Department performance was still aimed mainly at individuals and attitudes, rather than at the general lack of a well developed military professional culture or of a proper managerial organization to handle the incumbencies of modern industrial mass warfare.[37] Roosevelt thought that major impediments lay in the 'red tape bureaucratic' and 'unmilitary' nature of staff departments' personnel; this is the reason why he ardently supported the establishment of the 'detail system', with a four-year rotation between line and staff. This, as we have seen, was accomplished by Root in 1901, before Roosevelt took office, but only for positions below the rank of colonel, therefore leaving the powerful bureaux heads in place. While the President recommended its extension to higher ranks, he and Root had to face the reaction of the bureaux chiefs. They held that the new policy was harmful to the service, because the four-year rotation prevented the development of full professional competence; this was particularly true of the very 'technical' ordnance bureau.[38]

The bureaux' resistance on account of professionalism shows the ambivalence of the detail system policy. Although it intended to increase the efficiency of the logistical service by breaking up their red-tape routine and bringing them in closer contact with the real needs of the units, it also represented the outcome of long intra-service struggles between staff and line officers. Line officers wanted to abolish staff officers' privileges and establish the hegemony of the 'fighting men' within the service. Drive for innovation and backward disregard for the managerial dimension of modern warfare were mixed in the detail system. This shows how reform was also a cultural problem: in their proposals reformers blended European influences and practical considerations of peculiar features of the American military system; sometimes their knowledge of European models or their ideas about how they could be implanted in the US army were confused, partly because of the fact that the military world was in an age of radical transformation and innovation.

This was the case with Roosevelt and the general staff. The President was not unaware and unmindful of the necessity and functions of a general staff. He thought it should be a 'thinking agency' at the top of the army, which could elaborate war plans, coordinate army administration, predispose mobilization and supervise preparation for war in time of peace. In fact, he openly advocated the adoption of a general staff in the navy also, and in 1908 he clearly argued that it should have full authority above the staff departments.[39] But the general staff question was complex; it was a new institution, and it embodied the introduction into the American military system of methods which had been developed in a totally different institutional and cultural context. While in Germany the militaristic and authoritarian character of the Emperor's power made it easier for the general staff to exert its hegemony over the military establishment, in the United States the political system was based on a network of horizontal connections. The staff bureaux were connected to Congress, which controlled army expenditures, while the general staff was supposed to be strictly associated with the executive, which in turn had very little real power over peacetime military administration. Besides, the very reason of existence for a general staff – systematic preparation of war – was a new thing in American history, and it went against a tradition of ad hoc mobilization based on decentralized institutions and practices.

Just like other military men, including Root and his successor as secretary of war, William Howard Taft, Roosevelt had no clear ideas about how to establish the general staff as a working concern within the military establishment. He proved this, in the first place, by failing to provide it with effective leadership. In the first years of its existence, the President nominated as chiefs of staff several ageing officers who were neither able to set a firm course for their new office nor energetic enough to assert their authority. Roosevelt made these choices either because he felt the need to follow the seniority principle, or because he wanted to reward a good fighting record; he did not seem to understand the need to put a modern professional in charge of a modern professional institution. This changed to some extent only after several years, when, in 1906, John F. Bell became chief of staff.[40]

Most important, Roosevelt's relations with the general staff showed that he did not have a clear idea of what it should do. In 1903 he suggested to the first chief of staff, Samuel B. M. Young, a more realistic kind of cavalry training, including the setting up of 'dummies' as targets of the charge.[41] In 1905 he sent Taft a long list of subjects concerning the artillery service, upon which the chief of artillery should express an opinion and formulate legislative proposals.[42] Later the same year he wrote a long letter directly to the chief of staff Adna R. Chaffee, in which, after entertaining him extensively about the use of swords and bayonets *vis-à-vis* firearms with reference to the performance of the Japanese in the Russian–Japanese War, he asked whether the staff had 'prepared practical plans for embarking a division, for providing how to get the necessary provisions for an expeditionary army corps, and so forth and so forth', reminding him of 'the unutterable folly and confusion which we both saw at Santiago', and suggesting that the general staff set up practical rehearsals of amphibious operations.[43] In 1907 he pressed upon the new chief of staff the subject of promotion by merit, asking for new legislation proposals.[44] On several other occasions he addressed the general staff on matters of weaponry and equipment. In short, Roosevelt did use the general staff, sometimes bypassing the secretary, and at times he invested it with rather broad responsibilities. Often, however, he simply succeeded in reinforcing its tendency to devote too much time to administrative trivia and minor technical questions, which caused it to drift towards the adoption of clumsy and pedantic work habits.

The general staff performed effectively in the second intervention in Cuba in 1906, when Bell and Roosevelt managed to cooperate satisfactorily. The general staff, through the War College, had prepared plans for an invasion of Cuba, which Roosevelt asked them to modify slightly by including more cavalry in the expeditionary force before he would approve them. General staff officers coordinated the logistics of the expedition, and then served as American military authorities in Cuba. Although not flawless, their performance proved its usefulness; the President appreciated and profited from having a body of trained professionals to help him execute his policy.[45] However, this was not enough to establish the authority of the general staff firmly within the army. The bureaux, exploiting their congressional connections, continued to be largely independent, and the general staff went back to a kind of peacetime work involving mainly administrative and technical details. War-planning activities continued within the War College, but they had a rather narrow scope, focusing largely on tactical and operational aspects. Only gradually, as the international commitments of the United States grew, did the general staff develop its policy-making functions, embodying the growth of the military establishment as a self-conscious, large-scale organization and a significant part of the new twentieth-century state. An example of this was its working out, after 1911, of national military policy plans, envisioning enlargements of the regular army and the creation of a national reserve.[46]

Roosevelt, however, conceived the general staff more as a source of practical advice on specific issues and an instrument to coordinate and execute such single operations as the invasion of Cuba than as an authoritative institutional agency on which civil authorities should rely systematically for guidance on military matters, use as an exclusive communication channel with the army, or entrust, at least to some extent, with broad policy-making functions and control over the military establishment. His attitude had both historical and personal justifications: the American tradition of civil control over the military, his conception of a strong presidency, his taste for personal power, and his opinion of himself as a military expert fully entitled to interact with military professionals. Explicitly, he conceived the adoption of a general staff mainly as a way of re-establishing the supremacy within the army of the 'purely military' component (that is, the men who actually did the fighting) over the 'bureaucratic' component embodied by the staff bureaux.[47]

World War I

The contradictions within Roosevelt's ideas *vis-à-vis* the features of a fully developed progressive-like military doctrine and professional culture are clearly exposed by his behavior towards World War I. Before American entry into the war, Roosevelt had become a protagonist of the growth of the 'preparedness movement' and particularly of the 'Plattsburg movement' for universal military training led by his friend Leonard Wood, who in the meantime had become chief of staff. This movement presented broad political and cultural implications: social engineering, nationalism, professionalism, moralism, corporativism aimed at reconciling class struggle under the leadership of an élite class of public men, international activism and drive to hegemony, were all features of the preparedness campaign which strongly connected it with the mainstream of progressivism.[48] Roosevelt, although not immediately, strongly supported the preparedness movement, especially as an attempt to revive the old citizen-soldier virtues in the American public. At the same time, he bitterly attacked Wilson's neutrality policy. Faithful to his general views of war, he thought the United States should enter the conflict, both on account of her practical interests, and, even more, of her moral and spiritual responsibilities.[49] When at last, in 1917, the United States did take sides with Great Britain and France, Roosevelt saw the chance for a rebirth of his military self, with all the assumptions, beliefs and attitudes that went with it.

On 19 March 1917, after the United States had broken off diplomatic relations with Germany, Roosevelt sent Wilson's secretary of war, Newton D. Baker, an earnest telegram asking permission to raise a volunteer division 'for immediate service at the front'. To his great consternation, Baker declined: first, he communicated, Roosevelt personally lacked military training; second, with the advice of the general staff it was the intention of the administration to send to Europe an expeditionary force made up only of regulars and National Guard men; conscript units would be raised, but they would have to be trained for a long time (probably over a year) before they could be actually sent to the front. Only 'military considerations', Baker added, should govern the administration's action, meaning by this that he intended to follow standardized procedures fixed by military professionals, and not the old path of piecemeal, decentralized mobilization.[50]

Deeply hurt, Roosevelt started a correspondence with Baker, in which insistence for permission to be in the fight alternated with strong criticism of the administration's foreign and military policy. In his long, detailed, persistent and repetitious letters, the former President's ideas on the military came to new life, modified only slightly by experience and political developments.[51] In the first place, Roosevelt strongly defended his personal qualifications for active service; he reminded Baker that he had been commander-in-chief of the US army, and, more particularly, that he had seen combat service in the Spanish–American War, where he had thoroughly proved his 'fitness for command'. In fact, he accused Baker of sending to Europe generals who had 'only one tenth' of his experience, and extolled the value and the accomplishments of the Rough Riders, of which he had been a leader. His other arguments had a wider scope. Volunteer units, he thought, could be raised and sent to Europe at once. He would make sure that his division would enlist only 'the best type of fighting men' and put them 'in the right spirit which will enable ... [us] to get the best possible results out of them in the actual fight'; if this was the case, he claimed, only four months of training would make excellent troops out of them.

Showing how the political climate with respect to 'militarism' had evolved since his presidency, Roosevelt openly declared himself 'most heartily in favor of universal obligatory military training and service, not only as regards this war, but as a permanent policy of this government'. Even so, he insisted, volunteers should be used, because they represented a fast-ready resource, as effective as the regulars if properly selected and trained. It was a 'very grave blunder' on Baker's side to think that the 'belated adoption of the obligatory system' was a reason to reject the employment of volunteers. Immediate use of a large expeditionary force, such as could be raised only by patriotic volunteer effort, was indispensable to uphold and preserve the moral significance of US involvement in the conflict. If American participation was confined to a small professional expeditionary force because of the long time required for universal military service to put out trained troops, this would stain the country's honor and prove that the nation had lapsed into base materialism and was no longer able to rise up to its responsibility and historical mission. The administration policy amounted to suggesting that 'we shall pay billions of dollars to the Allies to do our fighting for us, while we stay here in comfort' – a course that was simply 'ignoble'.

Roosevelt's criticism then turned to the general staff. The military advisers to whom Baker referred were 'military men of the red tape and pipe clay school, who [were] hide bound by the pedancy of that kind of wooden militarism which is only one degree worse than its exact opposite, the folly which believes that an army can be improvised between sunrise and sunset'; they were the product of a calamitous seniority system, and had risen to their position owing 'more to the possession of a sound stomach than to the possession of the highest qualities of head and heart'. In brief, Roosevelt again displayed the full set of his tenets on war and military service: an heroic conception of war; the importance of individual instinctive qualities; the primary relevance of combat leadership; the relative irrelevance of professionalism and organization; a persistent faith in the ideal of the citizen soldier; and a general inability to grasp the full significance of the advent of modern industrial mass warfare.

Baker's words, as he countered Roosevelt's accusations, are indicative of a substantially different approach:

> [General Staff officers were] that part of our professional army of longest experience ... men of intense and discerning enthusiasm for their profession, filled with loyalty to their country, and very zealous so to train, equip and use our military forces as to make them most effective and to minimize to the utmost the inevitable losses of life ... Unless the whole theory of having a professional army is vicious, a portion of our professional army would be more efficient from a military point of view than such a hastily assembled force, and quite obviously, the long and systematic training to which the members of the Regular Army are subjected will have taught them better how to fight without needless exposure and how to protect their health and diminish their losses both in camp and in the field.[52]

Theodore Roosevelt's Military Thought: An Assessment

An assessment of Theodore Roosevelt's military thought must take into consideration the broader context of the military reform movement on one side, and of progressive political culture on the other. Although significantly connected with the main currents of progressivism, military reform in America at the turn of the century was not a simple battle between traditionalists and modernizers, with clear-cut and consistent ideologies; in part it sprang from intra-service conflict between line and staff, and it was affected by the way reformers understood – or misunderstood – European models and tried to reconcile them with American traditions and institutions. Although generally oriented towards a new, truly national, integrated and professionalized military establishment, reform plans included contradictory aspects such as an underestimation of the organizational dimension of modern warfare.

Theodore Roosevelt's military policy is a most significant example of such complexity. As a supporter of Root, and as a promoter of reform on his own account, he certainly contributed significantly to the modernization of the American military establishment; after Roosevelt's presidency, the 'Old Army' structure and cultural orientation had definitely been left behind, and a new military establishment was on its way to becoming a relevant component of the American national, political, social and economic scenario. However, it would be wrong to classify this accomplishment simply as an expression of Roosevelt's 'progressivism'. As a matter of fact, in the military field we can detect some of the differences separating his political approach from a more fully developed progressive political culture, such as the one outlined by Herbert Croly, Walter Lippmann, Walter Weyl and others. Even though they did not repudiate individualism altogether (on the contrary, they wanted to revitalize individual initiative, prostrated by the rise of corporations and political 'corruption'), these political thinkers relied on managerial organization, impersonal expertise, and the systematic application of social sciences as the main instruments for a regeneration of American society. The expansion of the functions of the state and the subsequent growth of its institutional structure were cardinal aspects of their program.[53]

Roosevelt shared this approach only to a certain extent. Although he sensed the increasing complexity of life in an urban and industrial America, and recognized the growing importance of large-scale 'combinations' and 'federations' (as he preferred to call them), such as trusts and trade unions, *vis-à-vis* traditional local, small-scale and individualistic institutions and practices, he did not fully appreciate the growth of a modern bureaucratic society. His conception of leadership was one of transition between the old model of the patrician and the new model of the 'public man', whose authority is based on professional expertise rather than superior moral fiber. Roosevelt's basic ideological tenets were rooted in the nineteenth-century tradition of individualism, voluntarism, and idealism. The growth and centralization of the military establishment during his presidency is a relevant aspect of the state-building process that characterized the Progressive Era, but Roosevelt was comparatively disregardful of its institutional aspects. His concern was focused more on other matters. Although he was an enthusiast of technological innovation (but so was Nelson A. Miles, the main adversary of military reform), his conception of military excellence assigned only a secondary relevance to systematized training and managerial ability.[54] His program to make the army more efficient by enhancing its 'purely military' character was in part ambiguous, as shown, for instance, by the weight he gave to personal considerations in the selection of officers.

To some extent, his views conflicted with the very ideas of the professionalist Uptonian reformers. Significantly, Roosevelt was not at all an unconditioned admirer of Emory Upton. Although his calls for reform and peacetime preparation sound very Uptonian, he criticized *The Military Policy of the United States*, Upton's major work, as 'one sided' in its constant attack on the citizen soldier and systematic praise of the regular; in many instances it was regular officers who had committed blunders, he remarked, and Upton should have remembered that 'mere length of service ... mere calling troops "regulars" amount to nothing whatever'.[55] This approach was rooted in Roosevelt's general foreign policy and strategic beliefs, which led him to underestimate the importance of the land forces. His real passion was the navy; it was to battleships, he thought, that the nation's security and strength was entrusted. And the navy appeared to him as a more modern and technological service than the army. In his opinion, while it took only brief training to the effectiveness of a good soldier, long training, constant practice, thorough familiarity with sophisticated naval weaponry and machinery were indispensable to the effectiveness of a naval crew. And while mobilization – though it required peacetime preparation – could be carried out on an ad hoc basis, a fleet could not be improvised.[56]

Roosevelt believed that American isolationism was over and that a war with a major European (Germany) or Asiatic (Japan) power was possible, but he thought it would be fought largely on the seas. Therefore, he did not think very deeply about how the army should be organized and used in a major conflict. Of course, hardly anybody in Roosevelt's time could foresee that the United States would be involved, as soon as 1917, in such a conflict as World War I, but while Uptonian reformers concerned themselves with the backwardness of the American land forces with respect to European standards and organizational models, Roosevelt seems to have believed that future wars on land could be fought without radically restructuring the system, or repudiating its spirit. The regular army should be ready to conduct efficient small-scale operations (such as Caribbean interventions) and to fight by itself in the early stages of a major conflict. Volunteer forces would then be raised, and provided that they were well-equipped and led, and that bureaucracy did not get in the way, their *élan* would eventually prevail. It is significant that, as President, while he constantly kept asking for more ships, Roosevelt often said that the regular army, apart from an increase in its officer corps, did not need to be enlarged.[57] A desire to avoid charges of militarism also accounts for these statements, but, at least until the preparedness campaign had taken off, Roosevelt basically thought that the country needed not so much a larger, but rather a better professional military force. Not surprisingly, then, he advised his son not to take up a military career: 'I have too much confidence in you', he wrote him, arguing that challenges were higher and opportunities for excellence better in civil life. He was being realistic, to be sure, but it is also clear that he did not consider professional soldiery as a value in itself.[58]

The cultural implications of Roosevelt's ideas on the military emerged very clearly in the heat of his attempt to participate in World War I. While other political leaders were devoting themselves to managing the war effort as a large-scale corporate state experiment, the former President strove to fight in another 'heroic' war – which we know was not heroic at all, and very different from the small expedition to Cuba to which he constantly referred to as the main source of his military wisdom. In spite of their cooperation in the push for the New Nationalism reform program, Roosevelt's political culture differed substantially from that of men like Croly, Lippmann, and Dewey. Their political programs all 'intersected', as Robert Wiebe has noted, in a common desire for a strong, united, organic nation, provided with an energetic leadership and pervaded by a new kind of patriotic spirit.[59] But this common goal was to be accomplished by different means and different approaches. To Croly, Lippmann, and Dewey, the collective dimension and the role of the state were primary. Talking about what he called 'the social problem', Croly stated: 'No voluntary association of individuals, resourceful and disinterested though they be, is competent to assume the responsibility [of solving the "social problem."] The problem belongs to the American national democracy, and its solution must be attempted chiefly by means of official national action.'[60] And to Dewey public education should not only favor the spontaneous development of individual character, but rather it should be a positive force, shaping individual character in such a way as it may be functional to a harmonious social life. To full-grown Progressives, society was going to be based more and more on organization, rationality, managerial methods, and technical specialization, all culminating in the rise of the new figure of the expert, 'a part of a great industrial machine', whose 'individuality tended to disappear in his work'.[61]

Roosevelt's approach, as shown in his military thought and policy, was different. To him the problem lay more in bringing forward the best individuals, liberating individual initiative from the restraints of bureaucracy and crystallized tradition, and rekindling the spirit of the frontier. As regards organization, he was aware of the need to expand the state and create new agencies, but he neither understood nor was very concerned with specific technical and institutional aspects, which, on the contrary, were essential. The concept of professional specialization, which is fundamental in organizational theory, was rather blurred to him. In fact, he thought that the essence of the function and authority of the general staff officers lay in their being men of military character, as opposed to the civil character of the bureaux officers, and in their being 'generalists', as opposed to the 'specialists' employed in the staff bureaux. Significantly, he thought of large organizations, such as corporations or trade unions, simply as giant individuals, which should be dealt with just like any other individual (for instance by requiring 'fairness' from them), thereby missing the qualitative change they represented in social life.[62]

In conclusion, Roosevelt shared with progressive political thinkers a concern for the major themes of nation, organization, and the individual, but with a distinctive conception of their ultimate nature, and reciprocal relation. In his eyes, individuality was still whole and primary; nation was still mainly a matter of ideal and will; organization was a condition and an instrument, but it did not represent a new essential aspect of social life, with a value of its own. Croly had declared that in the new industrial, urban America average citizens 'had ceased to be pioneers'; and Frederick Jackson Turner, together with other progressive intellectuals, had pointed to scientists, social engineers, and technical experts of all fields as the new pioneers.[63] Roosevelt's emphasis was differently placed; to him the ultimate champions of American civilization were still his military heroes, intended as pioneer-like, daring, energetic individuals, fighting for the noble American mission. As Richard Slotkin has recently pointed out, Roosevelt's beloved Rough Riders emerge in his writings as a sort of ideal 'microcosm of progressive order ... a utopia of meritocracy', in which 'the notion of consent envisioned in democratic theory' is substantially modified inasmuch as 'it is not obtained through political negotiation or the clash of asserted wills but through a training process that makes men accept the idea that consent to obey is implicit once superiority is recognized in a commander'.[64] It is an order based essentially on personal qualities, and led by a 'natural aristocracy' which is self-selected, at least in theory, on account of its superior character; it is not characterized by technical specialization, managerial abilities, or rational planning capacity; significantly, the Rough Riders perform their deeds in the jungle, not in urban industrial America, or even in the overcrowded, chaotic fronts of the European war. As he tried to prove in World War I, Roosevelt thought that the individual, as a volunteer citizen soldier, committed to the country's ideals, still had much to offer. Maybe the nation could no longer do without organization; but to Roosevelt, neither should she, nor could she, do without the individual.

Notes

1. For a brief overview of the debate on progressivism: Daniel T. Rodgers, 'In search of progressivism', *Reviews in American History* 10 (December 1982), pp. 113–32; Richard L. McCormick, 'Public life in industrial America, 1877–1917', in Eric Foner (ed.), *The New American History* (Philadelphia, Pa: 1990), pp. 93–118, esp. pp. 106f.; Martin Sklar, 'Periodization and historiography: studying American political development in the progressive era, 1890s–1916', *Studies in American Political Development* 5 (Fall 1991), pp. 173–213; William Deverell and Tom Sitton (eds), *California Progressivism Revisited* (Berkeley, Calif.: 1994), pp. 1–11.

2. Eldon J. Eisenach, *The Lost Promise of Progressivism* (Lawrence, Kan.: 1994); the general features of the Progressive Era and progressive political culture as I assume them are outlined in such fundamental works as Robert Wiebe, *The Search for Order* (New York: 1967); Alfred Chandler and Louis Galambos, 'The development of large-scale economic organizations in modern America', *Journal of Economic History* 30 (March 1970), pp. 201–17; Jerry Israel (ed.), *Building the Organizational Society* (New York: 1972); Stephen Skowronek, *Building a New American State: The Expansion of National Administrative Capacities, 1877–1920* (Cambridge: 1982).

3. In this essay the terms 'army' and 'military establishment' refer to the complex of the military land forces of the United States, including their institutional and legislative structure. On the reform of the military establishment: Russell F. Weigley, 'The Elihu Root reforms and the progressive era', in William Geffen (ed.), *Command and Commanders in Modern Warfare* (Office of Air Force History Headquarters USAF and United States Air Force Academy, 1971), pp. 11–27; Philip L. Semsch, 'Elihu Root and the general staff', *Military Affairs* 27 (Spring 1963), pp. 16–27; James E. Hewes, jun., 'The United States army general staff, 1900–1917', *Military Affairs* (April 1974); Marc Powe, 'A great debate: the American general staff (1903–1916)', *Military Review* 55 (April 1975), pp. 71–89; Peter Karsten 'Armed progressives: the military reorganizes for the American century', in Israel (ed.), *Building the Organizational Society*, pp. 197–307; Elbridge Colby, 'Elihu Root and the National Guard', *Military Affairs* 23 (Spring 1959), pp. 28–34; Louis Cantor, 'Elihu Root and the National Guard: friend or foe?', *Military Affairs* 33 (Fall 1969), pp. 361–73; Philip Jessup, *Elihu Root* (1938; Archon Books, 1964), vol. 1, pp. 215–407; Allan R. Millet and Peter Maslowski, *For the Common Defense: A Military History of the United States of America* (New York: 1984), pp. 299–327.

4. For an overview of Theodore Roosevelt's ideas, see the excellent anthology edited by Mario Di Nunzio, *Theodore Roosevelt: An American Mind* (New York: 1994), esp. pp. 166–201. Also, *Theodore Roosevelt: An Autobiography* (1913; New York: 1943).

5. For Roosevelt's conception of war, see for instance his assessment of the reasons for entering the Spanish–American War, in Roosevelt, *Autobiography*, pp. 208–9, and his views on World War I: *Theodore Roosevelt, America and the World War* (New York: 1915); see also Roosevelt's opinions

on disarmament and internationalism: Roosevelt to E. Grey, 22 October 1906, in Elting E. Morison (ed.), *The Letters of Theodore Roosevelt* (Cambridge: 1951), vol. 5, p.462; Roosevelt to White, vol. 5, pp.357–9; Roosevelt to E. Grey, vol. 5, pp.600–2. Hereafter Morison's work will be quoted as *Letters*.

6.   Howard K. Beale, *Theodore Roosevelt and the Rise of America to World Power* (New York: 1965); Serge Ricard, *Theodore Roosevelt et la justification de l'imperialisme* (Aix-en-Provence: 1986); Serge Ricard, *Theodore Roosevelt, principes et pratique d'une politique étrangère* (Aix-en-Provence: 1991); Alfred T. Mahan, *The Influence of Sea Power upon History* (1890; Boston, Mass.: 1918); Richard W. Turk, *The Ambiguous Relationship: Theodore Roosevelt and Alfred Thayer Mahan* (New York: 1987).

7.   On Roosevelt's navy policy: Gordon C. O'Gara, *Theodore Roosevelt and the Rise of Modern Navy* (Princeton, NJ: 1943), James R. Reckner, *Teddy Roosevelt's Great White Fleet* (Annapolis, Md.: 1988).

8.   Russell F. Weigley, *History of the United States Army* (New York: 1967), pp.265f.; Edward M. Coffmann, *The Old Army: A Portrait of the Army in Peacetime, 1784–1898* (New York: 1986), pp.268–87; Robert M. Utley, *Frontier Regulars: The United States Army and the Indians, 1866–1891* (New York: 1973); Raimondo Luraghi, 'Due secoli di politica militare degli Stati Uniti', *Politica Militare* 3 (1977), pp.7–23.

9.   Morgan H. Wayne, *America's Road to Empire: The War with Spain and Overseas Expansion* (New York: 1968), pp.70–1; Graham A. Cosmas, *An Army for Empire: The United States Army in the Spanish–American War* (Columbia, Mo.: 1971); Millet and Maslowski, *For the Common Defense*, pp.267–89.

10.   Theodore Roosevelt, *The Rough Riders* (1899; New York: 1923); Serge Ricard, 'L'Histoire mythifiée: Theodore Roosevelt et la conquête de Cuba en 1898', *Revue d'Histoire Moderne et Contemporaine* 34 (Oct.–Dec. 1987), pp.660–8; Weigley, *United States Army*, pp.309–12; Barrie Emert Zais, 'The struggle for a 20th century army: investigation and reform of the United States army after the Spanish–American war' (Ph.D. diss., Duke University, 1981), pp.127–38; Cosmas, *Army for Empire*, pp.264f.; also see the *Report of the Commission Appointed by the President to Investigate the Conduct of the War Department in the War with Spain* (8 vols, Senate Document N. 221, 56th Cong., 1st Sess., 1900).

11.   See note 3; also: Zais, 'Struggle for a 20th century army'; William R. Roberts, 'Loyalty and expertise: the transformation of the nineteenth-century American general staff and the creation of the modern military establishment' (Ph.D. diss., Johns Hopkins University, 1980); Louis Cantor, 'The creation of the modern National Guard: the Dick Militia Act of 1903' (Ph.D. diss., Duke University, 1963); James W. Pohl, 'The general staff and American military policy: the formative period, 1898–1917' (Ph.D. diss., University of Texas, 1967), pp.1–99; William A. Sherrard, 'The legislative origins of the twentieth century American army' (Ph.D. diss., University of Nebraska, 1993).

12.   'Annual Report of the President' (henceforth AR) for the years 1901–8, *The Works of Theodore Roosevelt: State Papers as Governor and President*

(New York: 1925), pp.142–6; 180–2; 231–3; 304–5; 359–60; 477–8; 547–54; 635–7; Roosevelt, *America and the World War*, *passim*; Roosevelt, *Autobiography*, *passim*.

13. Emory Upton, *The Armies of Asia and Europe* (New York: 1878); *The Military Policy of the United States From 1775* (Washington, DC: 1904); Stephen E. Ambrose, *Upton and the Army* (Baton Rouge, La.: 1964); James L. Abrahamson, *America Arms for a New Century* (New York: 1981), pp. 1–101; Weigley, *History of the United States Army*, pp.268–92; Skowronek, *Building a New American State*, pp.85–120; John M. Gates, 'The "new" military professionalism', *Armed Forces and Society* 11 (1985), pp.427–36.

14. Roosevelt, *Autobiography*, pp.227–32; Roosevelt to J. Hamilton, 5 January 1906, *Letters*, vol. 5, p.139.

15. AR 1902, p.181.

16. Roosevelt to L. Wood, 6 May 1901, *Letters*, vol. 3, p.70.

17. Roosevelt, *Autobiography*, pp.227–32, 247.

18. Roosevelt, ibid., p.227.

19. 'Annual Report of the Governor of the State of New York for the year 1899', *State Papers*, p.60; AR 1902, p.181; AR 1904, p.305; AR 1906, pp.479–80.

20. AR 1901, p.143; AR 1903, p.232; AR 1906, pp.476–7; AR 1907, pp.552–3; AR 1908, p.636; Roosevelt to J. F. Bell, 20 April 1907, *Letters*, vol. 5, pp.651–2.

21. *Army and Navy Journal* (11 January 1902), p.458; ibid. (26 March 1904), p.788.

22. 'Annual Report of the Governor of the State of New York for the year 1899', *State Papers*, p.59.

23. Roosevelt to A. L. Key, 10 April 1908, *Letters*, vol. 6, pp.999–1001.

24. See for instance Roosevelt to E. Root, 14 July 1899; 14 August 1899; 24 November 1900; 1 June 1901, Theodore Roosevelt Papers (Washington, DC: Library of Congress); from now on quoted as TRP.

25. Roosevelt to O. G. Villard, 25 July 1903, *Letters*, vol. 3, p.531; Roosevelt to L. Wood, 8 June 1904, *Letters*, vol. 4, pp.826–8; Mark Matthew Oyos, 'Theodore Roosevelt: Commander in Chief' (Ph.D. diss., Ohio State University, 1993), pp.106–22. Oyos's work is the only specific study available on Roosevelt's army military policy; it is very useful and well researched, although it is limited to Roosevelt's presidency, and does not study systematically the broad cultural and political implications of his actions.

26. Roosevelt, *Autobiography*, p.229; 'Annual Report of the Governor of the State of New York for the year 1899', *State Papers*, pp.17–19; 'Annual Report of the Governor of the State of New York for the year 1900', ibid., p.60.

27. AR 1901, p.146.

28. See for instance F. R. Coudert, 'The proposed reorganization of the national guard', *Journal of the Military Service Institution* 24 (March 1899), pp.239–45; 'Report of the Adjutant General', in *US Department of War, Annual Report of the Department of War for the year 1903* (Washington, DC: 1903), p.309.

29. Cantor, 'The creation of the modern national guard', pp. 215–62; Cantor, 'Elihu Root and the national guard: friend or foe?'; Colby, 'Elihu Root and the National Guard'; Martha Dertick, *The National Guard in Politics* (Cambridge, Mass.: 1965), pp. 22f.; Jim Dan Hill, *The Minute Man in Peace and War: A History of the National Guard* (Harrisburg, Pa.: 1964), pp. 175–90; John K. Mahon, *History of the Militia and the National Guard* (New York: 1983), pp. 137–41; Jessup, *Elihu Root*, vol. 1, pp. 265–8; Skowronek, *Building a New American State*, pp. 216–18; Elihu Root, 'The Militia Act of 1903', in Robert Bacon and James B. Scott (eds), *The Military and Colonial Policy of the United States: Addresses and Reports by Elihu Root* (Cambridge, Mass.: 1926), pp. 137–51.

30. 'Remarks of President Roosevelt to the members of the Interstate national guard Association at the White House', 22 January 1906, Elihu Root Papers (Washington, DC: Library of Congress).

31. See notes 3 and 10; see also the extracts from Elihu Root's annual reports as secretary of war included in 'The general staff', Bacon and Scott (eds), *The Military and Colonial Policy of the United States*, pp. 417–40.

32. Roosevelt to F. V. Green, 25 July 1899, TRP; Roosevelt to H.C. Lodge, 9 March 1899, *Selections from the Correspondence of Theodore Roosevelt and Henry Cabot Lodge, 1884–1918* (New York: 1925), vol. 1, pp. 393–4; H. C. Lodge to Roosevelt, 15 March 1899, ibid., vol. 1, pp. 395–6.

33. AR 1901, p. 143.

34. Roosevelt implicitly recognized Root's leading role, especially as far as the transformation of generic calls for reform into actual legislation was concerned. In a letter to O. G. Villard, for instance, he referred to 'the Army bill, to which Root has given such thought and effort', 22 March 1902, *Letters*, vol. 3, p. 147.

35. T. Roosevelt to C. J. B. Bonaparte, 28 November 1906, *Letters*, vol. 5, p. 514.

36. T. Roosevelt to A. L. Key, 10 April 1908, *Letters*, vol. 6, pp. 999–1001.

37. Roosevelt, *Autobiography*, pp. 219f.

38. 'Report of the Chief of Ordnance', *US Department of War, Annual Report of the Department of War for the year 1906* (Washington, DC: 1906), p. 3; 'Report of the Chief of Staff', *US Department of War, Annual Report of the Department of War for the year 1908* (Washington, DC: 1908), pp. 368–9; Otto L. Nelson, *National Security and the General Staff* (Washington, DC: 1946), pp. 106–7.

39. AR 1908, p. 639.

40. Nelson, *National Security and the General Staff*, pp. 81–2; Oyos, 'Theodore Roosevelt: Commander in Chief', pp. 174–7.

41. Roosevelt to S. B. Young, 8 August 1903, *Letters*, vol. 3, p. 546.

42. Roosevelt to the secretary of war, 13 March 1905, *Letters*, vol. 4, p. 1138.

43. Roosevelt to A. R. Chaffee, 3 July 1905, *Letters*, vol. 4, p. 1260.

44. Roosevelt to J. F. Bell, 20 April 1917, *Letters*, vol. 5, p. 652.

45. A. Millett, 'The general staff and the Cuban intervention of 1906', *Military Affairs* 32 (Fall 1967), pp. 113–19; on the relationship between Roosevelt and Bell: E. F. Raines, 'Major General J. Franklin Bell and military reform' (Ph.D. diss., University of Wisconsin-Madison, 1976), pp. 117–21.

46. 'Annual Report of the Chief of Staff' in *US Department of War, Annual Report of the Department of War*, for the years 1904f. (Washington, DC: 1904f.). The first major military policy statement from the general staff, entitled 'The Organization of the Land Forces of the United States', appears as an appendix to the 'Report of the Secretary of War', *US Department of War, Annual Report of the Department of War for the year 1912* (Washington, DC: 1912), pp. 71–128.

47. AR 1908, p. 639.

48. John C. Clifford, *The Citizen Soldiers: The Plattsburg Training Camp Movement, 1913–1920* (Lexington, Ky.: 1972), esp. pp. 34–5, 84–9; Michael Pearlman, *To Make Democracy Safe for America: Patricians and Preparedness in the Progressive Era* (Urbana, Ill.: 1984); John P. Finnegan, 'Military preparedness in the progressive era, 1911–1917' (Ph.D. diss., University of Wisconsin, 1969); Leonard Wood, 'The inevitability of a citizen army', in Russell F. Weigley (ed.), *Towards an American Army* (New York: 1962), pp. 199–221.

49. For Roosevelt's views on Wilson, his war policy, and on World War I, see 'America and the World War', in *The Works of Theodore Roosevelt* (National Edition), 20 vols (New York: 1926), vol. 18, pp. 3–185; and Ralph Stout (ed.), *Roosevelt in the Kansas City Star: Wartime Editorials by Theodore Roosevelt* (Boston, Mass.: 1921); see also Serge Ricard, 'Anti-Wilsonian internationalism: Theodore Roosevelt in the Kansas City Star', in Daniela Rossini (ed.), *Theodore Roosevelt to FDR: Internationalism and Isolationism in American Foreign Policy*, vol. 2 of European Papers in American History (Keele: 1995), pp. 25–44.

50. Roosevelt to N. D. Baker, 19 March 1917, TRP; Roosevelt to N. D. Baker, 25 March 1917, TRP. As to the political aspects of American mobilization in previous wars, suffice it to remember that William McKinley repeatedly modified the legislation regulating the call for troops to be employed in the Spanish–American War, under pressure from different political lobbies such as the National Guard Association.

51. The information included in the following paragraph is based on the following letters, part of the TRP: Roosevelt to N. D. Baker, 12 April 1917; Roosevelt to N. D. Baker, 22 April 1917 (an eighteen-page-long letter containing the bulk of Roosevelt's arguments); Roosevelt to N. D. Baker, 8 May 1917.

52. N. D. Baker to Roosevelt, 5 May 1917, TRP.

53. Edward A. Stettner, *Shaping Modern Liberalism: Herbert Croly and Progressive Thought* (Lawrence, Kan.: 1993); Robert Crunden, *Ministers of Reform: The Progressives' Achievements in American Civilization, 1889–1920* (New York: 1982); Charles Forcey, *The Crossroads of Liberalism: Croly, Weyl, Lippmann, and the Progressive Era, 1900–1925* (New York: 1961); John A. Gable, *The Bull Moose Years: Theodore Roosevelt and the Progressive Party* (Port Washington, NY: 1978).

54. Oyos, 'Theodore Roosevelt: Commander in Chief', pp. 261–313.

55. Roosevelt to E. Root, 16 February 1904, *Letters*, vol. 4, pp. 731–2.

56. See for instance AR 1901, pp. 135–41, esp. p. 137; AR 1905, p. 361. While Roosevelt was President, he consciously reduced the regular army

to the minimum size allowed by the law: Roosevelt to H. White, 14 August 1906, *Letters*, vol. 5, p.358; Roosevelt to E. Grey, 22 October 1906, *Letters*, vol. 5, p.463; a significant episode occurred in 1902, when Elihu Root had to fight back Roosevelt's attempt to take away from the army, and assign to the navy, the building of coastal fortifications in the Philippines: Elihu Root to the President, 7 January 1902; Elihu Root to the secretary of the navy, 28 February 1902, Root Papers; Lewis L. Gould, *The Presidency of Theodore Roosevelt* (Lawrence, Kan.: 1991), pp.122–3.

57.   AR 1904, p.305.

58.   Roosevelt to Theodore Roosevelt, jun., 11 January 1904, *Letters*, vol. 3, pp.694–5.

59.   Wiebe, *The Search for Order*, p.190.

60.   Herbert Croly, *The Promise of American Life* (1909; New York: 1964), p.24.

61.   Ibid., p.103.

62.   '[T]he line as between different corporations, as between different unions, is drawn as it is between different individuals; that is, it is drawn on conduct, the effort being to treat both organized capital and organized labor alike; asking nothing save that the interest of each shall be brought into harmony with the interest of the general public, and that the conduct of each shall conform to the fundamental rules of obedience to law, of individual freedom, and of justice and fair dealing toward all', AR 1903, pp.199–200.

63.   Tiziano Bonazzi, 'Frederick Jackson Turner's frontier thesis and the self-consciousness of America', *Journal of American Studies* 27 (1993), pp.1–23.

64.   Richard Slotkin, *Gunfighter Nation: The Myth of the Frontier in Twentieth Century America* (New York: 1993), pp.102–3.

7

World War I, the Campaign for Compulsory Health Insurance, and the Transformation of Progressive Social Thought

Axel R. Schaefer

The political, cultural, and intellectual significance of the pre-World War I campaign for compulsory health insurance goes well beyond the position of the movement in the pantheon of progressive reform. The sudden rise and precipitous decline of the campaign in the United States reveal both the depth and the dilemma of progressive causes which drew their symbols and inspiration from European social reform. The fate of the insurance movement exemplifies the extent to which the war separated the development of the American welfare state from European models of reform. World War I, while initially reviving hopes for health insurance reform, ultimately undermined the transnational, cultural, and intellectual foundations of the movement. Hailed in the early teens of the twentieth century as the next step in social progress, the campaign was utterly defeated by 1920. Its opponents, insurance reformer Isaac M. Rubinow bemoaned, were 'strong enough to kill even the agitation, the very thought of it, for many years to come'.[1] The cultural and political obstacles that the war put in the way of compulsory health insurance, because of its association with foreign models of reform, are discussed in the first part of this paper.

The fate of the movement also reveals that the 'end' of progressivism after the war was not primarily the result of the dismantling of wartime government agencies. In fact, wartime government intervention itself had already legitimized a model of state action that was at odds with the progressive ideal. Despite their rapid disintegration after the war, these federal agencies established precedents for the postwar extension of government police powers that were embraced by many progressives in the 1920s. These neo-liberal models of state intervention, however, were significantly different from the cultural-organicist conception of the state which had been the basis of the pre-war health insurance reform movement. The second part of this paper takes a closer look at this intellectual transformation of the movement during and after the war.

The main organization pushing for compulsory health insurance in the United States after the turn of the century was the American Association for Labor Legislation (AALL), which was founded in 1906, and which 'created and sustained the organized social insurance movement'.[2] It was dominated by professionals and reformers who had either been trained at German universities, or were avid students of German social reform. They included the physician and actuary Isaac M. Rubinow, Chicago sociologist Charles R. Henderson, the social workers Florence Kelley and Edward T. Devine, Johns Hopkins political economist Richard T. Ely, and labor advocate John Graham Brooks.[3] In 1916, the AALL issued a model health insurance bill, which became the centerpiece of the campaign for commensurate legislation. It called for the elimination of private insurance, to be replaced with local, self-governed funds, jointly managed by employers and employees under public supervision and regulation. In this regard the bill followed the German precedent that had been established after the 1911 insurance revisions.[4] In a departure from the German model, the committee suggested that funds be contributed not only by employers and employees, but also by the state. The AALL bill specified that cash benefits should amount to two-thirds of the wages, beginning on the fourth day of illness. This amount, the reformers argued, was 'not likely to cultivate malingering', but also 'not so small as to cause a breakdown of family standards'.[5] The Progressives were confident that the bill would work well 'based upon observation of its success in Germany'.[6] The AALL plan was not restricted to males; it also extended to female workers. It granted benefits as a right, without means tests or questions of fault. It included maternity benefits which did not differentiate between illegitimate and legitimate children. However, health insurance was mainly geared toward restoring health and productivity to male workers. It did not address the problem of women facing discrimination because of pregnancy, left the care of invalids to charity, and excluded casual, farm, and domestic workers.[7] The Progressives emphasized that compulsory health insurance was not the same as state insurance. They noted that the local, self-governed funds would promote self-help, thrift, and providence among workers, and 'furnish the sort of training, both moral and intellectual, which is indispensable to the most efficient social reform'.[8]

In 1916, the AALL succeeded in introducing its model bill in three industrial eastern states: New York, Massachusetts, and New Jersey. In fifteen other states bills were introduced in 1917. By 1920, twenty states had considered the model health bill. Commissions or legislative committees had been appointed in nine states, and the majority reported in favor of compulsory insurance. In California and New York, health care legislation was almost passed. Enthusiasm for broad-based insurance reform was, however, for the most part confined to academic and professional supporters. Powerful insurance interests took up the fight against health insurance reform, challenged by the funeral and maternity benefits included in the AALL bill, which threatened the profitable life insurance business.[9] They forged alliances with such diverse groups as the American Medical Association (AMA), the National Association of Manufacturers, the National Civic Federation, and the American Federation of Labor (AFL).[10] The labor movement remained split on the issue, fearing that compulsory insurance deductions would cement lower wages. While John Mitchell of the United Mine Workers, and William Green of the AFL supported the plan, Samuel Gompers emerged as one of its most vocal critics. A believer in voluntarism, Gompers lambasted compulsory insurance as another misguided scheme to 'rivet the masses of labor to the juggernaut of government'.[11]

The reformers were also stymied by political considerations. Worried about the two million dollar share that insurance would impose on the State of California, Progressive Governor Hiram Johnson withheld his support from the AALL bill and proposed a referendum on the issue to be held in 1918. The insurance companies mustered a considerable force against the plan by setting up the California Research Society of Social Economics, which, according to its employees, neither conducted research nor studied economics. Instead, it busied itself with distributing pamphlets that showed a picture of the Kaiser over the words 'Made in Germany. Do you want it in California?' When Californians went to the polls in November, they soundly defeated the initiative for compulsory health insurance.[12] Likewise, the New York campaign eventually faltered. Although the bill had garnered bipartisan support of Democrats and progressive Republicans and included many changes demanded by physicians and labor, it was killed in the assembly. 'By 1920 health insurance was dead, and subsequent discussions did nothing to revive it'.[13] The pre-war reformers' heavy reliance on an idealized image of Germany and German social reform had contributed to the demise of the movement. The Progressives promoted this image as a way of legitimizing reform in the United States, which, however, proved to be fatal, as wartime hysteria replaced the popular perception of Germany as a well-governed civil service state with images of an autocratic militaristic regime.

The Progressives had tapped into the image of a United States hatching ideas that were bred in Europe. Despite their misgivings about the paternalism of the German state, many Progressives, such as Frederic Howe, regarded Germany as 'a democratically-minded country ... organized on the ideas of Frederick the Great, but guided by the scientific idea of the twentieth century'.[14] Many German-trained reformers defined their mission as the application of European social ideas through a self-styled middle class of administrators, academics, and civil servants. This emphasis on the transnational aspect of reform was part of an attempt to fight the three genuinely American manifestations of social welfare policies in the early twentieth century: the Progressives rejected the spoils element in the Civil War pension system;[15] they resented the urban political machines, which offered jobs and a measure of social security to a working-class clientèle in exchange for votes and loyalty; they objected to the paternalistic social policies advocated by big business, which often made benefits dependent on worker behavior and threatened the loss of payments in case of job changes.[16] In addition, the reformers condemned the pitfalls of large-scale, impersonal, self-propelling bureaucracies that marked private insurance and gobbled up high premiums for administrative outlays. At the same time, they made a determined attempt to present compulsory health insurance as genuinely American in character. They regarded the scheme as a means of creating a system of collective security based on a social right. Yet, they defended insurance reform by invoking the older rhetoric of self-help, individual providence, moral benefits, and the producer-class ideology. The reformers maintained that the decentralized, self-governing features of the AALL insurance plan, and the absence of large-scale government intervention, suited American traditions and customs. As Charles Henderson remarked, the German insurance system retained the features of 'personal moral bonds', which added a 'human touch', but also diminished the 'temptation to malingering'.[17] The feature of compulsion in the insurance reform proposal was, the reformers insisted, in compliance with American history and culture. Henderson pointed out that school-attendance laws, taxation, road maintenance, and police functions were well established and accepted.[18]

Although justified on progressive terms and with progressive rhetoric, the war ultimately reversed this imagery. The high moral fervor of Wilsonian idealism made the war into a crusade to bring the American knight in shining armor to rescue the European damsel in distress. Pro-war propagandists tapped into older American myths depicting American military involvement as a campaign against 'all that Europe historically represented in the American mind: coercive government, irrationality, barbarism, feudalism'.[19] Opponents of insurance reform branded the scheme a Hun-inspired master plan of the Kaiser to turn Americans into slaves of autocratic government. George Creel's powerful Committee on Public Information commissioned a series of articles exposing German insurance as a fraud against workers. In the words of one of the most outspoken opponents of compulsory health insurance Frederic Hoffman, the 'German cause of world conquest was largely conditioned by the German conception of so-called social or compulsory insurance'.[20] As a result of this opposition, the Progressives increasingly renounced the foreign influences on the reform campaign. The immigrant roots of mutuality, namely the immigrant German sickness funds, English fraternal orders, Italian societies, and Jewish lodges, eloquently

defended by Rubinow, now proved a burden in promoting health insurance reform.[21] The reformers learned the lesson that 'the less identification with Europe, the better the prospects of social insurance'.[22]

Initially, however, the war revived hopes and aspirations for reform.
Many Progressives were taken in by the wartime vision of relative social
harmony achieved through regulation of business, rationalization, price
fixing, and social planning.[23] Wartime health needs and the public outcry over the devastating effects of venereal diseases, tuberculosis, typhus,
deep wounds, and alcohol catapulted health care to the forefront of
public debates. During this time the federal government extended its
activities into the field of social insurance. The War Risk Insurance Act
of 1917 eventually insured four million American soldiers and sailors.
The act, drawn up with the help of progressive reformers, mirrored
the wartime extension of insurance benefits in Europe. It offered life
insurance, medical care, vocational education, and disability benefits
for war-related injuries or death. It also forced enlisted men to send
home a family allowance, which was subsidized by the government.[24]

During the war, the campaigners for insurance reform began to
embrace this expansion of federal power in addition to pushing self-
governed mutual insurance funds. Samuel McCune Lindsay, president
of the AALL in 1919, expected health insurance to result from 'a new
concept of governmental duty and opportunity growing out of our
recent experiences in preparing the nation for the part which it took in
the war'.[25] The Progressives believed that the federal programs revealed
that 'the true American spirit of independence and self-help' had joined
with 'the government in its efforts to do justice in the emergencies
created by this war'.[26] They expected that the government, in cooperation with private insurance companies, would extend insurance coverage
to all workers.[27] However, wartime government intervention did not
contribute to the expansion of the social welfare responsibilities or
redistributive powers of the state. In general, the only departments
that broadened their power base were traditional repressive agencies,
such as those of justice and the interior. In the public mind the war
legitimized the use of the state as a restrictive police power. As Uriel
Rosenthal concluded, the war revealed that the traditional repressive
element in the American state was better institutionalized than the
welfare complex.[28]

The insurance field was a point in case. Wartime insurance reformers
shifted from advocating decentralized and self-governed mutual funds,
to urging a broader national public health policy, preventive safety
measures, compulsory physical examinations, and the amendment of
existing workmen's compensation acts.[29] This forestalled any reform in
the direction of broader democratic participation of workers, since the
workmen's compensation systems were not based on the principle of

effective worker representation.[30] As Rubinow noted, American work-men's compensation laws favored 'straight out-and-out state insurance against the democratic self-government type'. Citing laws in California, Ohio, Colorado, Washington, and other states, he found that 'the "un-American" institution of state insurance in the field of compensation has become more extensive in the United States than it has ever been in Europe'.[31] The extension of government insurance programs to government workers in the 1920s created privileges for an interest group, not a broad-based system of social security. Although federal programs for medical care, vocational rehabilitation, and compensa-tion for disability continued to grow after the war, the government life insurance program was allowed to lapse.[32] Thus, the war cemented the selective, exclusionary, and reward-based foundation of American social insurance, following the precedent set by the Civil War pension system. 'Are we ready to admit that a life full of toil is of less social value than a life full of play and parade, with a few occasional battles thrown in?', Rubinow asked in 1904.[33] The war revealed that the ques-tion had been answered in the affirmative. Workers and soldiers would continue to be treated according to different standards. In fact, progres-sive rhetoric itself had, to some extent, encouraged a debate that focused on the themes of fault, dissimulation, malingering, 'playing sick', and the distinction between the deserving and the undeserving poor. Charles Henderson promoted health insurance as a means of protecting working men, while 'dependents, defectives and other parasites belong to another social group which exists by means of alms and theft'.[34] Although the AALL health bill, reflecting Rubinow's revisionist social democratic approach, attempted to exclude the moralistic considerations that haunted the American debate, many Progressives were not able to free themselves from the mental shackles of the poor law tradition.

The postwar reliance of reformers on the police power of the state and business support, exemplified by Herbert Hoover's idea of the 'asso-ciative state' and John R. Commons's emphasis on employer cooperation in Wisconsin, was indicative of a larger intellectual shift within the Progressive movement, to be discussed in the second part of this paper.[35] It marked the acceptance of neo-liberal ideas of the associative state and welfare capitalism in the reform discourse in American society. Contrary to Richard Hofstadter's classic dictum, war had not proven the nemesis of liberalism. Instead, it effectively contributed to the destruction of the philosophical middle ground that had developed between liberalism and socialism. Pre-war Progressives had formulated a cultural-organicist social theory as a genuine intellectual alternative to both *laissez-faire* liberalism and revolutionary socialism.

In his seminal book on progressivism, James Kloppenberg saw reform thought as 'a body of ideas cut loose from its moorings in the liberal tradition', because the reformers 'renounced the atomistic empiricism, psychological hedonism, and utilitarian ethics associated with nineteenth-century liberalism'.[36] Kloppenberg detected 'genuinely radical impulses' in progressive social reform, although they 'filtered into the political process in a way that has enabled systems of welfare capitalism ... to perpetuate themselves'.[37]

Kloppenberg regarded progressive reform as part and parcel of a fundamental transformation of Western conceptions of knowledge, ethics, democracy, and social action. Rejecting *a priori* economic laws, the Progressives opened up the field for pragmatic experimentation with reform, he claimed. Their theory of voluntary action, he argued, emphasized man's ability to shape his environment and create an ethical society. Many Progressives opposed the liberal model of man as an autonomous, acquisitive, and self-interested being, whose freedom was grounded in private property.

Progressive social theory was the result of a fertile cross-cultural exchange of ideas. It was to a large extent inspired by the teachings of the German Historical School of Economics, and the ideas of American pragmatism. The cultural-organicist undercurrent in progressive reform was not narrowly moralistic, but cosmopolitan and relativistic. German scholars introduced their students to a philosophy that embraced the uncertainty of truth, the interconnectedness of existence, the potential of the creative human will, and the significance of ethics in society. Gustav Schmoller, Adolf Wagner, Wilhelm Roscher, Johannes Conrad, Lujo Brentano, and other German economists were frequently mentioned by leading German-trained Progressives as their most influential teachers.[38]

The progressive emphasis on public ownership, civic centers, and, last but not least, mutual insurance funds was part and parcel of the reformers' attempt to define American democracy as an ethical community, rather than as a community of interest. John Dewey reasoned that extended avenues of public participation would allow individuals to recognize that their freedom and happiness were intrinsically tied to their social being. Democracy, which relied on the participation of all individuals based on equal rights, 'is the effective embodiment of the moral ideal of a good which consists in the development of all the social capacities of every individual member'.[39] Other German-trained thinkers, such as Simon Nelson Patten and Albion Small, further elaborated on the cultural-organicist ideal of a society defined as a social organism striving for ethical advancement.[40]

Compulsory health insurance exemplified the ethical and organicist, even revivalistic, elements of progressive social thought. New civic institutions, such as mutual insurance funds, were more than simply mechanisms of imposing administrative order for the purpose of making health provisions more predictable and rational. They were designed to awaken intrinsic moral feelings in order to advance the ethical level of society through social participation.

This process consisted of three steps. First, progressive social thinkers regarded each social institution as an expression or objectification of a historically and culturally constituted moral sentiment. Many scholars of progressivism interpreted this ethical concern primarily as hiding more immediate economic and status considerations, or as an expression of a narrow moralistic point of view.[41] However, the reformers' emphasis on ethics was an integral part of their intellectual departure from orthodox liberalism. Ethical precepts, as John Graham Brooks maintained, should be the basis of social reform, since it was 'against this "ethical" function of the state that political radicals and orthodox economists alike directed their sharpest fire'.[42] The concept of the objectification of ethical impulses in institutions was a legacy of romantic thought and Hegelian idealism. As Gustav Schmoller, the leading advocate of the Historical School, put it, the economic organization of a society was the product of the 'ethical and customary views on what is right and just in the relationship between social classes'.[43] Many Progressives regarded ethics as historically and culturally constituted, rather than as reflections of absolute moral ideas. Likewise, they did not consider modern society to be the result of objective, natural processes, but rather of specific, historical institutions consciously created to realize evolving ideas of justice.

Historicists and Progressives alike substituted historical relativism for the liberal belief in the universal operation of Malthus's law of population growth, the iron law of wages, and the dictates of self-interest. The character of business organization, Thorstein Veblen declared, conformed 'to the circumstances of the time, not to any logical scheme of development from small to great or from simple to complex'.[44] Frederic Howe decried the American obsession 'with the idea that the laws of commerce are like the laws of nature. We assume that they cannot be controlled or aided by man', while Germany 'takes it as a matter of course that many things must be done by the state in order to protect its life and develop industry'.[45]

Second, the reformers argued that the power and significance of a new institution, such as an insurance fund, rested in its role in transforming moral feelings into conscious ethical principles. The Progressives evoked the Jeffersonian idea of virtue residing in 'the people', which they could easily reconcile with the historicist faith in the customs and ethics of the *Volk*. Thus, the reformers embraced new social institutions that allowed for the greatest measure of mutuality, democratic participation, self-government, and public control, because they regarded them as commensurate with the tradition and customs of

American society. Although many German-trained Progressives considered the state to be an ethical institution expressive of a sense of mutual responsibility permeating society, they rejected the notion of the leviathan state and large-scale bureaucratic control. Schmoller summed up the creed: 'Every larger undertaking whenever it united continuously a certain number of men for a common purpose reveals itself as a moral community.' He noted that, in the wake, 'the relations of those concerned necessarily exchange a merely economic for a generally moral character'.[46] The social sciences were an important element in the progressive social conception, because they operated on the assumption that society was not an aggregation of autonomous individuals, but an organism, where freedom, individuality, and morality were dependent on institutional organization and social customs. Albion Small, Dewey's colleague at the University of Chicago, demanded that sociology be 'a moral philosophy conscious of its task, and systematically pursuing knowledge of cause and effect within this process of moral evolution'.[47] In Dewey's eyes, the social sciences were a means to a moral end of developing 'the welfare of society as an organized community of attainment and endeavor'.[48]

Third, the Progressives assumed that participation in the insurance funds, to use the example at hand, would not only refine individual morality by replacing the motivation of self-interest and calculating reason with the dictates of an inner moral sense. It would also yield new moral feelings, born of experiences and sentiments that developed from the newly attained level of social interaction. This, the Progressives thought, would lead to the further development of social ethics. The revivalistic undercurrent of progressive reform is most visible in this concept. The Progressives envisioned reform as a process of awakening and conversion. They also juxtaposed their conception of the living social organism with the lifeless, meaningless, and deadening laws of orthodox liberalism. Charles Richmond Henderson explained that the United States was 'still struggling with its atomistic and self-centered notions born of primitive conditions of frontier life where man was separated from man, and where institutions have not had time to develop'. America, he argued, had not yet come to 'accept the principle of national solidarity and obligation for the welfare of all citizens'.[49]

In the same vein, John Dewey declared that under modern conditions 'individual achievements and possibilities require new civic and political agencies if they are to be maintained as realities'. Individualism meant 'inequity, harshness, and retrogression to barbarism', unless it was 'a generalized individualism which takes into account the real good and effective – not merely formal – freedom of every member of society'.[50]

Many pre-war Progressives thought that social control would be the result of an inner moral awakening through increased social interaction and participation in institutions of self-government. The moral growth of the individual, they argued, would control the unreflected emotional action that they believed to be the basis of revolutionary upheaval. Thus, the joint administration of the health insurance funds, the AALL stated, 'means that the organization will not be dominated by a small coterie of radical workers who may not be guided by sound business principles', but neither would it 'rest with a group of business men eager to cut down benefits'.[51] The concept of social control through imposing restrictive regulations had been put on the back burner.

While wartime rhetoric also invoked an image of social cohesion and harmony, government intervention was not designed to further ethical self-development, but to enforce a culturally exclusive and politically repressive consensus. Governmental powers were expanded into the realm of social insurance, while the idea of self-governed mutual funds came to naught. The goal of wartime insurance reform, AALL President Irving Fisher suggested in 1918, was the 'cementing of the labor element to the government', not the expansion of political participation.[52] When the Progressives embraced the extension of governmental powers during the war, they broke with a significant part of their own political tradition, which embraced local self-government, decentralized decision-making, and the extension of the public sphere of control. The neo-liberal strain of thought that gained prominence in the postwar period, however, had already been an undercurrent in pre-war progressive discourse. Political economist Henry Carter Adams, for example, who had studied under Wagner and Knies in the late 1870s, developed a liberal restrictionist model of government intervention. He called for state 'conditioning' of economic relations and for restrictions on the accumulation of profits.[53] In the words of the German-trained social worker Edward T. Devine, the state was obligated to 'fix the levels below which the exploitation of workers and consumers would not be tolerated', and above which 'the principles of free competition might safely and advantageously be left free to operate'.[54]

In conclusion, wartime opponents of reform effectively exploited the declining public image of Germany to set up insurmountable cultural and political obstacles for the insurance reformers. However, it was the internal intellectual transition from a cultural-organicist conception of new social institutions to a neo-liberal model of state police powers that spelled the death of pre-war progressivism. During and after the war many Progressives embraced either the restrictive moralism of prohibition and immigration control, or pursued closer ties with business. In the field of public health, prohibition, measures against public smoking, and litigation suits proved more successful in stirring up reformist fervor than full-fledged attempts to reform the insurance business. To employ Norman Furniss's and Timothy Tilton's categories, the United States developed into a corporate-oriented positive state, rather than a social security state that emphasized minimum standards, or a social welfare state that operated on radically democratic and egalitarian principles.[55]

Whether the campaign for compulsory health insurance would have been more successful if World War I had not interfered remains a difficult question to answer. On the one hand, a number of factors that contributed to the movement's failure would have existed despite the war. The federal political structure of the United States, for example, hampered the development of social welfare policies. It gave states wide discretion over taxation, regulation, and social programs, and contained no provision for revenue-sharing. As a result, states 'behaved much like business firms in a competitive market', where the 'most marginal competitors will tend to cut unnecessary costs in order to attract business', through low taxes and limited social expenditures.[56] Likewise, the power of the courts often stymied the development of social legislation. In addition, opposition from insurance interests, business, and some parts of organized labor was vocal and well-funded. On the other hand, wartime attacks on the alleged Germanic origins of the insurance movement, combined with widespread ignorance about the workings of the compulsory system, were sufficient to provide opponents of reform with the necessary means of turning the tide.[57] Wartime propaganda and hysteria were instrumental in undermining support for the movement, since the AALL had made significant inroads into both labor and business circles, and had initially succeeded in gaining the support of the AMA. In addition, wartime insurance programs, though supported by progressive reformers, limited the range of reform and forestalled the development of broad-based programs for social security.

Notes

1.   Isaac M. Rubinow, *The Quest for Security* (New York: 1934), p. 209.
2.   Roy Lubove, *The Struggle for Social Security, 1900–1935* (Cambridge, Mass.: 1968), pp. 29, 67.
3.   The number of American students of the social sciences at German universities increased dramatically after 1880. Germany remained the first choice for most American students going to Europe. In 1885, two hundred Americans were enrolled at the University of Berlin, while only thirty American students attended the Sorbonne in Paris. See Jurgen Herbst, *The German Historical School in American Scholarship: A Study in the Transfer of Culture* (Ithaca, NY: 1965), p. 8. The legislative influence of German-trained American social scientists, Herbst points out, was

larger than their scholarly impact (p. 202). See also Jack C. Myles, 'German Historicism and American Economics: A Study of the Influence of the German Historical School on American Economic Thought' (Ph.D. diss., Princeton University, 1956).

4.   Committee on Social Insurance, 'Health Insurance: Tentative Draft for an Act', *American Labor Legislation Review* 6 (June 1916), pp. 250f. The German revisions reduced the original two-thirds majority of workers in the insurance funds, established in the 1883 laws, to equal representation. In turn, they limited workers' contributions to 50 per cent.

5.   John B. Andrews, 'Social Insurance', *Annals* 69 (January 1917), p. 47.

6.   Henry R. Seager, 'Plan for Health Insurance Act', *American Labor Legislation Review* 6 (March 1916), p. 24.

7.   For a recent study on gender and race issues in progressive reform see Linda Gordon (ed.), *Women, the State, and Welfare* (Madison, Wis.: 1990).

8.   John Graham Brooks, *Compulsory Insurance in Germany* (Washington, DC: 1895), p. 288.

9.   For a discussion of the significance of the funeral benefit, see Paul Starr, 'Transformation in Defeat: The Changing Objective of National Health Insurance, 1915–1980', in *Compulsory Health Insurance: The Continuing American Debate*, Contributions in Medical History, no. 11 (Westport, Conn.: 1982), p. 123; Rubinow later argued that the health insurance movement signed its own death warrant by including the funeral benefit. See Rubinow, *Quest for Security*, p. 213.

10. For a closer look at the ambiguous stance of the AMA towards compulsory health insurance, see Ronald L. Numbers, *Almost Persuaded: American Physicians and Compulsory Health Insurance, 1912–1920* (Baltimore, Md.: 1978). For a discussion of the National Civic Federation, see Hace Sorel Tishler, *Self-Reliance and Social Security, 1870–1917* (Fort Washington, Md.: 1971). Although Edward Berkowitz and Kim McQuaid claim that the private sector provided the conceptual models for public welfare programs, the health insurance campaign revealed the power of insurance interests to limit the development of social reform beyond the narrow confines of welfare capitalism. See Berkowitz and McQuaid, *Creating the Welfare State: The Political Economy of Twentieth-Century Reform* (Lawrence, Kan.: 1992).

11. Quoted in J. Lee Kreader, 'America's Prophet for Social Security: A Biography of Isaac M. Rubinow' (Ph.D. diss., University of Chicago, 1988), p. 251. See also Samuel Gompers, 'Labor versus its Barnacles', *American Federationist* 23 (April 1916), p. 270. For the role of the social insurance campaigns in creating a tenuous coalition between labor and Progressives, see Irwin Yellowitz, *Labor and the Progressive Movement in New York State, 1897–1916* (Ithaca, NY: 1965), pp. 138f.

12. Numbers, *Almost Persuaded*, p. 81. For a discussion of the California campaign, see Arthur J. Viseltear, 'Compulsory Health Insurance in California, 1915–1918', *Journal of the History of Medicine* 24 (April 1969), pp. 151–82.

13. Clarke Chambers, *Seedtime of Reform: American Social Service and Social Action 1918–1933* (Minneapolis, Minn.: 1963), p. 158.

14. Frederic C. Howe, *Socialized Germany* (New York: 1915), p. 7.

15. See Theda Skocpol and John Ikenberry, 'The Political Formation of the American Welfare State in Historical and Comparative Perspective', in Richard F. Tomasson (ed.), *The Welfare State, 1883–1983*, Comparative Social Research, no. 6 (Greenwich, Conn.: 1983); in addition, Isaac Rubinow, who was deeply interested in race issues, attacked the pension system for excluding blacks and immigrants. See Kreader, 'Prophet of Social Insurance', p. 183.

16. For a closer discussion, see Berkowitz and McQuaid, *Creating the Welfare State*.

17. Charles R. Henderson, 'The Logic of Social Insurance', *Annals* 33 (March 1909), p. 268.

18. Charles R. Henderson, *Industrial Insurance in the United States* (Chicago, Ill.: 1909), p. 12.

19. David M. Kennedy, *Over Here: The First World War and American Society* (Oxford: 1980), p. 42.

20. Frederick L. Hoffman, 'Some Lessons of the German Failure in Compulsory Health Insurance', in *Facts and Fallacies of Compulsory Health Insurance* (2nd edn; Newark, NJ: 1920), p. 186.

21. Isaac M. Rubinow, *Social Insurance: With Special Reference to American Conditions* (New York: 1913), p. 283; see also J. Joseph Huthmacher, 'Urban Liberalism in the Age of Reform', *Mississippi Valley Historical Review* 49 (September 1962), pp. 231–41.

22. Lubove, *Social Security*, p. 115; see also pp. 168–70.

23. For a detailed discussion see, for example, Allen F. Davis, 'Welfare, Reform, and World War I', *American Quarterly* 19 (Fall 1967), pp. 516–33.

24. See Samuel McCune Lindsay, 'The Soldiers' and Sailors' Insurance Acts', *Proceedings of the National Conference of Social Work* (1918), pp. 392–5.

25. Samuel McCune Lindsay, 'Next Steps in Social Insurance in the United States', *American Labor Legislation Review* 9 (March 1919), p. 110.

26. Lindsay, 'The Soldiers' and Sailors' Insurance Acts', p. 395.

27. Lindsay, 'Next Steps in Social Insurance', pp. 112–13.

28. Uriel Rosenthal, 'Welfare State or State of Welfare?', in Tomasson (ed.), *Welfare State*, p. 295.

29. See, for example, National Industrial Conference Board, 'Sickness Insurance or Sickness Prevention', *Research Report* 6 (March 1918), p. 22. In 1919, the Illinois Health Insurance Commission decided against compulsory insurance, recommending instead that the 'authority and power of the state Department of Public Health be enlarged', *Report of the Health Insurance Commission of the State of Illinois* (Springfield, Ill.: 1919), p. 167.

30. Workmen's compensation laws became a fundamental element of the rudimentary welfare state created during the early twentieth century. They enjoyed widespread support in business circles because they averted the threat of litigation. See, for example, Berkowitz and McQuaid, *Creating the Welfare State*, p. 43; Gaston Rimlinger, *Welfare Policy and Industrialization in Europe, America, and Russia* (New York: 1971), p. 120; see also Lubove, *Struggle for Social Security*, p. 57.

31.   Isaac M. Rubinow, 'Health Insurance through Local Mutual Funds',
      American Labor Legislation Review 7 (1917), pp. 74–5.
32.   See Chambers, *Seedtime*, p. 156.
33.   Isaac M. Rubinow, 'Labor Insurance', *Journal of Political Economy* 12
      (June 1904), p. 372.
34.   Charles R. Henderson, 'Workingmen's Insurance', *World Today* 10 (Feb-
      ruary 1906), p. 148.
35.   See Robert D. Cuff, *The War Industries Board: Business–Government
      Relations during World War I* (Baltimore, Md.: 1973); Ellis W. Hawley,
      'Herbert Hoover, the Commerce Secretariat, and the Vision of an
      "Associative State", 1921–1928', *Journal of American History* 61 (June
      1974), pp. 116–40; John R. Commons and John B. Andrews, *Principles of
      Labor Legislation* (New York: 1920).
36.   James Kloppenberg, *Uncertain Victory: Social Democracy and Progressivism
      in European and American Thought, 1870–1920* (New York: 1986), p. 298.
37.   Ibid., p. 11.
38.   Henry W. Farnam, 'Deutsch–amerikanische Beziehungen in der Volks-
      wirtschaftslehre', chap. 18 in *Die Entwicklung der deutschen Volkswirt-
      schaftslehre im neunzehnten Jahrhundert: Gustav Schmoller zur siebenzigsten
      Wiederkehr seines Geburtstages* (Leipzig: 1908), p. 29; see also Herbst,
      German Historical School, p. 134.
39.   John Dewey and James Tufts, *Ethics* (New York: 1908), p. 474.
40.   See, for example, Simon N. Patten, *The New Basis for Civilization* (New
      York: 1907); Albion Small, 'The Significance of Sociology for Ethics',
      University of Chicago Decennial Publications 4 (1903), pp. 113–49.
41.   See, for example, Mary O. Furner, *Advocacy and Objectivity: A Crisis in
      the Professionalization of American Social Science, 1865–1905* (Lexington,
      Ken.: 1975).
42.   Brooks, *Compulsory Insurance*, p. 36.
43.   'Die Volkswirtschaftliche Organisation jedes Volkes ist kein Naturprodukt,
      wie man so lange gefaselt, sie ist hauptsächlich ein Produkt der jeweiligen
      sittlichen Anschauungen über das, was im Verhältnis der verschiedenen
      socialen Klassen zu einander das Rechte, das Gerechte sei.' Gustav
      Schmoller, 'Die sociale Frage und der preußische Staat', in *Zur Social-
      und Gewerbepolitik der Gegenwart: Reden und Aufsätze* (Leipzig: 1890),
      pp. 55–6.
44.   Thorstein Veblen, 'Gustav Schmoller's Economics', in *The Place of Science
      in Modern Civilization and Other Essays* (New York: 1932), p. 278; the
      essay originally appeared in 1901.
45.   Frederic C. Howe, 'City Building in Germany', *Scribner's* 47 (May
      1910), p. 611.
46.   Gustav Schmoller, 'The Idea of Justice in Political Economy', *Annals* 4
      (March 1894), p. 23; the German original appeared in 1881.
47.   Albion W. Small, 'Technique as Approach to Science: A Methodological
      Note', *American Journal of Sociology* 27 (March 1922), p. 650, quoted in
      Chris Bernert, 'From Cameralism to Sociology with Albion Small',
      Journal of the History of Sociology 4 (Fall 1982), p. 54.
48.   Dewey and Tufts, *Ethics*, p. 473.

49.   Charles R. Henderson, 'The German Social Policy', *Chautauquan* 52 (November 1908), p.397.
50.   Dewey and Tufts, *Ethics*, p.472.
51.   'Brief for Health Insurance', *American Labor Legislation Review* 6 (June 1913), p.229.
52.   Irving Fisher, 'Health and War', *American Labor Legislation Review* 8 (1918), p.13.
53.   Henry C. Adams to James B. Angell, 25 March 1886; Henry C. Adams, 'Berlin Diary', 20 December 1878, p.17, and 4 January 1879, p.31, Henry C. Adams Papers, Bentley Historical Library, University of Michigan, Ann Arbor.
54.   Edward T. Devine, *When Social Work Was Young* (New York: 1939), p.4.
55.   Norman Furniss and Timothy Tilton, *The Case for the Welfare State: From Social Security to Social Equality* (Bloomington, Ind.: 1977), p.x.
56.   David Brian Robertson, 'The Bias of American Federalism: The Limits of Welfare State Development in the Progressive Era', *Journal of Policy History* 1 (1989), p.272.
57.   As Ronald Numbers has shown, many physicians remained ignorant about and apathetic towards the movement for compulsory health insurance. See Numbers, *Almost Persuaded*, p.51; see also Rubinow, *Quest for Security*, p.213.

8

Maritime Strategy and the Crucible of War: The Impact of World War I on American Naval Policy, 1914–1921

Michael Simpson

Despite a proud history dating back to the Revolution and a brief Civil War expansion, the US Navy in 1914 was as much a 'new navy' as those of Germany and Japan, its transformation from a heterogeneous collection of sailing frigates and coastal monitors into a distant water battlefleet dating from the 1880s. The rise of Latin American navies and the development of great power rivalries in the Far East, renewed interest in an isthmian canal, and a more assertive nationalism suffused by social Darwinism, combined with burgeoning trade and a healthy Treasury surplus to foster the rapid growth of a modern fleet.[1] Furthermore, Admiral Stephen B. Luce and his acolyte Captain Alfred T. Mahan taught the navy to think and to study; officers were schooled in strategy and high command at the Naval War College (1884), while the Naval Institute (1873) enabled them to develop their professional interests further.[2] The cheap triumphs of 1898 enhanced the navy's profile. President Theodore Roosevelt, who sought to integrate foreign and defense policies, instigating war plans against Germany (*Black*) and Japan (*Orange*), built up a state-of-the-art, 'blue water' dreadnought battlefleet, second only to the Royal Navy.[3] However, his successor, William Howard Taft, lacked both interest in and understanding of sea power and his relative neglect of the navy coupled with the naval race between Britain and Germany led to the latter eclipsing the US fleet.[4]

Woodrow Wilson also evinced little interest in defense, appointing Josephus Daniels, who shared the President's pacifistic sympathies, as secretary of the navy.[5] However, the young Franklin D. Roosevelt, who was fascinated by all things maritime, became the assistant secretary and, scornful of Daniels, identified himself with the admirals.[6] FDR shared his cousin Theodore's belief that '[i]f a nation desires any weight in foreign policy ... then it must possess the means to make its words good by deeds'.[7] Both Roosevelts supported the recommendations of the navy's general board (established in 1900) for a fleet strong enough to uphold the Open Door policy and the Monroe Doctrine, and defend the freedom of the seas and the ban on Asiatic immigration. Nevertheless, Daniels sought only to maximize political support by following

the golden mean between those like FDR who agitated for four
battleships a year, and most Democrats who, in the interests of peace
and retrenchment, wanted none.[8]

Though the United States possessed a substantial battlefleet in 1914,
it was in a poor state of readiness due to its ill-conceived employment
in the coercion of Mexico. Moreover, the politicians' obsession with
battleships left the navy's deficiencies in flotilla craft, logistic support
and well-defended bases unaddressed. Its air arm was vestigial, and its
submarine branch grossly inefficient. Short of officers and skilled manpower, it also lacked adequate reserves.[9] Furthermore, its war plans
were quite impractical. War plan *Orange* (1911) assumed a clean sweep
of America's Pacific possessions by Japan and an exhausting campaign
to recover them, involving (before the opening of the Panama Canal in
1914) a repetition of the 1907 voyage of the Great White Fleet to the
orient through the Mediterranean, conjuring up images of a second
Tsushima – 'a grand strategy for a war of illusions'.[10] Indeed, when a
crisis with Japan developed in 1913 – though a bellicose FDR barked
'It's war – and we're ready!' – the administration, advised by the navy
that victory over Japan was doubtful, forbade any warlike moves.[11] War
plan *Black* was equally absurd – 'a fabulous tale of future Teutonic
perfidy'.[12] It envisaged the German fleet sailing into the Caribbean,
threatening the Panama Canal and landing an army on the shores of
the Gulf states. American strategy was to defeat the German fleet
far out in the Atlantic.[13] Aside from the fact that the British would
not have tolerated an armada roaming the Atlantic, German logistic
problems in the Caribbean would have been as insuperable as those of
America in the Pacific. Moreover, in one of his more perceptive
observations, Mahan pointed out 'the tendency towards such an equi-
librium of naval force in Europe as will render it increasingly difficult
for any one Power to divert a large detachment of its navy so far from
home shores'.[14] Anglo-German naval antagonism actually made America
more secure in the Atlantic.

When war broke out in 1914, therefore, the US Navy lacked a clear
development policy, a balanced fleet, realistic plans, sufficient manpower
and adequate training. Furthermore, the initial effect of the war was
regressive. Wilson, proclaiming American neutrality, attempted to
mediate the conflict on the basis of 'peace without victory'. To avoid
provoking the belligerents, he suspended the Army–Navy Joint Board
(established in 1903) on the grounds that it might be tempted to
prepare for war. Daniels halted revision of the war plans, and officers
were forbidden to visit war zones or to write about the conflict. While
Wilson, Bryan and Daniels thus earned the plaudits of the prominent
peace movement, Daniels's chief naval adviser, Admiral Bradley Fiske,
lamented that '[t]he people of the United States are developing an

anti-military spirit'.[15] At the end of 1914, the navy was even less ready for action than it had been at the beginning of the year.

By early 1915, however, the persistence of the war strengthened offi-cers' demands for a naval general staff, their developing professionalism clashing with Daniels's fear of 'Prussianization'. Whereas '[t]he German naval machinery was immeasurably better than ours', the US Navy was still burdened with the antiquated bureau system of 1841.[16] When Fiske attempted to remedy this by colluding with congressman Richmond P. Hobson, a naval hero of 1898, to insert in the 1915 estimates provision for a chief of naval operations (CNO) with a supporting staff, Daniels, perceiving that the secretary would become a mere cypher, amended it to read: 'There shall be a Chief of Naval Operations ... who shall, under the direction of the Secretary of the Navy, be charged with the operations of the fleet and with the preparation and readiness of plans for its use in war.'[17] Sandwiched between the powerful Navy Depart-ment bureaus and fleet commanders, the CNO thus held responsibility without power. Moreover, the first CNO, William S. Benson, an obscure captain, stolid, dependable and loyal, who had evinced no interest in strategy, lacked Fiske's drive, originality, talents and apparent lust for power. Fiske observed that he was 'one of the last men who should have been selected for such a job', adding perceptively: 'It is probable this was the reason he *was* selected.'[18] Nevertheless, while Benson offered no threat to Daniels's continued domination, the distant drums of war had brought into the high command a new post, which, as a result of hostilities, came to dominate the civilian officers, the bureaux and the fleets.[19]

More importantly, the longer the war dragged on, the more likely became American belligerence, and this prospect stimulated a 'prepared-ness' movement. Led by Republicans such as Theodore Roosevelt, Henry Cabot Lodge, Elihu Root and A.P. Gardner, it was supported chiefly by the Anglophile East Coast establishment. Theodore Roosevelt, castigating Wilson for 'drifting "stern-foremost"' into war, 'advocated preparation for war in order to avert war', claiming that 'a proper armament is the surest guarantee of peace'.[20] Lodge believed that '[t]he ocean barrier which defended us in 1776 and 1812 no longer exists. Steam and electricity have destroyed it', while his son-in-law Gardner declared: 'The United States shall never be at the mercy of any other nation.'[21] FDR, disdainful of the pacifist, isolationist and arbitrationist elements dominating the Democrats, stormed, '[t]he country needs the truth about the Army and the Navy instead of a lot of soft mush about everlasting peace', and disloyally furnished the opposition with damaging facts about the navy.[22] The campaign was endorsed by the Navy League, the League to Enforce Peace, the National Security League, the US Chamber of Commerce, labor leaders and the Plattsburg movement. Leading journals pointed out that America's battlefleet was outnumbered 4:1 and 2.3:1 by those of Britain and Germany respectively, while Japan was engaged on a major expansion. Professional opinion naturally supported expansion and now demanded parity with the Royal Navy. Fiske complained that the American people had not thought out their international role and corresponding maritime requirements, while Darwinist assumptions prevailed in the naval hierarchy: 'The present world war has emphasised the fact that survival of the fittest is as much a law of nature as ever.' Moreover, since '[m]odern science and invention have annihilated space', it was foolish to believe that the victors would leave America alone.[23]

Nevertheless, Wilson, drawing strength from the equally clamorous and substantially more numerous peace lobby, was unmoved by the preparedness campaign until the summer of 1915, when he called abruptly on his secretaries of war and the navy to draw up major expansion programs. The President remained vague on his dramatic conversion to deterrence and possible overseas intervention; but he was exercised by Germany's tardiness in settling the *Lusitania* affair, by Japan's seizure of German territories in the Pacific and by her Twenty-One Demands on China, by Allied agreements on postwar territorial and commercial adjustments, and by the need to defend America's mushrooming trade and merchant marine.[24] Exasperated by Britain's cavalier treatment of American shipping, he exclaimed to his close adviser Colonel Edward M. House: 'Let us build a bigger navy than hers and do as we please!', but he desired also to regain the political initiative from the Republicans.[25] In February 1916 he declared indiscreetly: 'There is no other navy in the world that has to cover so great an area of defense as the American navy, and it ought, in my judgment, to be incomparably the greatest in the world.'[26] Wilson's conversion to Rooseveltian big-stick diplomacy disconcerted the moderate chairmen of the congressional naval committees, Senator Tillman and Lemuel Padgett, and the Democratic House Leader, Claude Kitchin, lamented that 'the war goblins and jingoes have caught' the President.[27]

Responding to the President's conversion to preparedness, the general board, which harbored the nightmare of a two-ocean war, argued that '[o]ur present Navy is not sufficient to give due weight to the diplomatic remonstrances of the United States in peace nor to enforce its policies in war', and drew up a program for 16 capital ships and 140 other vessels.[28] Though peace groups regarded this 1916 program as a large step towards war and *The New Republic* castigated it as 'armament without limit', continued international turmoil and the timely battle of Jutland swept it through Congress.[29] Moreover, the supposedly subservient Benson also subtly reinserted the substance of the CNO proposals rejected by Daniels in 1915; even Fiske commented that the

CNO's office was 'now as good as a general staff'.[30] Other war-induced steps included the purchase of the Danish West Indies, the establishment of a technical naval consulting board and an advisory Council of National Defense, the refinement of the war plans, and improved logistic support in the Pacific. However, naval aviation, the submarine service and the defense of overseas bases remained low priorities. FDR's call for a national security council went unheeded, and foreign and defense policies thus remained uncoordinated.[31]

Nevertheless, *World's Work* claimed justifiably that '[w]e have seriously undertaken the business of organizing a Navy worthy of the Nation', but America was catapulted into belligerency before the 'navy second to none' got under way.[32] Moreover, even after Germany resumed unrestricted submarine warfare in February 1917, Daniels resisted calls to mobilize the navy, though FDR and Benson did what little they could.[33] America's 'isolationist' tradition left the nation ignorant of the European diplomatic and military situation, of the probability of her intervention on the side of the Allies, and the likelihood that she would have to fight in Europe. The fleet of 1917 still lacked balance and its war plans were inapt. Continued emphasis on the battlefleet meant that the navy was ill-equipped to meet the challenge of the U-boats, which by 1917 were the greatest maritime threat to Allied survival, yet in 1914 Fiske had prophesied accurately that war with Germany would come about through interference with American shipping in the eastern Atlantic.[34] *The New Republic*, observing that 'ever since the day the *Lusitania* was sunk, our one known specific prospective enemy has been Germany and its submarine', had called in 1916 for 'a horde of anti-submarine boats'.[35] The visits in 1915–16 of German cargo submarines and U-53, which sank vessels in sight of the coast, testing American reactions to war on her doorstep, 'destroyed forever the ridiculous idea that 3,000 miles of ocean furnishes an insurance against war'.[36] However, the navy, unaware of the true extent of U-boat depredations, noted complacently: 'It is apparent that the submarine is not an instrument fitted to dominate naval warfare.'[37] The acute shipping crisis in the spring of 1917 swiftly transformed the navy's programs, commands and attitudes.

The seriousness of the U-boat threat to Britain's Atlantic lifeline was quickly revealed to Rear-Admiral William S. Sims, ordered to London by Wilson in March 1917 to liaise with the Admiralty. On his arrival on 8 April, the Anglophile Sims, tactful, resourceful, dynamic and inspiring, was informed by the First Sea Lord, Admiral Jellicoe, that 'our present policy is heading straight for disaster', for U-boats were sinking one in every four ships leaving Britain; only one in ten were being replaced and the Germans were well on course to force Britain (and hence the Allies) into an unsatisfactory peace by September 1917, long before America's immense potential could be realized.[38] By May, Britain was down to 10 days' supply of sugar, 21 of grain and 42 of oil. Sims cabled at once that 'control of the sea is actually imperilled' and transmitted British requests for six million tons of merchant shipping and the despatch of all available American destroyers and light craft to the western approaches to the British Isles, the focal point of the naval war.[39] The British wished to integrate American forces into the Royal Navy's command structure for maximum effectiveness. In response, Sims told Washington that:

> The military situation is very grave indeed on account of the success of the enemy submarine campaign ... If the shipping losses continue as they have done during the past four months ... the Allies will be forced to very dire straits indeed, if they will not actually be forced into an unsatisfactory peace.[40]

Sims's pleas, supported by Ambassador Page, were treated with caution in Washington; both men were regarded as hopelessly pro-British.[41] Moreover, both Daniels, a notoriously 'slow decider', and Benson were unable to comprehend either the nature of the new form of sea warfare or the gravity of the situation.[42] Like most senior officers, Benson still thought in terms of surface fleet actions. He feared an imminent Allied defeat, leaving America exposed to an unimpaired German fleet, reinforced by surrendered ships, and possibly also by the Japanese. This nightmare strengthened Benson's determination to retain strong forces in American waters.[43] Furthermore, even an Allied victory might lead to economic and diplomatic pressure on the United States. Thus the Navy Department refused to curtail battleship construction in favor of a crash program of 200 destroyers; it took months of British pressure (supported by Sims and Page), a telling report by Benson's assistant, Captain Pratt, and Wilson's insistence (he observed that battleships were 'not of much value' in the war) to get dreadnought building suspended and the destroyer program under way.[44]

The crisis of the battle of the Atlantic led to the despatch to Europe of every available American anti-submarine vessel, but further adjustments to American maritime strategy were soon to follow. Encouraged by Sims and with the prospect of American reinforcements, Jellicoe, 'convinced the convoy system is a necessity and the only method left to us', ordered its institution in the North Atlantic.[45] As Sims pointed out: '[t]his convoy system is looked upon as an offensive measure ... the enemy would be forced to seek us' and, even if submarines did locate convoys, 'our losses would not be so great as at present'. He recommended that the US Navy 'should lend every possible support to ensure success'.[46] In Washington, the convoy system found favor with civilians rather than with the Navy Department, Wilson telling Sims that: 'I do not see how the necessary military supplies and supplies of food and fuel oil are to be delivered at British ports in any other way ... than under adequate convoy.'[47] Benson, however, rejected convoys, favoring armed merchant vessels sailing alone, to which Sims replied: 'Guns are no defence against torpedo attack.'[48] Benson agreed reluctantly to cooperate, and by September 1917 it was clear that 'Convoy was an unqualified success, and [one] to which the Germans had discovered no counter.' Only 0.59 per cent of ships in convoy were sunk and by the end of the war 93 per cent of shipping was escorted. The success of the convoy system was demonstrated further by the fact that from mid-summer of 1918 new construction was expected steadily to outweigh sinkings.[49]

American hesitation in extending maximum help to the Allies arose in large part from reservations about their strategy. As Wilson told Sims in July 1917: 'From the beginning of the war I have been greatly surprised at the failure of the British Admiralty to use Great Britain's naval supremacy in an effective way.'[50] He expostulated to Atlantic Fleet officers – 'We are hunting hornets all over the farm and letting the nest alone' – and stated that he was 'willing to sacrifice half the navy Great Britain and we have together, to crush that nest, because if we crush it the war is won'.[51] The American journalist Winston Churchill told the President that creative talent in the Royal Navy had been stifled, that the Sea Lords were all conservative, and that the Admiralty did no forward planning.[52] Graduates of the rather rigid, Mahanite Naval War College posted to London found the Admiralty slack, backward, haphazard, pessimistic and bleakly defensive. Benson complained further that America had not been taken into 'full partnership' and that the British assumed the Americans would fall in meekly with prevailing Allied strategy.[53] American exasperation exemplified the difference in military traditions. Historically, the British favored a cautious, indirect, long-term strategy. They pointed out that the whole Allied position hinged on the Royal Navy's command of the seas; over 10 million troops and their supplies had been transported, virtually without loss. These commitments and the Grand Fleet's distant blockade of Germany left inadequate resources for offensives; moreover, modern technology (mines and torpedoes) favored defenses.[54] The American military tradition was to aim at once for the enemy's jugular vein. However, when Benson declared, 'I think it better to lose some of our older battleships and other fighting craft than to remain on the defensive' and stressed the 'extreme urgency' of 'a definite Naval Policy based upon a concrete plan of operations' for the spring of 1918, Jellicoe patiently listed the practical obstacles to these 'odd ideas', calling the Americans' bluff by asking for twenty obsolescent vessels to help block German ports.[55] As Sims made clear, such operations would play to the enemy strategy of attrition.[56] Admiral Mayo, commander-in-chief of the Atlantic Fleet, and Benson, who visited Jellicoe in September and November respectively, were convinced by the Admiralty that such assaults were impracticable.[57] Baulked by the Admiralty's opposition to aggressive action, the Americans attempted to gain some leverage on Allied maritime strategy by insisting on an Allied Naval Council (formed in September 1917) to coordinate naval effort and decide a definite plan of offensive operations. They discovered, however, that Allied policies were set in concrete, that events dictated strategy, and that America's naval contribution was too hesitant and limited to gain her significant influence.[58]

Nevertheless, the resourceful and energetic Franklin Roosevelt, who supported full and immediate anti-submarine assistance to the Allies, sought ceaselessly for opportunities to seize the initiative in the maritime war. He was a tireless advocate of a mine barrage between Scotland and Norway, designed to pen the U-boats into the North Sea, claiming it as a sovereign remedy which, 'if it works ... will be the biggest single factor in winning the war'.[59] Initially, the British were characteristically sceptical, but by September 1917 Jellicoe had conceded that it was practicable. Logistic, technical and other problems delayed its laying until the spring of 1918, but by the end of the war it was 230 miles long, 30 miles wide, and consisted of nets and 70,000 mines (mostly American). Though formidable, it was neither complete nor impenetrable; between four and eight U-boats were destroyed – not a cost-effective return.[60]

FDR was also an enthusiast for hunting groups, being largely responsible for the construction of several hundred 'bantam' submarine chasers, which, equipped with listening gear and depth charges and led by destroyers, were intended to seek and destroy U-boats. Feeling that 'the enemy has maintained the initiative in the submarine war from the beginning', and dismissing convoys as a 'palliative', naval planners hoped to 'devote the maximum possible anti-submarine force to offensive operations'.[61] Unfortunately, the hydrophone was of more use to the submerged prey than to the surface hunter, the sub-chasers were unseaworthy, and the assistant chief of the British naval staff commented that: 'There is no more futile offensive measure than that of employing Destroyers in so-called hunting operations. ... Convoy is a bait which must attract enemy submarines.'[62] In any case, most American destroyers were diverted to escort American Expeditionary Force (AEF) transports; there would have been severe political repercussions had thousands of troops been lost. Hunting, severely curtailed by other demands on resources, achieved absolutely nothing, much to the Americans' chagrin.[63]

Roosevelt also entered the Mediterranean imbroglio with characteristic zest, self-confidence and brashness. Despite considerable naval
superiority in the Mediterranean, the Allied navies failed to coordinate
their forces (due largely to Franco-Italian antipathy) and suffered huge
losses to U-boats. In the Allied Naval Council, the Americans called
for the bombing of enemy submarine bases, amphibious assaults on the
Austrian Dalmatian coast, and mine barrages in the Sicilian Narrows,
the Adriatic and the Aegean, proposing also an 'Admiralissimo' to exercise supreme command.[64] Though the Americans had but a handful of
decrepit gunboats at Gibraltar and a squadron of the worthless chasers
at Corfu, FDR followed up these proposals. Visiting Rome in the
summer of 1918, he blithely took it upon himself to galvanize Allied
Mediterranean strategy. Declaring that 'we have no ultimate designs in
the Mediterranean', the even-handed Roosevelt pressed 'for more
actual offensive work against the Austrians on the Dalmatian coast';
unfortunately, the Italian '[n]aval people at the top are thinking more
about keeping their fleet intact at the end of the war than of winning
the war itself'. Moreover, his unauthorized diplomacy antagonized
the French, and Wilson and the American attempt to energize the
Mediterranean petered out.[65]

The American maritime tradition of bold and decisive strokes, executed with dash and courage in the spirit of John Paul Jones, Farragut
and Porter, was therefore ill-suited to the situation facing the United
States and its partners in 1917–18. For the most part, the war was a
monotonous, unglamorous defensive battle against the submarine. In
these circumstances, the expensive battleships of the Atlantic Fleet
seemed redundant, but even when, in the spring of 1917, the British
requested a division of American dreadnoughts to relieve some Grand
Fleet ships, the Navy Department refused. Benson, afraid of a German
victory and her possible alliance with Japan, concluded that: 'The strategic situation necessitates keeping the battleship force concentrated.'[66]
Once again, however, events and pressures in Europe overturned
Mahanite doctrine. Following his visit to Britain in November 1917,
Benson recommended the despatch of a division, though less on strategic than on political grounds. The battleships were the only idle US
vessels; a refusal to send them 'will be invoked in future against the building of large vessels'. Furthermore, a division working with the Grand
Fleet might prevent a British defeat, participate in a victory, gain
valuable experience, raise Atlantic Fleet morale and efficiency, and
strengthen American influence. Benson concluded that: 'It is of the
first importance to our present and future prestige that the Navy of the
United States shall act in a principal role in every prominent event.'
The division served with the Grand Fleet, entirely under British strategic control, but saw little action.[67]

In the one theatre in which the Americans could dictate strategy – the western hemisphere – little of moment happened. To Benson's credit, when German submarines undertook a spasmodic offensive off the eastern seaboard in the spring of 1918, designed to panic America into recalling its destroyers from Europe, he refused to rise to the bait; defensive measures and German logistic difficulties led to few sinkings.[68]

The American contribution to victory at sea was embarrassingly small in quantitative terms. At the Armistice, the US Navy was supplying only 3 per cent of the warships in British waters and only 6 per cent of those in the Mediterranean. There were 375 US ships in European waters, with 80,000 men, 45 bases, 570 aircraft and 23 air stations. The vaunted 'bridge of ships' to Europe failed to materialize, and naval shipbuilding was also sluggish; of the 267 destroyers ordered in 1917, only 44 were completed during the war. US naval aviation was slow to take off, only a handful of units being operational by the end of the war. Half of the AEF was transported in British liners and most of the escorts were British.[69] As late as October 1918, it was estimated that: 'The United States will continue to be a naval liability on the Alliance until the end of 1919, that is to say, her demands for transport protection will exceed the contribution she makes in light craft for escort purposes.'[70] Nevertheless, the accession of US destroyer strength was a major factor in the introduction of North Atlantic convoys, the crucial factor in Allied success. The US Navy provided useful support elsewhere, and its units were generally keen and efficient, while in Sims it boasted an outstanding theatre commander, highly respected by the Allies. That the American naval effort was only just becoming effective by November 1918 was due to the unsuitability of Daniels and Benson to head a fighting service in wartime, the lack of preparedness for war (and for an anti-submarine campaign in particular), the inevitable absence of a sense of urgency in a country 3,000 miles from the war's epicentre, and the failure to develop an effective naval staff, balanced fleet construction program, and realistic operational plans in good time. Apart from a few individuals like Franklin Roosevelt, the government had little conception of the demands of total war, either at the front or at home. The Germans estimated correctly that it would take the United States eighteen months to mobilize its awesome potential strength.[71]

Hostilities therefore had a devastating impact on the US Navy. The core of the fleet, the mighty dreadnoughts, had done almost nothing to justify their expensive existence. War plan *Black* was exposed as a total nonsense. The assumption that maritime warfare was a matter of conclusive fleet engagements, decisive descents upon enemy coasts and individual heroics was quickly dissipated, as the navy sought frantically for any small vessel suitable for the dreary but vital duty of convoy escort. Nor did the navy effectively control its own forces in the war zones. Moreover, while the US Army deployed some 1.5 million men – an independent force of comparable size to those of the Allies – on the Western Front, the navy was a minor player in the war at sea. The war had also revealed shortcomings in Navy Department organization and command structures.

While in many ways the wartime experience was something of a disappointment and shock to American naval leaders, it also expanded their horizons. They had gained in the CNO's office something akin to the general staff for which they had agitated unavailingly in peace time. They seized on the swelling demand for preparedness to promote parity of naval strength with Britain and, though the immense 1916 program had to be shelved for the duration of the war before most of the ships had been even ordered, the goal of equality with the world's largest navy was fuelled by the further experience of the war, and it was this conse-quence of hostilities which dominated postwar naval policy and led to more than a decade of prickly rivalry with the Royal Navy once the guns fell silent.

The Armistice came about with dramatic suddenness and posed the problem of the immediate future of the German Navy, which was prac-tically intact. Whereas the British naturally sought the total destruction of German sea power, including all U-boats and fortifications, the Americans agreed only with the elimination of the U-boats. A draco-nian settlement would not only be inconsistent with Wilson's Fourteen Points, it would probably provoke German revanchism. Moreover, 'the effect would be to leave Great Britain the absolute naval master of Europe'. US naval planners argued that '[t]he presence in Europe of the German Fleet is a balance wheel governing any undue or arbitrary ambition' on the part of Britain, and recommended that Germany should cede no more than ten dreadnoughts.[72] Should there be a wholesale distribution of German battleships, America would be con-fronted by an Anglo-Japanese concentration of 76 capital ships against America's 17, reviving the nightmare of a two-ocean war. However, by the spring of 1919 the practical and financial difficulties of absorbing foreign ships persuaded the US Navy to agree to the emasculation of the German Navy; both British and American naval leaders were relieved when the greater part of it scuttled itself in the summer.[73]

While an Anglo-American dispute over the German fleet was thus averted, the peace conference brought about a 'naval battle of Paris' between them. The specifically naval issues, which were intertwined, were freedom of the seas in peace and war (the second of the Fourteen Points, the *casus belli* with Germany and the cause of much acrimony with Britain between 1914 and 1917), and parity of naval strength. Naval experts, naturally adversarial, warned:

Four Great Powers have arisen in the world to compete with Great Britain for commercial supremacy on the seas – Spain, Holland, France and Germany. Each one of those powers in succession has been defeated by Great Britain and her fugitive Allies. A fifth commercial power, the greatest one yet, is now arising to compete for at least commercial equality with Great Britain. Already the signs of jealousy are visible. Historical precedent warns us to watch closely the moves we make or permit to be made.[74]

Wilson, echoing these concerns, remarked: 'Many nations, great and small, chafed under the feeling that their seaborne trade and maritime development may proceed only with the permission and under the shadow of the British Navy.'[75] On arrival in Paris, he declared: 'I cannot consent to take part in the negotiation of a peace which does not include freedom of the seas.'[76] Lloyd George affirmed that Britain would not abandon her principal strategy but he added: 'If the League of Nations is a reality, I am willing to discuss the matter.'[77] While feelings rose high, Wilson knew that ultimately he needed Britain's support to inaugurate the League of Nations and, noting that '[u]nder the League of Nations there are no neutrals', he dropped the matter.[78]

Parity was incapable of a swift solution, for in this case passions were even more inflamed. Daniels was described in London as 'a resurrected Tirpitz', Britain's insistence on supremacy was likened in America to Prussian militarism and '[t]he sailors arrived at the conference breathing fire'.[79] Lloyd George was determined to maintain Britain's primacy at sea, affirming that she 'would spend her last guinea to keep a navy superior to that of the United States or any other power', though since the United States had long been ruled out as a potential enemy, there was no sound strategic reason for the British to oppose parity.[80]

The American demand for parity grew directly out of the war, arising partly from Britain's high-handed rejection of freedom of the seas between 1914 and 1917, Benson explaining that: 'We do not intend to remain in a naval position where we may be compelled to accept the British doctrine of maritime rights.'[81] Moreover, in the League of Nations, no one power should be able to impose its will by means of absolute naval superiority. Daniels and FDR pointed also to America's long coastlines and lines of communication, her swelling commerce and shipping, and her island possessions, as further justifications for parity. American naval planners insisted on a 'commanding superiority' in the Pacific and a 'defensive superiority' in the Atlantic.[82] The underlying reason for parity, however, was America's war-induced position as the most powerful nation in the world and the concomitant professional pride among the officer corps which argued that her naval strength should match this status. Captain Pratt remarked that '[t]he son had grown up and wished equal representation with the father', while the flimsy strategic cloak around the demand was revealed when America blithely advised Britain to determine the size of navy she required and the Americans would then build up to it.[83]

The British were worried both by American objectives and the knowledge that they could no longer compete. They considered that the American program 'is probably aimed at Japan, for the belief in an eventual struggle with that country is deeply rooted in the minds of many Americans', but since America's was 'now the only fleet which is a potential rival, and consequently menace to ours, [it] must be a matter of great concern to us'.[84] However, an exhausted Britain was helpless, for as Colonel House expressed it haughtily and brutally: 'We had more money, we had more men, our resources were greater.'[85] The Americans intensified the crisis by introducing a new three-year program, effectively repeating that of 1916. This had the dual object of forcing Britain into sharing Neptune's trident and of frightening Congress and the people into ratifying the peace treaty and League Covenant – or arming America to the teeth. Even the 1916 program would bring the British and American battlefleets virtually into balance by 1924; that of 1919 would give America 'incomparably the greatest [navy] in the world'.[86]

However, the war also produced countervailing influences; the Republicans, who gained control of Congress in 1918, were anxious to satisfy the rising clamour for a 'peace dividend': lower taxes. Moreover, Theodore Roosevelt, who felt that freedom of the seas would have resulted in a German victory, told the British that the Republicans would not support the 1919 program. Anti-League senators declared that America had no obvious enemies, that modern technology doomed the dreadnought, and that the United States should take the lead in disarmament.[87] World's Work argued that: 'For their own sakes and that of the world, "Britain and America" should cultivate the spirit of the most amicable co-operation.'[88] The log-jam was broken by 'two men of goodwill', House and Lord Robert Cecil, in April 1919. The United States undertook to consider postponing its program if the League came about; the British agreed to the inclusion of the Monroe Doctrine in the Covenant and to join the League.[89] In London a month later Daniels exuded conciliation: 'It would be a blunder, a calamity equal to a crime, if Great Britain and the United States should enter upon competitive naval building.'[90] With the effective cessation of America's great program, the British could claim victory but, as Paul Kennedy has pointed out, the triumph was brief, for the British had few cards to play. When the Washington Conference on naval limitation took place in 1921, the British were thankful to get away with parity.[91]

Though there were definite limits to the public's 'spread-eaglism', the war also expanded American maritime horizons in other directions. Naval leaders sought a chain of bases in the Caribbean and Pacific, if necessary by the acquisition of new territories, casting covetous eyes on British possessions in the western hemisphere, but the British were averse to the Caribbean becoming 'a *mare clausum* to European Nations' and would have demanded a *quid pro quo*.[92] Rear-Admiral Dunn, wartime US commander in the Portuguese Azores, thought America should purchase them, and Sims told him: 'when the final settlement comes the islands will fall naturally into our hands'.[93] Sims's post of Force Commander, US Naval Forces in European Waters, with headquarters in London, was retained at flag rank for several years and American squadrons were despatched to help solve the Trieste and Chanak disputes. Vice-Admiral Huse advised Daniels in October 1920 to retain US battleships in Europe to assist in maintaining peace, while if the US Navy were deployed worldwide, it 'would not only benefit American trade relations but would unquestionably make for a policy of justice and altruism in the world'. There were proposals also to internationalize the Marshall and Caroline Islands, which Japan had seized from Germany in 1914, compensating the Japanese with eastern Siberia, and diverting their ambitions away from American possessions. The war thus reinforced the navy's Darwinist, confrontational, determinist mentality and its territorial and material expansionism.[94]

In Washington, the halting response to the crisis of 1917 had demonstrated the need for a more effective and adequately staffed professional leadership in the Navy Department, but Daniels continued to hold out against 'the persistent agitation to reorganize and militarize the Navy Department'.[95] However, Benson's successor as CNO, Admiral Coontz, quietly extended his authority.[96] The Army–Navy Joint Board, the forerunner of World War II's joint chiefs of staff, was resuscitated in 1919 and promptly called for a 'national security council':

The efficient and effective co-operation in the execution of our national policies demands the close co-ordination of the State, War and Navy Departments. The policy and strategy of a nation are inter-related and neither can be carried on efficiently without due regard for the other.

The development of the War Plans of the Army and Navy should be based upon the national policies they are to support. Conversely, the policies of the nation should take into account the armed forces which are available for their enforcement.[97]

Franklin Roosevelt endorsed the plea, but Secretary of State Charles Evans Hughes peremptorily scorned this approach and a national security council was not formed until the onset of the cold war: American policy thus continued to fail to balance ends and means.[98]

The war's strategic and technical lessons were intensively debated within the navy. Sims accused the Navy Department of gross inefficiency, complacency and a criminal refusal to help the Allies in the crisis of 1917. The resulting Senate enquiry, while not endorsing Sims's charges that Daniels's incompetence had prolonged the war for four months, at a cost of 500,000 lives and 2.5 million tons of shipping, discovered organizational shortcomings, but the enquiry was highly partisan and had little effect on the navy.[99]

The war had brought three new elements into naval warfare: mines, aircraft and submarines. Their rapid development led some to believe that dreadnoughts had become dinosaurs, a view apparently endorsed by General Billy Mitchell's somewhat dubious bombing experiments, but the naval establishment, arguing that progress in armor, underwater protection, speed and anti-aircraft armament largely nullified the threats, successfully preserved the battlefleet as the navy's core. Though Sims and Fiske argued that 'sea power must inevitably be dependent on air power in the future' and that 'air forces and airplane carriers constitute the most powerful weapons of the future', only two experimental carriers were ordered.[100] There was ambivalence also about the submarine; after an initial call for a universal ban, it was recognized that the German underwater *guerre de course* offered a means of destroying Japan's vital and vulnerable carrying trade, thus forcing her to starve or surrender. Long-range patrol submarines were developed and successfully employed in this role in World War II. Nevertheless, though the *New York Times* observed presciently that '[w]hile the 1916 program was appropriate when we were at war and before the naval lessons of the war were digested it may be inappropriate to peace times and does not take adequately into consideration airplane and submarine developments'; naval aviation and undersea warfare remained Cinderellas until the 1930s.[101]

The war had thoroughly discredited war plan *Black*, but American rejection of League membership led to the preparation of war plan *Red* against the British Empire, chiefly for war games and programmatic purposes, though naval planners warned also that: 'The British may be forced into a war to maintain their commercial supremacy.'[102] However, given the vulnerability of British possessions, mutual economic interests, sentimental ties, imperial pressures to avoid conflict, and the lack of any substantial animus, war was virtually inconceivable. Moreover, the Foreign Office was bent on appeasing America, conscious that in a future war US economic, if not military, assistance would be essential.

The war had enhanced Japan's position and navy, in turn rendering the United States more vulnerable in the Pacific. Postwar versions of

war plan *Orange* assumed an American riposte across the ocean from
Pearl Harbor, island-hopping through the new Japanese mandates,
and had a cultural and racial basis. Military leaders and propagandists
in both countries stigmatized the other as evil and there were disputes
over Yap, Shantung, the Open Door, and the treatment of Japanese
nationals in the United States. Japan believed that the western powers
adopted a double standard on empire, and saw America as a malign
influence and an interloper in Asia. She had tripled her naval budget
between 1917 and 1921, partly in response to America's 1916 program.
Japanese strategy focused on limited-risk warfare, based on fast strike-
and-retire operations (for which carrier forces were ideal), seeking to
hold off enemy counter-attacks until basic objectives had been obtained
and accepting battlefleet engagements only on favorable terms.[103] *World's
Work*, observing that Japan was 'compelled to expand or starve', felt it
was 'of vital interest to the United States to turn Japan towards the
continent of Asia'.[104] However, Sims dismissed the Japanese threat, for
'she can only make a raid',[105] while others argued that America was
'strong enough to render any warlike aggression against us by Japan
highly unwise except Japan be in alliance with a strong European
power'.[106] Thus, after Germany was defeated, the Americans became
paranoic about the Anglo-Japanese alliance, despite British assurances
that it was not directed against the United States. The British, aware of
Japan's restlessness with the alliance's constraints, and imperial and
American dislike of it, were ready for a general Pacific settlement.
Moreover, they desired a halt to the 5-handed naval race, 40 dreadnoughts being under construction.[107] *World's Work* remarked that '[t]he
United States has everything to gain from disarmament and nothing to
lose', and when Senator Borah introduced a resolution in December
1920, calling upon the President to convene a general disarmament
conference, the US Navy entered the 'Treaty era'; naval limitation, to
the chagrin of the sailors, dominated policy from then until 1937.[108]

Between 1880 and 1914, the US Navy moved from a Jeffersonian to
a Hamiltonian conception of sea power. At the beginning of World
War I, it was built around a battlefleet and its war plans focused on
deep-water dreadnought actions. The Wilson administration, almost
totally unmilitary in outlook, initially adopted the popular policy of
America as the peaceable giant, which, by example and earnest endeavor,
would restore the lost peace, in the meantime dampening the ardor of
the admirals. Events then conspired to swing the President himself into
the camp of the preparedness movement, which argued that influence
and even peace came at the end of a gun. Precipitated into hostilities
before it was ready, the navy found its war plans and its principal
weapon redundant in a war fought an ocean away, a remorseless and
unheroic defensive grind of convoy and patrol in which 'the militia of

the sea', flotilla craft, were the priceless naval currency. Thus the US Navy could not satisfy its craving for the offensive first and last; it was compelled to sublimate its preferred strategy to the defensive mode adopted by the Allies. America's contribution to the victory at sea was significant rather than crucial.

Following the Armistice, a brief bout of 'spread-eaglism', arising from wartime economic buoyancy and pride in victory, prompted an ill-considered dispute with Britain, when an Anglo-American condominium should have been the object. However, during the transitional stage in American foreign policy, from the parochial attitudes of the nineteenth century to the fully developed internationalism of the 1940s, clear thinking about America's relationships with power blocs elsewhere was rare; there was little attempt to determine realistically how and where America might go to war, nor were foreign and defense policies coordinated.

The war had demonstrated starkly the need for professionalism, which was second nature to other great powers, but which in America was resisted by a powerful residual political influence which warned, prophetically, of a 'military-industrial complex'. Furthermore, the lessons of the first battle of the Atlantic were forgotten also, partly because it was assumed to be unrepeatable and partly because the postwar naval hierarchy returned almost uncritically to the 'gunlaw' of the dreadnought; the Allies paid dearly for American amnesia in the first six months of 1942. Finally, the Wilson administration's drive for naval 'overkill capacity' sat oddly with its Fourteen Points, and the Republicans, in calling the Washington Conference of 1921–2, ended a generation of continuous naval expansion, mental as well as material. It took a second immersion in the crucible of war and the alarming and apparently imminent prospect of a third before the technological, organizational and strategic lessons of World War I were absorbed fully and America became a 'national security state'.

Notes

1. George T. Davis, *A Navy Second to None* (New York: 1940); Harold and Margaret Sprout, *The Rise of American Naval Power* (Princeton, NJ: 1939); Robert W. Love, jun., *History of the U.S. Navy* (Harrisburg, Pa.: 1992), 2 vols.
2. C.S. Alden and R. Earle, *Makers of the Naval Tradition* (Boston, Mass.: 1925); John A.S. Grenville and George B. Young, *Politics, Strategy and American Diplomacy* (New Haven, Conn.: 1969), pp. 1–37, 297–336.
3. Henry Cabot Lodge (ed.), *Selections from the Correspondence of Theodore Roosevelt and Henry Cabot Lodge* (New York: 1925), vol. 1, pp. 63, 220, 267, 277, 294, 287; G.C. O'Gara, *Theodore Roosevelt and the Rise of the*

Modern American Navy (Princeton, NJ: 1943); R.D. Challener, *Admirals, Generals and American Foreign Policy, 1898–1914* (Princeton, NJ: 1973), pp. 50, 111–18, 235–61; Robert G. Albion, *Makers of Naval Policy, 1798–1947* (Annapolis, Md.: 1980), pp. 212–15; William R. Braisted, *The U.S. Navy in the Pacific, 1909–1922* (Austin, Tex.: 1971), pp. 12–36, 49, 59; Michael Vlahos, 'The Naval War College and the Origins of War Planning against Japan', *Naval War College Review* 33, 4 (July 1980), pp. 23–41 (hereafter *NWCR*).

4.   William Taft, *Presidential Addresses and State Papers* (New York: 1910), vol. 1, pp. 34–5, 442–3, 475; *Message of the President on Fiscal, etc., Affairs, 6 Dec 1912* (Washington, DC: 1912), pp. 20–2; S.W. Bryant, *The Sea and the States* (New York: 1967), p. 39; Challener, *Admirals*, pp. 265–81, 344–63.

5.   Josephus Daniels, 'The Navy: A Power for Peace', *World's Work* (May 1914), pp. 62–3; Burton J. Hendrick, 'The Case of Josephus Daniels', *World's Work* (July 1916), pp. 281–396; E. David Cronon (ed.), *The Cabinet Diaries of Josephus Daniels* (Lincoln, Nebr.: 1963); Arthur S. Link et al. (eds), *The Papers of Woodrow Wilson* (Princeton, NJ: 1979), vol. 30, pp. 145–8 (hereafter *Wilson Papers*); Albion, *Makers of Naval Policy*, pp. 217–23; Paola Coletta, 'Josephus Daniels', in Coletta (ed.), *The Secretaries of the Navy* (Annapolis, Md.: 1980), vol. 2, pp. 525–6; Jonathan Daniels, *The End of Innocence* (Philadelphia, Pa.: 1954), p. 17.

6.   Frank B. Freidel, *Franklin D. Roosevelt* (Boston, Mass.: 1952), vol. 1, pp. 28, 160; Elliott Roosevelt (ed.), *The Letters of Franklin D. Roosevelt, 1905–1928* (New York: 1948), pp. xvii, 232–8, 245, 270.

7.   Theodore Roosevelt, quoted in *Review of Reviews*, January 1898, p. 206.

8.   Sprout, *American Naval Power*, p. 307; Albion, *Makers of Naval Policy*, p. 85; J.L. Morison, *Josephus Daniels: The Small-d Democrat* (Chapel Hill, NC: 1966).

9.   Lt-Cdr J.P. Jackson, 'Preparedness – A Vital Necessity', *US Naval Institute Proceedings*, vol. 42 (1916), pp. 1571–2 (hereafter *USNIP*); Lt-Cdr W.P. Cronan, 'The Greatest Need of the U.S. Navy', *USNIP*, vol. 42 (1916), p. 1140.

10. Vlahos, *NWCR* (1980), p. 31. See also Michael Vlahos, *The Blue Sword: The Naval War College and the American Mission, 1919–1941* (Newport, RI: 1980), pp. 113–27; Thomas A. Bailey, *Theodore Roosevelt and the Japanese–American Crises* (Stanford, Calif.: 1934), p. 291; Grenville and Young, *Politics, Strategy and American Diplomacy*, pp. 317–19.

11. Quoted in Frank B. Freidel, *Franklin D. Roosevelt: A Rendezvous with Destiny* (Boston, Mass.: 1990), p. 28. See also Cronon, *Cabinet Diaries*, pp. 52–66; David F. Houston, *Eight Years with Wilson's Cabinet* (Garden City, NY: 1926), pp. 60–6; Burton J. Hendrick, 'A Navy Weak in Battle Line', *World's Work* (February 1915), pp. 445–6; Braisted, *US Navy*, pp. 127–32; Challener, *Admirals*, pp. 367–78.

12. Vlahos, *NWCR* (1980), p. 27.

13. Sprout, *American Naval Power*, p. 253; Davis, *A Navy*, p. 163.

14. Capt Alfred T. Mahan, *The Interest of America in International Conditions* (Boston, Mass.: 1910), pp. 191–2.

15. R-Adm Bradley A. Fiske, 'The Paramount Duty of the Army and Navy',

USNIP, vol. 40 (1914), p. 1073. See also Albion, *Makers of Naval Policy*, p. 354; Gerald E. Wheeler, *Admiral William V. Pratt* (Washington, DC: 1973), p. 93; Mary Klachko and David F. Trask, *Admiral William S. Benson: First Chief of Naval Operations* (Annapolis, Md.: 1987), p. 27; on World War I generally, see Paul G. Halpern, *A Naval History of World War I* (London: 1994).

16.   R-Adm Bradley A. Fiske, *From Midshipman to Rear Admiral* (New York: Century, 1919), p. 530. See also Cdr W.S. Crosley, 'The Naval War College, the General Board, and the Office of Naval Intelligence', *USNIP*, vol. 39 (1913), p. 969; George Meyer, 'Are Naval Expenditures Wasted?', *North American Review* (February 1915), pp. 248–53; John B. Hattendorf, 'Technology and Strategy: A Study in the Professional Thought of the U.S. Navy, 1900–1916', *NWCR* 24, 3 (November 1971), pp. 25–48; Jonathan Daniels, *The End of Innocence*, pp. 90–4; Paola Coletta, *Admiral Bradley A. Fiske and the American Navy* (Lawrence, Kan.: 1979), pp. 137–8, 150–4, 171.

17.   *Annual Report of the Secretary of the Navy, 1915* (Washington, DC: 1915), p. 9. See also Josephus Daniels, *The Wilson Era*, vol. 1, *The Years of Peace* (Chapel Hill, NC: 1944), pp. 239–45; Albion, *Makers of Naval Policy*, p. 219; Klachko and Trask, *Admiral William S. Benson*, pp. 28–9; Paul Y. Hammond, *Organizing for Defense* (Princeton, NJ: 1961), pp. 74–7.

18.   Fiske to Sims, 26 December 1918, Box 46, Sims Papers, Library of Congress. See also David F. Trask, 'William S. Benson', in Robert W. Love, jun. (ed.), *The Chiefs of Naval Operations* (Annapolis, Md.: 1980), p. 5; Klachko and Trask, *Admiral William S. Benson*, pp. 26–40.

19.   Coletta, 'Daniels', in Coletta (ed.), *Secretaries of the Navy*, vol. 2, p. 539.

20.   Theodore Roosevelt, *America and the World War* (New York: 1915), p. xiii; and idem, *National Strength and International Duty* (Princeton, NJ: 1917), pp. 5, 15.

21.   Lodge, quoted in John M. Cooper, jun., *The Vanity of Power: American Isolationism and the First World War, 1914–17* (Westport, Conn.: 1969), pp. 24–5; Augustus P. Gardner, 'If I Were Caesar', *North American Review* (September 1915), p. 359.

22.   Elliott Roosevelt, *FDR Letters*, pp. 256–7. See also Freidel, *Roosevelt*, vol. 1, pp. 236–52, 260–4; Grenville and Young, *Politics, Strategy and American Diplomacy*, p. 328.

23.   Jackson, *USNIP* (1916), pp. 1559, 1562. See also Burton J. Hendrick, 'Do We Need a Strong Navy?', p. 440, and 'A Navy Weak in Battle Line', pp. 445–6, both in *World's Work* (February 1915); 'Congress and the Navy', *The Outlook*, 17 February 1915, pp. 353–4; R-Adm Bradley A. Fiske, 'Naval Defense', *North American Review* (February 1915), p. 225; Fiske, 'National Preparedness', *North American Review* (December 1915), pp. 847–57; General Board statement, *Annual Report of the Secretary of the Navy, 1915*, pp. 73–4; Sprout, *American Naval Power*, pp. 319–20.

24.   *Wilson Papers*, vol. 34, p. 514; Arthur S. Link, *Wilson: The Struggle for Neutrality* (Princeton, NJ: 1960), pp. 372–5, 588–9, and *Wilson: Confrontations and Crises* (1964), pp. 15, 25–8, 45–8, 334–7; O. J. Clinard, *Japan's Influence on American Naval Power, 1897–1917* (Berkeley, Calif.: 1947),

p. 171; Sprout, *American Naval Power*, p. 332; Albion, *Makers of Naval Policy*, p. 221; Braisted, *U.S. Navy*, pp. 186–8.

25. Charles Seymour, *The Intimate Papers of Colonel House* (hereafter *House Papers*), vol. 2, *From Neutrality to War* (London: 1926), pp. 316–17.

26. Wilson, address at St Louis, 3 February 1916, *Wilson Papers*, vol. 36 (1981), pp. 119–20.

27. A.M. Arnett, *Claude Kitchin and the Wilson War Policies* (Boston, Mass.: 1937), pp. 68, 56–7, 64, 86–97. See also Tillman–Wilson correspondence, 14 February 1916, pp. 173–5, and House to Wilson, 17 May 1916, pp. 64–5, *Wilson Papers*, vol. 37 (1981).

28. General Board statement, *Annual Report of the Secretary of the Navy, 1915*, pp. 73–4.

29. *The New Republic* (8 January 1916), p. 234. See also Albion, *Makers of Naval Policy*, pp. 222–3; Klachko and Trask, *Admiral William S. Benson*, pp. 49–50; Coletta, *Fiske*, p. 179; Hammond, *Organizing for Defense*, p. 61; 'Expert Opinion on the Naval Bill', *The Outlook*, 21 June 1916, pp. 402–3; American Union against Militarism to Wilson, 8 May 1916, *Wilson Papers*, vol. 36, p. 633.

30. R-Adm Bradley A. Fiske, 'The Next Five Years of the Navy', *World's Work* (January 1917), p. 275.

31. Franklin D. Roosevelt, 'The Naval Plattsburg', *The Outlook*, 28 June 1916, pp. 495–501; Albion, *Makers of Naval Policy*, p. 359; Grenville and Young, *Politics, Strategy and American Diplomacy*, p. 321; Charles C. Tansill, *The Purchase of the Danish West Indies* (Baltimore, Md.: 1932); D.D. Creque, *The U.S. Virgins and the Eastern Caribbean* (Philadelphia, Pa.: 1968).

32. 'An American Navy at Last', *World's Work* (October 1916), p. 609.

33. Paolo Coletta, *The Naval Heritage in Brief* (Washington, DC: 1980), p. 260; Grenville and Young, *Politics, Strategy and American Diplomacy*, pp. 326, 334.

34. Fiske, quoted in *USNIP*, vol. 42 (1916), pp. 2038–42.

35. 'Armed Insecurity', *The New Republic*, 1 January 1916, p. 210.

36. 'Lessons of the U53', *World's Work* (December 1916), p. 120.

37. General Board statement, *Annual Report of the Secretary of the Navy, 1915*, pp. 73–4.

38. Jellicoe to Sir Edward Carson, 27 April 1917, in A. Temple Patterson (ed.), *The Jellicoe Papers* (Aldershot: 1968), vol. 2, p. 162. See also Arthur J. Marder, *From the Dreadnought to Scapa Flow*, vol. 4, *1917: Year of Crises* (Oxford: 1969), chapters 4 and 5. On Anglo-American relations, 1917–19, see Adm William S. Sims, *The Victory at Sea* (Garden City, NY: 1921); David F. Trask, *Captains and Cabinets: Anglo-American Naval Relations, 1917–1918* (St Louis, Mo.: 1972); William B. Fowler, *British–American Relations, 1917–1918: The Role of Sir William Wiseman* (Princeton, NJ: 1969); Michael A. Simpson (ed.), *Anglo-American Naval Relations, 1917–1919* (Aldershot: 1991).

39. Sims to Daniels, 14 April 1917, Box 100, Daniels Papers, Library of Congress.

40. Ibid., 29 June 1917, US Congress, Senate, *Naval Investigation, 1920*, p. 48, Franklin D. Roosevelt Library, Hyde Park, New York.

41. Burton J. Hendrick, *The Life and Letters of Walter Hines Page* (London: 1924), pp. 277, 284.

42. Lt R. Emmet to Sims, 22 June 1917, Box 55, Sims Papers. See also Elting E. Morison, *Admiral Sims and the Modern American Navy* (Boston, Mass.: 1942), p. 396.

43. Trask, *Captains and Cabinets*, pp. 58, 96.

44. *House Papers*, vol. 3 (1928), p. 70. See also Braisted, *U.S. Navy*, pp. 293–300.

45. Jellicoe to Capt Gaunt, 29 June 1917, ADM 137/656, Public Record Office, London.

46. Sims to Daniels, 16 June 1917, Box 5, Benson Papers, Library of Congress; and Sims to Wilson, 4 July 1917, Box 91, Sims Papers.

47. Wilson to Sims, 4 July 1917, Navy Subject File (hereafter *NSF*), TD, National Archives, Washington, DC.

48. Sims to Daniels, 28 June 1917, *Senate Naval Investigation*, p. 86; and Gaunt to Jellicoe, 1 July 1917, ADM 137/656.

49. Henry Newbolt, *History of the Great War: Naval Operations* (London: 1931), vol. 5, p. 337. See also Admiralty Memorandum, 11 July 1918, ADM 116/1810; Page to Wilson, 9 June 1917, *Wilson Papers*, vol. 43, p. 47; Sims to Adm Bayly, 5 May 1918, Box 47, Sims Papers.

50. Wilson to Sims, 4 July 1917, *NSF*, TD.

51. Wilson to Atlantic Fleet officers, 11 August 1917, in Joseph P. Tumulty, *Woodrow Wilson as I Know Him* (Garden City, NY: 1921), p. 297, and *House Papers*, vol. 3, p. 176.

52. Winston Churchill (United States) to Wilson, July 1917, 22 October 1917, Box 51, Sims Papers.

53. Gaunt to Admiralty, 5 July, and to Jellicoe, 10 September 1917, ADM 137/1437.

54. Jellicoe to Northcliffe, 10 July 1917, *NSF*, TT.

55. Benson to Sims, 24 September 1917, Box 5, Benson Papers; Jellicoe to Beatty, 9 November 1917, *Jellicoe Papers*, vol. 2, pp. 225–6. See also V-Adm Sir M. Browning to Jellicoe, 20 July 1917, ADM 137/657; Adm Mayo to Daniels, 8 September 1917, Box 5, Benson Papers; Jellicoe to Browning, 7 July, and to Beatty, 31 July 1917; Browning to Jellicoe, 31 July 1917, *Jellicoe Papers*, vol. 2, pp. 181–2, 191–2.

56. *House Papers*, vol. 3, p. 176.

57. Mayo to Benson, 5 September 1917, *NSF*, TT; Mayo to Daniels, 8 September 1917, Box 5, Benson Papers, 'U.S. Naval Policy', November 1917, Box 42, Benson Papers.

58. Trask, *Captains and Cabinets*, pp. 175–80.

59. Roosevelt to Daniels, 29 October 1917, Assistant Secretary of Navy File 15, Roosevelt Papers. See also FDR, memorandum on 'Submarine Situation', 24 May 1917, Assistant Secretary of Navy File 15; Roosevelt to Wilson, 5 June 1917, Box 100, Daniels Papers.

60. Jellicoe to Benson, September 1917, *Jellicoe Papers*, vol. 2, p. 210. See also Trask, *Captains and Cabinets*, pp. 154–6, 216–18; Love, *History of U.S. Navy*, vol. 1, p. 512.

61. Memorandum by Admiralty Plans Division, 28 August 1918, ADM 137/2709; US Memorandum to Allied Naval Council, 12 March 1918,

NSF, TX. See also Joint British and US Plans Divisions memorandum, 30 August 1918, *NSF*, TX.

62. Minute by ACNS on Admiralty Plans Division memorandum, 28 August 1918, ADM 137/2709.
63. Daniels to Sims, 28 July 1917, Box 100, Daniels Papers; Cronon, *Cabinet Diaries*, p. 145; Adm William V. Pratt, unpublished autobiography, p. 219, Pratt Papers, Naval History Collection, Washington, DC.
64. US memorandum to Allied Naval Council, 12 March 1918, *NSF*, TX; Paul G. Halpern, *The Naval War in the Mediterranean, 1914–1918* (Annapolis, Md.: 1987), and ibid., *The Royal Navy in the Mediterranean, 1915–18* (Aldershot: 1987).
65. Roosevelt to Daniels, 2 August 1918, Assistant Secretary of Navy File, 93, Roosevelt Papers.
66. Benson to Sims, 20 August 1917, Senate Naval Investigation, 67. See also Northcliffe to War Cabinet, 5 July 1917, *NSF*, TT; Dean C. Allard, 'Anglo-American Naval Differences during World War I', *Military Affairs* (April 1980), p. 77; Russell F. Weigley, *The American Way of War* (New York: 1973), p. 187.
67. Benson, 'U.S. Naval Policy', November 1917, Box 42, Benson Papers.
68. Simpson, *Anglo-American Naval Relations*, part 8, 'The Western Hemisphere'.
69. General Board statement, *Annual Report of the Secretary of the Navy, 1919*, p. 41; Sims to OpNav, 13 November 1918, *NSF*, WV; Intelligence Secn., US Naval Forces in European Waters, memorandum, 3 August 1918, ADM 137/1964; Sims to Bayly, 31 January 1918, Box 47, Sims Papers; *House Papers*, vol. 3, p. 74; Fowler, *British–American Relations*, p. 8.
70. Admiralty memorandum for War Cabinet, October 1918, and also British Naval Mission to United States, memorandum, 22 September 1918, ADM 137/2710.
71. Sims, *Victory at Sea*, p. 291; Coletta, 'Daniels', in Coletta (ed.), *Secretaries of the Navy*, vol. 2, p. 553; Dudley W. Knox, *A History of the U.S. Navy* (New York: 1948), p. 418.
72. 'U.S. Comments on Adm. Fremantle's Memorandum', October 1918, *NSF*, TX.
73. 'U.S. Naval Interests in the Armistice Terms', October 1918, *NSF*, TX.
74. Ibid.
75. Sir Eric Geddes, 'Notes of an Interview with the President', 16 October 1918, ADM 116/1809. See also Fowler, *British–American Relations*, p. 198; J.J. Safford, *Wilsonian Maritime Diplomacy, 1913–1921* (New Brunswick, NJ: 1960).
76. *House Papers*, vol. 4, p. 168.
77. Ibid., pp. 163–4.
78. Klachko and Trask, *Admiral William S. Benson*, p. 138. See also E.B. Parsons, *Wilsonian Diplomacy: Allied–American Rivalries in War and Peace* (St Louis, Mo.: 1978), p. 172; Seth P. Tillman, *Anglo-American Relations at the Paris Peace Conference of 1919* (Princeton, NJ: 1961), pp. 49, 50; Arthur Walworth, *America's Moment: 1918* (New York: 1977), pp. 59, 62.

79. Michael G. Fry, *Illusions of Security: North Atlantic Diplomacy, 1918–1922* (Toronto: 1972), pp. 37, 38, and *House Papers*, vol. 4, p. 179.

80. *House Papers*, vol. 4, p. 180; see also pp. 418–23, and J.K. McDonald, 'Lloyd George and the Search for a Post War Naval Policy, 1919', in Alan J.P. Taylor (ed.), *Lloyd George: Twelve Essays* (London: 1971), p. 191.

81. Benson, memorandum, May 1919, Box 66, Daniels Papers. See also US Naval Advisory Staff, memorandum, 7 April 1919, *NSF*, UP.

82. Daniels, quoted in *Daily Telegraph*, 2 May 1919; Roosevelt, quoted in *Daily Mail*, 23 January 1919; US Planning Section, memorandum, May 1918, *NSF*, TX.

83. Pratt, quoted in OpNav to Benson, 25 October 1918, Box 10, Benson Papers; Adm Sir W. Lowther Grant to War Cabinet, 25 February 1919, ADM 116/1773.

84. Deputy Chief of Naval Staff, minute, 12 November 1918, ADM 137/2709.

85. *House Papers*, vol. 4, p. 160.

86. Admiralty memorandum for War Cabinet, 7 May 1919, ADM 116/1773; General Board statement, *Annual Report of the Secretary of the Navy, 1920*, p. 2.

87. Adm Grant to War Cabinet, 25 February 1919, ADM 116/1773; Braisted, *U.S. Navy*, pp. 422–42; William H. Harbaugh, *The Life and Times of Theodore Roosevelt* (New York: 1975), pp. 184–6.

88. 'No American Navy Greater than England's', *World's Work* (July 1919), pp. 239–40.

89. Marder, *Dreadnought*, vol. 5, p. 233. See also Braisted, *U.S. Navy*, p. 440.

90. Daniels, quoted in *Daily Telegraph*, 2 May 1919.

91. Paul M. Kennedy, *The Rise and Fall of British Naval Mastery* (London: 1983), p. 263.

92. Geddes to War Cabinet, 4 September 1917, ADM 116/1768.

93. R-Adm Henry O. Dunn to Sims, 29 December 1918, and Sims to Dunn, 31 December 1918, Box 55, Sims Papers.

94. V-Adm Henry P. Huse to Daniels, 21 October 1920, Box 545, Daniels Papers. See also R-Adm Philip Andrews to Sims, January 1920, Box 46, Sims Papers; Love, *History of U.S. Navy*, vol. 1, pp. 521–2; R.W. Curry, *Woodrow Wilson and Far Eastern Policy, 1913–1921* (New York: 1957), pp. 258–9, 319–20.

95. General Board statement, *Annual Report of the Secretary of the Navy, 1918–1919*, p. 207.

96. Trask, 'Benson', in Love (ed.), *Chiefs of Naval Operations*, p. 28.

97. Albion, *Makers of Naval Policy*, pp. 267–8.

98. Ibid., pp. 268–9, Braisted, *U.S. Navy*, p. 470.

99. Albion, *Makers of Naval Policy*, p. 111; Morison, *Sims*, chapter 23; Coletta, 'Daniels', in Coletta (ed.), *Secretaries of the Navy*, vol. 2, p. 568; Coletta, *Naval History in Brief*, pp. 276–7; Wheeler, *Admiral William V. Pratt*, p. 152.

100. Fiske to Sims, 4 October 1919, Box 57, and Sims to Cone, 3 December 1921, Box 52, Sims Papers. See also Fiske to Sims, 7 February 1920, Box 57, Sims to Fullam, 7 January, 17 January, 9 December 1921, Box 59, Sims to Land, 5 December 1921, Box 69, Sims Papers; US Planning Section, 'Building Program', early 1919, Box 39, Benson Papers.

101. 'Rusticating Sims', *New York Times*, 3 November 1921. See also Davis, *A Navy Second to None*, pp. 238–9.
102. Vlahos, *Blue Sword*, pp. 100–10.
103. Davis, *A Navy Second to None*, pp. 238–9, 252; Braisted, *U.S. Navy, passim*; Vlahos, *Blue Sword*, pp. 127–30.
104. 'The Necessity for Disarmament', *World's Work* (March 1921), p. 429.
105. Sims to Fiske, 8 October 1920, Box 69, Sims Papers.
106. US Planning Section, 'Building Program', early 1919, Box 39, Benson Papers.
107. Davis, *A Navy Second to None*, pp. 262–3; Long to War Cabinet, 13 February 1920, ADM 1/773; Armin Rappaport, *The Navy League of the United States* (Detroit, Mich.: 1962), pp. 83–5; Fry, *Illusions of Security*, pp. 68–79.
108. 'The Necessity for Disarmament', *World's Work* (March 1921), pp. 428–9.

9

Psychological Warfare and the Building of National Morale during World War II: The Role of Non-Government Agencies

Daria Frezza

At the outbreak of World War II many professional and institutional organizations sprang up throughout the country in order to help mobilize the entire population of the United States into a total war effort. Among the many existing civilian and religious associations, the Council for Democracy and the Committee for National Morale deserve particular attention, as they recruited the most qualified social scientists, including anthropologists, sociologists, social psychologists, political scientists and experts in advertising, press, radio and cinema.

Although not all their programs were enacted, examination of their relationships with official government agencies and consideration of the cultural perspective of their work is significant in two respects:

(i) their ambivalent relationship toward Nazism, which, though attentively scrutinized as the foremost enemy, at the same time influenced their approach to the problem of propaganda;
(ii) the analysis of ethnic groups and race relations oriented to achieving national unity as opposed to Nazi propaganda's aim of dividing ethnic minorities.

The problem of aliens and foreign-born citizens was confronted in the framework of a national process of Americanization. That cultural approach becomes particularly significant in the light of present historiographical debates about multiculturalism.

The Home Front

The term 'morale' as applied to personal or group status (in the army, the factory, the community) had been increasingly used during the 1930s in the fields of sociology and social psychology, but it was only at the outbreak of World War II that the word became widely used in public discourse outside academic circles. Shortly after the Pearl Harbor attack, the psychologist Gordon Allport wrote about its meaning:

The popularity of a term ... is proportional to its vagueness. When
asked what he meant by morale, an army officer replied: 'It is the
assurance you have while walking down the street that when you
wink at a girl she will wink back to you' ... Somewhat more
adequate and equally brief is the definition of Rundquist and Sletto,
who regard morale as 'one's confidence in one's ability to cope with
whatever the future may bring.'[1]

Apart from what Allport called 'a crisp definition', the concept of
morale gave rise to wide discussions from many conflicting points of
view. The goal of national unity in front of impending war emergency
represented one of the Roosevelt administration's chief problems. As
the majority of the American people was anti-interventionist at the
outbreak of war in Europe, approval of the Lend Lease Bill received
the support of only half of the population, because it was perceived as
increasing the risk of involvement in the war. As late as the summer of
1941, the proposed extension of the draft law, prolonging military duty
for the duration of national emergency, was met by bitter opposition
inside and outside Congress.[2] It was not until the Pearl Harbor attack
that 97 per cent of the population approved the congressional declaration of war.[3] But during the years of hostilities backing for the war
effort was never as unanimous, and varied along class, gender and race
lines. From a more general political point of view, 'the country was not
united. It was split two ways ... and the fissures ran across each other.'[4]
Isolationists and interventionists did not coincide with conservatives
and liberals, 'Old Dealers and New Dealers'. The deep changes provoked by war affected all social institutions with consequent reciprocal
interactions.

At the economic level, in was only with rearmament that the problem
of unemployment was being resolved. The general shift from 'Dr New
Deal to Dr Win the War', according to Franklin D. Roosevelt's famous
expression, implied a basic restructuring of the country's economy.
The mobilization of big industry, traditionally hostile to Roosevelt's
administration, and of war-geared manpower under the newly established Office of Production Management, inevitably caused economic
and social tensions between those industries geared towards the needs
of war and those still operating for civilian production. The whole
system had to be readjusted for military production aims. All other
industrial and civilian needs, like the need for raw materials in the
automobile industry or the housing shortage in the construction
industry, were subordinated to military production planning.[5] Inter-
industrial conflicts as well as head-on collisions between civilian and
military agencies were compounded by social conflicts between management and labor in the factories.

At the social level, the displacement of large groups of the population and the abnormal growth of boom-towns around the new or expanded military material production sites, together with housing, medical and school shortages, increased social unrest in multi-ethnic communities which thereby suffered from chronic disorganization.[6] Families were deeply affected by the absence of men and by the new role of women as factory workers, who had to leave their children in the care of community institutions or, at times, to their own devices, with a consequent increase in juvenile delinquency. Rationing and price controls changed family life customs, and small communities became more isolated because of gasoline rationing and the absence of medical assistance.[7] A relevant part of the population, foreign-born citizens, as well as the so-called 'aliens', were fearful of legal and social discrimination, along the lines of what had happened during World War I. Afro-Americans resented discriminative policies in the defense programs, on the home as well as on the war front.[8]

For most people, such striking social changes demanded a drastic reorientation of values. One of the most visible changes in social attitudes noted by sociologists was the relaxation of social restraints:

> War develops its own characteristic psychology – an accumulation of kaleidoscopic change of ideas, impressions and emotions. War is ushered in usually on a wave of sentimentality and hysteria. This is succeeded by a sense of instability which breeds insecurity in turn … The customary relations between cause and consequence become uncertain and fallacious … Life becomes a carnival in which nothing remains true to itself. There is no apparent relation between what man does and what happens to him.[9]

But in the opposite direction war also brought about – not only on the military front – increased regimentation through rationing, price controls and pressure buying of bonds. As sociologist James S. Bossard remarked:

> War, like all crises, is a selective factor operating on a gigantic scale … It disturbs most things, it dislocates and disorganizes many, it sweeps away some, it breaks others. On the other hand it is harbinger of much that is new … in other cases war but facilitates the secular trend, releasing that which was straining at the leash.[10]

National Morale Agencies

Inside the administration, many committees were set up in order to deal with the problem, but the result was a great confusion and proliferation of agencies, often with overlapping powers.[11] The first of the new organizations was the Office of Government Reports. Established in 1939 under the direction of Lowell Mellett, it soon had to face mounting criticism from hostile Republican congressmen and from isolationists inside and outside Congress. The Division of Information of the Office of Emergency Management, set up in March 1941 under former Scripps-Howard director, Robert Norton, was more successful as a clearing house for official information material, but its work often conflicted with army and navy information sections. In the same period the Office of Civilian Defense, under the guidance of the New York Major, Fiorello La Guardia, was charged with civilian protection. Within this new organization, a subcommittee, 'a sort of bally-hoo Committee', according to La Guardia, was supposed to deal with the national morale problem. The Office of Fact and Figures, headed by the Librarian of Congress, Archibald MacLeish, was set up as a separate agency in July 1941, in order to gather and analyse data about public opinion attitudes and at the same time distribute official information. According to La Guardia, its purpose was also to give some 'sugar-coated, colored, ornamental matter, otherwise known as "bunk", but very useful'.[12] At the same time Colonel William S. Donovan was appointed as head of the Office of the Coordinator of Information, which dealt with national security problems. The President's method of setting up a new committee to cope with the inefficiency of a pre-existing one, without canceling it, gave rise to this large proliferation of agencies, with conflicting interests, caused by political disagreements and different cultural approaches.

The establishment in June 1942 of the Office of War Information (OWI) represented the government's solution to the entire information and intelligence problem inside and outside the country. The OWI, as it has been remarked, 'was created in response to rapidly mounting indignation over the inadequate and often contradictory items concerning the war, supplied by the myriad government press agents and spokesmen ... The OWI, it was expected, would bring order out of chaos.'[13] It would have been very difficult to fulfill this hope, given the great number of responsibilities with which the new agency was charged. In 1943 'the allocations for its domestic branch were reduced so sharply that its program was severely curtailed'.[14] Within the domestic branch, nevertheless, the Bureau of Motion Pictures, headed by Lowell Mellett, continued to perform a most important role throughout the war years.

Besides government's activity in this field, many private groups were set up throughout the country for the specific purpose of studying appropriate means for strengthening national morale. Among the most lively and interesting institutions in this field, relevant work was accomplished by the Committee for National Morale. It was formed by some of the most prominent figures in the fields of anthropology, social psychology, public opinion, political science: Gregory Bateson, Margaret Mead, Gordon W. Allport, Hadley Cantril, George Gallup, Carl Friedrich and many others. The committee's president was Arthur U. Pope, a professor of Persian art at Harvard University. The committee was part of the larger Council For Democracy which, under the presidency of James R. Angell, a New York lawyer, was composed mainly of outstanding social science scholars, such as Alvin Johnson and Max Ascoli of the New School for Social Research, together with such writers as Robert Sherwood, journalists, editors, labor and business representatives. The need to participate in the political process was strongly felt in the social sciences. 'This is no time for social researchers to sit in their ivory towers', wrote Dwight Sanderson in his presidential address for the annual meeting of the American Sociological Society planned for December 1942. The demand is for sociology to give 'fundamental contributions to the urgent demand that science be applied to the complex problems of human relations which now face us in realizing our faith in democracy'.[15]

In a letter to the Secretary of the Interior, Harold Ickes, Carl Friedrich, professor of government at Harvard University and chairman of the Executive Committee of the Council for Democracy, had stressed the opportunity for the government to take advantage of the great 'strides in the last two decades ... in the various fields pertaining to morale problems such as psychology, psychiatry, anthropology, sociology and political science and the more concrete fields of advertising, press, radio and cinema'. He remarked further:

America's resources in this respect are probably greater than those of any other country or combination of countries. The Axis have turned over to us many of the ablest specialists in this field that, when added to America's outstanding talent, constitute one of the country's most important resources in the present conflict. The struggle for the mind of mankind can and should be won by this country.[16]

In military circles too, government action in this sector was strongly called for. Assistant Secretary of War, John J. McCloy, wrote of this to Ickes: 'We are the greatest advertisers in the commercial field and organizers in the social, religious and political field in the world ... all of which is practical propaganda in other forms. And yet nationally we have done little about the present situation.'[17]

The possibility of a coordinated effort towards setting up a department of public information and morale in the executive branch of the federal government was proposed in March 1941 to Ickes by Pope on behalf of the most important cultural institutions of the country. These

included the National Research Council, the American Council of
Learned Societies, the Social Science Council, and the American
Council for Education.[18] The necessity of coping with the problem
and its relevance in confronting the critical national situation was
broadly affirmed both inside and outside government circles.

Robert S. Allen, director of a Washington, DC daily newspaper,
wrote to Ickes: 'In all parts of the country I get an awfully sour picture
about the general state of mind of the public. The overwhelming
majority are pro-British and behind the president's anti-Axis policy but
they are not steamed up about it. They don't have any real awareness
of the extreme gravity of the situation.' He went on to suggest that
'a conscientious and determined effort must be launched at once to
invigorate national morale and keep it pepped-up. By that I don't mean
whoop-te-do or carnival stuff, but serious enlightened building.' Of
course, he was aware of the priority of the defense production program, but 'production won't be worth a damn, if the spirit and will of
the people go to hell!'[19]

The importance of winning 'the war of the mind along with the war
of steel'[20] was also affirmed by an 'American Defense Harvard Group',
formed by psychologists, sociologists and psychiatrists interested in
analyzing public opinion trends and in giving suggestions to mass-media
operators. Moreover the link between civilian and military aspects was
reaffirmed in every public document: 'An Army fights as a people
think' was one of the most frequent slogans, as well as a quotation from
Hitler's *Mein Kampf*: 'Victory is won by destroying enemy morale …
Totalitarian war therefore always begins on the psychological front,
long before military operations start.'[21]

Notwithstanding Pope's repeated requests and his committee's
analysis of particular topics, the existing agencies inside the administration continued to refuse to take into account the work of this group
of 'academicians' who, in Lowell Mellett's words, 'demonstrate beau-
tifully Dewey's concept of "trained incapacity"'.[22] The establishment
of such a 'highly academic organization within the Government' was
considered highly unrealistic on a practical basis. One of Ickes's con-
sultants, working for the Division of Information in the Department of
Interior, gave a similar negative evaluation of the committee's plan,
even after a long discussion with one of its most representative figures,
Margaret Mead. He ended up warning against the committee's critical
analysis of words like 'censorship' and 'propaganda' as a risk of 'going
off into cloud banks'.[23] Lowell Mellett's advice was that the group
'should confine itself to making such studies … and passing the results
… [to] those actively engaged in the defense program'. He ended up
warning that 'only confusion would result if the group's activities went
further'.[24] Mellett's suggestion in the end prevailed, notwithstanding

Ickes 'and the formidable crowd who pressed upon the President for action'. Ickes had to admit his defeat: 'I have never worked on him with more determination in my life and I got precisely nowhere at all'.[25] Again, in September 1941, Ickes warned the President in an alarming letter about the state of the nation:

> I had 'highly resolved' that I would never again mention to you the question of national morale ... However ... one cannot read or listen to people ... without becoming frightened ... We are being drawn nearer and nearer to actual warfare but the people of the U.S. have no conception of the issues involved ... Lacking this they have no wish to fight and lacking a wish to fight they have no will of victory without which no people however strong and resourceful can hope to win.[26]

The committee itself reacted with anger at the government's inactivity: 'The majority of our Committee want to go into opposition, when the Committee represents the best brains America can mobilize on the subject, it is approaching the proportion of a scandal.'[27] The different contradictory opinions on this question within the administration barred the possibility of official government support. The non-government agencies continued anyway to be active with research work and with specific undertakings at community level, whenever this was possible. The Committee for National Morale abandoned the previous idea of a single morale agency in favor of a more eclectic choice: 'A certain duplication and overlapping are not to be deplored. A mechanically imposed unity is more to be feared ... it might pervert the very demo-cratic institutions that we are trying to safeguard.'[28]

Propaganda and Education

On one point there was almost unanimous consent: the example of the Committee on Public Information (CPI) of World War I had to be avoided in every way. Nothwithstanding George Creel's intervention in the debate, with an accurate description of the extraordinary infor-mational work accomplished by the CPI, the idea that its aim was 'not lies, not deceit, and not "goose stuffing", but the formation of public opinion through information'[29] was strongly questioned on all sides. Creel himself failed to find a place in Roosevelt's administration. The more widespread opinion was that Creel's techniques had left a long shadow of criticism and disillusionment throughout the nation. In 'A Plan for National Morale' the committee had worked out a clear estimate of the CPI:

Creel's Committee contributed materially to the winning of the war
but they didn't 'win the peace' ... A legacy from propaganda of the
last war is the cynicism and apathy of large sections of the American
people and it is hardly too much to say that a return to the propa-
gandistic techniques of the last war would precipitate a morale crisis
in the nation.[30]

Referring to propaganda methods of World War I, Ruth Benedict
recalled the 'Americanization' campaign which had to be 'sudden,
complete and bitter', and the widespread climate of 'hysteria and
witch-hunting' characterized by such extreme episodes as those that
were happening in New York City, where Germans were being
'thrown off street-cars for talking their own language'.[31] Propaganda
had become, since then, one of the most controversial concepts.[32]
Ralph D. Casey, director of the School of Journalism of the University
of Minnesota, writing on this subject at the outbreak of World War II,
remarked that 'unhappily, propaganda has been credited with too great
results in many episodes of our contemporary history at the expense of
more fundamental economic and political causes'.[33] The debate about
propaganda was focused on the term itself. With the rise of fascism and
Nazism, a sharper distinction had to be made between propaganda on
the one hand, and, on the other, education, which was considered more
suited to democratic rules. In 1938 an Institute for Propaganda Analysis
was set up in New York, with the aim of teaching students and citizens
alike how to detect propaganda techniques, thus helping to shape a
democratic educational process. At the outbreak of war a group of well-
known journalists and scholars, coordinated by William Y. Elliott,
professor of government at Harvard,[34] was strongly in favor of a kind
of propaganda that might give rise to active participation on the part of
the citizens, such as in the Defense Saving Bonds Program, a campaign
from this viewpoint that was 'peculiarly adapted to the democratic
pattern of American life',[35] as a 'propaganda of the act'.

In the Conference on Propaganda Committee held by Ickes, the government's contradictory position was repeatedly pointed out: if, on the
one hand, there was the willingness 'to create an agency to analyse and
combat propaganda', on the other hand the aim was to set up another
agency to propose propaganda. The problem was posed more on a nomi-
nalistic than on a substantial basis. According to Ickes, it was necessary
'to avoid using the words which the opposition will seize upon to our
disadvantage'. Secretary of War Henry Stimson connected 'the sinister
aspect of the word propaganda' with the common idea that 'it isn't true',
or that it is 'put over by devious methods'. It was therefore necessary to
avoid the term in the administrative language, in favor of 'more respectable' expressions such as 'positive attitudes toward our system'.[36]

If the methods to be adopted for the establishment of a propaganda campaign were under discussion, what was unanimously called for was, in substance, 'the recreation of that sort of propaganda in the country to set up democracy as something worth fighting for, worth dying for, something that comprised every thing that we held dear'.[37] According to the writer Gilbert Harrison, who worked for the committee, the difference of 'War Generation number 2' lay in having acknowledged the disillusionment of the previous generation. He recalled Scott Fitzgerald's novel *All the Sad Young Men*, described as having been 'swept up into the systematized hysteria of war', with no faith in the possibility of linking war to democratic values: 'All the Sad Young Men are being dressed in the uniform of warriors for democracy after having been trained to detect the mote in the eye of our own democracy.'[38] The gulf between the two experiences was mainly due to 'the ravages of the Great Depression'[39] which had undermined any optimistic faith in the democratic system. In a long series of causes contributing to the serious deterioration of American morale the committee had listed 'the obvious failure of democracy to fulfil its own promise, a failure keenly resented by the underprivileged and the unemployed'.[40]

One of the founders of modern advertising, Edward E. Bernays, stressed the importance of overcoming 'defeatism and cynicism', as a consequence of the weakening of 'our morale, our faith in the future of democracy', caused by the Depression,[41] because of which there had spread a tendency, as Peter H. Odegard had remarked, not only 'among the underprivileged, but in an even greater degree among those more fortunately placed, to gasp in amazement and admiration at Hitler's "ending of unemployments", Stalin's "liquidation of illiteracy", Mussolini's "making the trains run on time"'.[42]

During the past decade an analysis of the real functioning of the democratic system had been one of the most controversial issues among social and political scientists; it was when faced with the threat of a new world war that they urged an 'ideological rearmament' around the basic values of democracy, 'together with the military one'.[43]

The Enemy's Example

There was a risk of fueling political opponents by setting up an agency which might recall not only past war experiences, but also the techniques of the enemy. Nazi propaganda methods had, in fact, raised a great deal of interest among social scientists since the early 1930s. Social psychologists such as Leonard Doob and Hadley Cantril, as well as anthropologists, had carefully studied Nazi methods of mass persuasion, and had found analogies with American techniques. Max Lerner's remarks in 1933, at the rise of the Nazi regime, are particularly significant: 'The most damning blow the dictatorships have struck at democracy has been … in taking over and perfecting our most prized techniques of persuasion and our underlying contempt for the credulity of the masses.'[44]

The great attention paid by sociologists, social psychologists and anthropologists to the Nazi propaganda machine had given rise, together with the intellectual resources offered by exiled refugees, to a considerable amount of knowledge. The Committee on National Morale could draw from this in order to make a precise and accurate analysis of the Nazi war machine. Ladislas Farago's *The Axis Grand Strategy*[45] was one of the first successful publications undertaken by the committee. A book entitled *German Psychological Warfare*, comprising a critical survey with bibliography, was prepared by major experts in the field and 2,500 copies were sold to government specialists and educators; a project for an encyclopedia of Nazism was undertaken in 1941, though it was never completed, and a film project was also proposed, to be distributed among the nation's most important movie-theatres. A film called *The Enemy We Face* aimed to trace the rise of fascism within Axis countries from available documentary source material, filmed by such directors as Joris Ivens. But besides these important aspects of the committee's work, another result of the study of Nazi propaganda was a realization that Max Lerner's observations on how dictatorships had exploited mass-persuasion techniques could be put to the advantage of democratic countries: democratic societies should learn from authoritarian regimes how to use public ceremonies as 'a source of strength' for their own system, as had been remarked by many, including the famous economist John Maynard Keynes.[46] From this perspective, the use of German mass meetings in a different democratic context was seen by David Riesman as a possible way of nurturing 'a critical democratic spirit' in the average American citizen.[47]

Inside the military and civilian agencies of government there was also a great awareness of the successful Nazi propaganda machine. Secretary of the Navy Frank Knox had remarked that 'every totalitarian power has found one of its most effective weapons in what they call a ministry of information, and sometimes they add … and propaganda'. This opinion was shared by Ickes: 'This propaganda is one of the most effective agencies of totalitarian states.'[48] Therefore, according to W. Onslow, assistant director of information in the Department of Interior: 'It is futile to argue that should the nation become engaged in war, it cannot indulge in certain successful propaganda and morale techniques simply because they have been used by totalitarian nations. In many instances we can fight fire with fire.'[49]

The projects of the committee, and of the Council for Democracy, although only partially enacted, are significant as a cultural attempt to find possible ways of reaching a mass audience through nationwide undertakings that were symbolically meaningful for the majority of the American people. An interesting example, among others, is the committee's project for the use of national monuments as powerful stimuli for national morale, since 'instruction cannot have the graphic force of an historical monument which can actually be touched, walked through and explored'. The memorandum gives some general suggestions about how to 'convey the living continuity of our national life through the exhibition of such monuments'; it then remarks: 'It is interesting to note that these possibilities have not escaped the attention of the dictatorships. The Ordensburgen are ostentatiously modelled after the fortresses of the Medieval Teutonic Knights. Surely the historic monuments of democracy can be put to a better use.'[50] Among other noteworthy projects was a scenario for an exhibition on democracy and the war, prepared by the committee for the Museum of Modern Art in New York, and a hymn of democracy, for music was considered an important factor in the strengthening of national cohesion. The National Music Council had undertaken, together with the committee, a project for the promotion of noon-hour concerts of popular as well as classical music, at war industry plants and at community centers, churches, museums, libraries, et cetera. A rally pageant, with Eleanor Roosevelt among its speakers, was planned as a campaign for collecting for the army 25,000 copies of books which had been burned in the Axis countries. A 'Patriotic Sunday Driving', with the distribution of blue, white and red national windshield stickers, encouraged, by force of 'patriotic public opinion', driving in shifts in order to reduce gasoline consumption.[51] However, the most brilliant exploitation of Nazi propaganda techniques was achieved within the film sector by Frank Capra, who was working for the Special Services branch of the Navy and Army Department. The *Why We Fight* documentary film series was produced in 1942 in response to widespread concern among the military high command over the confusion among draftees about the international situation and American involvement in the war. 'Morale and combat effectiveness are, – as Secretary of War Henry Stimson told public relation officers – a reflection of the aptitudes of the "people at home".'[52] Capra wanted to shoot a five-minute sequence with President Roosevelt speaking from the screen to the new recruits.[53] This project was not actually realized, but what was set up in the first *Why We Fight* documentary film, called *Prelude to War*, was a systematic use of the most famous Nazi propaganda film, *The Triumph of the Will* by Leni Riefenstahl. Nazi techniques of blending commentary, images and sound in documentary films were greatly admired by Hollywood producers and directors.[54] 'Capra's tactic of choice was to hijack the Nazi's own images'[55] for the great American public, to whom the film was eventually shown in 1943.

Democratic Morale

Since the almost unanimous agreement that the pattern of a 'Creel–
Goebbels type of propaganda bureau' had to be avoided,[56] the term
'morale' was more widely accepted, but 'It was not until the summer
of 1940 that morale seemed almost overnight to become the most
fashionable and arresting of terms – the theme of countless lectures,
conferences, articles.'[57]

Studies on 'the nature of morale', its specific features and the main
factors influencing civilian and military morale had been undertaken
by social scientists.[58] Here too, comparisons had to be made with
authoritarian regimes.[59] As the psychoanalyst Harry Sullivan remarked:
'The army of a democracy cannot be democratic … There is no con-
ceivable place for an equal voice in the government; and often no
freedom of decision but rigid discipline and unquestioning execution
of orders.'[60] According to sociologist Robert Park, similarities were to
be found in the special relationship between the leader and the group
which might be established in wars or emergencies or, on the other
hand, in authoritarian regimes. In these cases the restoration of group
morale, according to Park, could be explained by resorting to anthropological concepts, such as the use of magic. He recalled the effect
on mass opinion of Franklin D. Roosevelt's famous radio speech of 12
March 1933. Following Bronislaw Malinowski's studies, he explained
'the essence of magic' as 'the effects brought about by words and
symbols'.[61] More often, though, sociologists or social psychologists
turned to anthropological concepts in order to explain the relationship
in the Nazi regime between Hitler and the masses. Hitler was very
often perceived as a modern Genghis Khan or 'the medicine man',
with 'hypnotic' capacities over the masses.[62] Park himself referred to
ceremonies and rituals in the Nuremberg rallies as kinds of 'religious
revivals' where every rational faculty of the individual was inhibited.

The committee distinguished between democratic morale building
and authoritarian morale by drawing on the findings of social scientists:
the difference consisted mainly in the opposition of 'rationalism' to
'irrationalism'. In this specific aspect was grounded the main distinction between the two regimes, for the concepts of rationality and
liberty were the cornerstones of democracy: 'Morale supported by
a principle of reason ceases to be a matter of either hope or fear and
becomes a morale force.'[63] The committee stated that:

> The German Propaganda Machine is relevant to us not only as a
> serious threat but as an example … We have to plan a service which
> shall be as appropriate to American character and American poli-
> tical ideas as that of Germany is to Nazi ideology … While Nazi

technique lays on 'crude emotional appeal ...' the alternative way is to obtain the full human assent, both emotional and understanding.[64]

Within the conceptual framework of democratic morale, its mental character was particularly emphasized, in the sense that knowledge, as opposed to irrational fear or panic, was far more effective in mastering future events, especially in the case of some unforeseen or unprecedented situation. Mass panic following Orson Welles's 'War of the Worlds' broadcast had been studied in this sense by Hadley Cantril as an emblematic situation arising from failure to cope with the commonly accepted system of values and meanings.[65] Knowledge as a cognitive structure related to the social environment is what the sociologist Kurt Riezler had called 'the universe of discourse', through which single phenomena can be interpreted and an explanation can be found, which permits action: without a universe of discourse no public discussion can take place and there is no possibility of establishing a democratic system. According to Riezler: 'transition from the democratic to totalitarian system is easy when indefinite fear paves the way ... Despair cannot be expected to produce a democracy of respectable people.'[66]

Among the many different definitions of morale, the most widely accepted ones included five points:

1. The definition of a common goal;
2. Togetherness, the sense of a shared purpose;
3. The knowledge of a common danger;
4. The conviction of having some resource adequate to meet the threat;
5. The sense of advancement.[67]

The five points were discussed at the meetings of the American Psychological Association in September 1941 by experts in the field, such as Paul Lazarsfeld, Gregory Bateson, and Goodwin Watson. Within this general framework, great emphasis was placed on the concept of 'time perspective': the importance of setting a 'psychological future' for individual as well as collective expectations. 'A potent source of poor morale in the U.S.A. before our entry into actual fighting' was ascribed by these scholars 'to uncertainty about the future'.[68] The problem of 'winning the peace', besides 'winning the war', involved, therefore, the drawing of a plan for the future world, where democracy had to be conceived more 'as a process than a mere mechanism ... which will evolve in the future as it has in the past'.[69] In the committee's program, again, this concept was restated: 'Democracy is not an event but a process, not an achievement but a hope and a program, not a gift, but a challenge.' It was important, then, 'not to idealize the *status quo* but urge values to be realized as well as defended'[70] for mobilization of social minorities and lower income social groups in the total war program.[70]

The Strategy of Truth and the Community Projects

To this end, informational activity had to be attuned to what Carl Friedrich called 'the strategy of truth'. The constant stressing of this concept had a strong rhetorical appeal, but, according to Friedrich, 'indeed no such simple formula will do the trick'. What he was actually proposing was a more articulate plan, according to the latest scientific results in the field of public opinion, for which there would be preliminary research on 'prejudice or ignorance or other ground obstructing the likelihood of the action' for which the people should be prepared; there should then be the 'channelling out of information in such amounts as will overcome these obstructions'; after which, research should be conducted 'to determine whether the information is being absorbed'.[71] It would thus be possible to feel the 'pulse of the people' and consequently to orient it in the desired direction. On the other hand, in the committee's plan an important point was 'to provide avenues through which this grass-roots initiative could be implemented' as one of the most distinctive aspects of American democracy: 'while leadership is essential, it is no less essential that initiative shall spring from the people and the local communities'.[72] The committee's proposal was to set up at a community level 'citizen centres': the setting-up of an education and information department to furnish material to men's and women's clubs, civic groups, schools and churches, thus creating 'channels of public influence and education'.[73]

The most complete and articulated project was set up by a research group of anthropologists on a stereotyped kind of community, fictitiously called Ameriton. This was the last of a series of research programs organized by W. Lloyd Warner of Harvard University for the study of contemporary American society. The broad aim of the project was based on the preliminary consideration that:

> The morale of a society at war upon which so much hangs, can no longer under conditions of modern warfare be left to its own force ... It must be fortified through all the best skills of educational propaganda. For such ends it must be understood. Its ... peculiarities must be studied continuously and diagnosed systematically.[74]

Methodological interest lay in applying anthropological tools from 'the study of simple societies ... to fuller understanding of the prodigious complex American society'. Focus was to be placed on the concept of 'community', scrutinized as an entire, integrated entity, which would become 'a sample microcosm of American macrocosm'. In their remarkable work, through sophisticated methodological techniques, light was shed on community behavior by focusing on different aspects of the identification process between the individual and the group's symbolic values from a particular perspective: the geographical 'proximity of war'. In 1944, again, Lowell Mellett, director of the film section of the OWI, focused on the geographical distance of the war from the general domestic perception. Answering to the council's president, Angell, he remarked about the differences between the Allies' home front situation:

> Without decrying the great leadership of Churchill and Stalin ... I think it is fair to say that neither has had ... so difficult a domestic problem as the President has ... The war hit the people of those countries right in their own homes, they didn't have to be told, they saw. The American people have been made to understand to a degree that makes possible an immense war effort on our part but still not to the degree that the British and Russian people understand. In spite of all that is said and written in America the war still seems very far ...[75]

Radio broadcasts such as 'Nightmare at Noon'[76] by Stephen Vincent Benet were, in fact, programed by the Council for Democracy in order to bring the war dimension closer to the American public. The 'Nightmare' consisted of a Nazi invasion from the air, recalling Orson Welles's famous 'War of the Worlds'. To this end, as was emphasized in the research program about Ameriton, the cinema was the most powerful medium for 'catching and holding fast the mass of American population now withdrawing from the minimal symbolic participation in the war'.[77]

'Americans All'

The last relevant point which deserves particular attention is the cultural orientation towards ethnic groups and foreign-born citizens. The presidential order of 8 December 1941, which defined as enemy aliens all foreign-born immigrants coming from enemy countries and halted naturalization proceedings, gave rise to strong resentment among minority groups and increased racial and social tensions in large metropolitan areas such as New York.[78] Sociologists, anthropologists and other scholars involved in this problem attempted to find workable

ways towards integration and assimilation. Again, the point of reference was World War I, an experience which was generally perceived
as a failure. As Ruth Benedict had remarked: 'In 1917 the alien was to
be picked up by patriots and thrown into the merrily boiling melting
pot; in 1920 he was to be picked up by police and thrown into jail. In
both cases he was an article to be pushed around at the will of the
dominant groups.'[79] The process was now perceived in a more articulated way, by taking into account the point of view of the 'minorities'.
But the very concept of minority had a self-devaluative meaning: 'Such
groups are held in lower esteem, are debarred from certain opportunities
or are excluded from full participation in our national life.'[80] Although
attention had to be given to their different cultural backgrounds, the
main issue should remain the 'Alien will-to-become American'. It
was necessary, then, in view of the war emergency, to find nationwide
points of social cohesion which could cut across ethnic lines.

The whole problem of the foreign-born citizen was 'a peculiarly American one' – as remarked by Harold Hoskins, an expert on this subject
who worked for the State Department: 'The handful of aliens or first
generation foreign-born citizens in France or England offered no large
problem to them.'[81] In the United States, 'the aliens together with the
foreign-born citizens represented approximately one third of the entire
population'.[82] Among these, the Italians were the largest group with
1,600,000, followed by Germans with 1,200,000, while the Japanese
group was composed of 127,000 people, nearly two-thirds of whom
were native-born. Rumors following a statement on the part of Hugh
Drum, general commander of the Eastern Defence Command, interpreted as a possible extension of the mass evacuation policy of the type
already enacted against the Japanese to Italian-Americans and German-
Americans on the East Coast, were strongly opposed by the president
of the council, Ernest Angell.[83] Within the entire problem the anoma-
lous situation of refugees from Axis countries considered as 'enemy
aliens' was stressed by figures such as Thomas Mann, who demanded
'a clear and practical line' to be drawn 'between the potential enemies
of American democracy on the one hand and the victims and sworn
foes of totalitarian evil on the other'.[84] The whole problem, according
to the council's remarks, had to be expressed on different grounds: 'The
term enemy alien as well as all the administrative and legal machinery
built around older concepts of nationality and citizenship do not fit
this war. For this war is more than anything else a world civil war.'[85] The
policies enacted by the administration actually went in the direction of
lessening possible causes of social discontent, when on Columbus Day
1942 Italian-Americans were no longer classified as aliens.

Risks of social tension also came from other sources. Racial discrimination was under attack from African-Americans. The emotional

tension that had grown up around the promotion of an Afro-American March on Washington was relieved by the presidential executive order of 23 June 1941. A special committee was set up to deal with discriminatory practices in war employment. Social inquiries about African-American morale showed how the worsening of their social conditions and exclusion from job opportunities could not provide a positive basis for active support of a war perceived as 'the white man's war', according to the Afro-American press, together with a strong dislike of England because of its racist tradition. The war had to be transformed for African-Americans into a war of the darker races against white imperialist countries. The double-V campaign for 'Victory at home and Victory abroad', sponsored by the *Pittsburgh Courier*, would thus indicate their own struggle within the general context of war.[86]

The risk, as many social scientists remarked, was that collective insecurity and war strains, together with the increasing of ethnic group frictions according to country of origin, would reinforce race prejudices and deepen social and racial cleavages within domestic society. Moreover, the racist issue was considered by social scientists as a crucial issue in the war propaganda campaign against the Axis powers. An attempt was made to challenge Nazi racist theories on a scientific basis, as Franz Boas had done in establishing in 1939 an American Committee for Democracy and Intellectual Freedom, which tried to reach mass public opinion outside academic circles.[87] On the other hand, a major issue of American counter-propaganda was a focus on the Nazi policy of dividing one group against another. The enemy's propaganda inside the United States, mainly through shortwave broadcasts and fifth columns, was aimed at injecting and reinforcing racial prejudices, in order 'to make our minorities self conscious and to impregnate them with an oppression psychosis, but also to set one minority against the other'.[88] As Gordon Allport remarked: 'The primary psychological strategy of the Nazi is to divide and rule. It is fascinating to mark the course of Nazi dissolvent propaganda wherever there is a chance of cleavage, at the St. Lawrence, at the Mason Dixon Line, at the Hudson River.'[89] The same strategy was used inside the African-American community in Chicago, according to the warnings of Louis Ruppel.[90] As interracial conflict increased in 1942 and 1943, there was general concern about the outbreak of race riots in war-industry cities such as Detroit.[91] A detailed survey stressed the main lines that should be followed in order to overcome resistance to the application of the Fair Employment Practice Committee.[92] The report, based on effective ground experience, was made available to 2,500 members of the American Management Association and was the subject of many editorial comments and articles in newspapers and magazines.[93]

The main line of government policy, and the work of social scientists, was aimed at promoting 'an identification process' of the individual, not with his ethnic group but 'with the collective enterprise'. As Louis Wirth recognized: 'Considering the enemy we are fighting against and the doctrines the enemy espouses we, as a country that so obviously is of a mongrel origin, cannot embrace his policies by recognizing citizens of inferior grade.'[94] More than the effectiveness of the Nazi propaganda machine in reaching minority groups, the internal processes inside American society were considered potentially dangerous: 'Yesterday attacks upon the Jews lead to tomorrow attacks upon Catholics, Masons, Negroes ...'[95] For the Secretary of Agriculture Henry Wallace, 'an illustrative example of the method of drawing our people of different nationality together' could be that of the 'national gardens' from the Shakespearian to the Jewish to the German, et cetera, growing within the same park of the city.[96] The general metaphor to look at, according to Harold Hoskins, was: 'Not the melting pot, with its some-what mournful implication of uniformity, but rather in terms of an orchestra in which each racial group contributes with its special different tone to the rich ensemble of the whole.'[97] The classification of hyphenated Americans had to be dismissed in favor of the simple definition of 'American Citizen'.[98] The title of the newsreel produced at the council's suggestion for *The March of Times* series was, significantly, 'Americans All'.

Notes

1. New York Public Library, A.U. Pope Papers, Box 4, Committee for National Morale, G.W. Allport, 'Morale and its measurement'. The quotation is from E.A. Rundquist and R.F. Sletto, *Personality in the Depression* (Minneapolis, Minn.: 1936).
2. Allport, 'Morale and its measurement', p. 3.
3. H. Cantril, 'Public opinion in flux', *The Annals of the American Academy of Political and Social Science* 219–21 (January–May 1942), pp. 132–52.
4. B. Catton, *The War Lords of Washington* (New York: 1948), p. 16. See also R.W. Steele, 'Preparing the public for war: efforts to establish a national propaganda agency, 1940–41', *American Historical Review* 75 (October 1970), pp. 1640–53. For the impact of war on American society, see among others R. Polenberg, *War and Society: The U.S. 1941–45* (Westport, Conn.: 1972); J.M. Blum, *V was for Victory: Politics and American Culture in World War II* (New York: 1976).
5. Catton, *The War Lords*, pp. 66–99.
6. Polenberg, *War and Society.* See also: E.D. Tetreau, 'The impact of war on some communities in the South-West', *American Sociological Review* 10, 1–4 (1945) pp. 249–56; H.M. Kallen, 'The war and education in the

United States', *The American Journal of Sociology* 48, 6 (1943), pp. 331–42; N. Anderson and N.H. Rogg, 'The impact of the war on labor and industry', ibid., pp. 361–8; F.M. Williams, 'The standard of living in wartime', *The Annals* 225–7 (July–November 1943), pp. 117–27.

7. J.S. Bossard, 'War and the family', *American Sociological Review* 6, 6 (1941), pp. 330–44; E.R. Mowrer, 'Recent trends in family research', ibid., pp. 499–511; E.W. Burgess, 'The effect of war on the American family', *The American Journal of Sociology* 48, 6 (1943), pp. 343–52. For the role of women in World War II, see among others K. Anderson, *War-Time Women: Sex Roles, Family Relations and the Status of Women in W.W. II* (Westport, Conn.: 1981); M.R. Higonnet *et al.*, *Behind the Lines: Gender and Two World Wars* (New Haven, Conn.: 1987).

8. E.F. Frazier, 'Ethnic and minority groups in wartime, with special reference to the negro', *The American Journal of Sociology* 48, 6 (1943), pp. 369–77; H. Powdermaker, 'The channeling of negro aggression by the cultural process', *The American Journal of Sociology* 48, 6 (July 1942– May 1943), pp. 750–8; H. Mann Bond, 'Education as a social process: a case study of a higher institution as an incident in the process of acculturation', ibid., pp. 701–9; L. Wirth, 'Education for survival: the Jews', ibid., pp. 682–91. For recent works on Afro-Americans in the army and American culture, see T. Doherty, *Projections of War: Hollywood, American Culture, and World War II* (New York: 1993), pp. 205–26.

9. Bossard, 'War and the family', pp. 343–4.

10. Ibid., p. 344.

11. A.M. Winkler, *The Politics of Propaganda: The Office of War Information* (New Haven, Conn.: 1978); Steele, 'Preparing the public for war'; R.W. Steele, *Propaganda in an Open Society: The Roosevelt Administration and the Media, 1933–41* (Westport, Conn.: 1985). See also, as a useful source of information, G.E. McMillan, 'Government publicity and the impact of war', *Public Opinion Quarterly* 5, 4 (Fall 1941), pp. 383–98; S.F. Possony, 'Needed – a new propaganda approach to Germany', *Public Opinion Quarterly* 6, 3 (Fall 1942), pp. 335–50.

12. The quotation is in Steele, 'Preparing the public for war', p. 1649. For a more detailed information about OFF structure, see R.K. Lane, 'The O.F.F.', *Public Opinion Quarterly* 6, 2 (Summer 1942), pp. 204–20.

13. Catton, *The War Lords of Washington*, p. 193.

14. Polenberg, *War and Society*, p. 54.

15. D. Sanderson, 'Sociology a means to democracy', *American Sociological Review* 8, 1 (1943), pp. 7, 9.

16. Library of Congress, H.L. Ickes Papers, Box 379, War National Morale Folder, Letter of C.J. Friedrich to H.L. Ickes, 8 March 1941.

17. Ibid., Letter of J. McCloy to H.L. Ickes, 8 February 1941.

18. Library of Congress, Ickes Papers, Box 379, WNM, A.U. Pope to H.L. Ickes, 9 March 1941.

19. Ibid., R.S. Allen to H.L. Ickes, 20 March 1941.

20. New York Public Library, A.U. Pope Papers, Box 4, CNM, memorandum: 'How do you feel about the war?', American Defense – Harvard Group, March 1942, p. 2.

21. Ibid., A Plan for national morale submitted by the Committee for National Morale, 21 February 1941.

22. Library of Congress, Ickes Papers, Box 379, WNM, 1941, memorandum on Committee for National Morale, p. 2.

23. Ibid., M. Strauss, memorandum to Ickes, 22 March 1941.

24. Ibid., L. Mellett to H.L. Ickes, 13 March 1941.

25. Ibid., H.L. Ickes to H.B. Swope, 5 August 1941; for Ickes's opinion on this subject, see also H.L. Ickes, *The Secret Diary of Harold L. Ickes* (New York: 1954), vol. 3, pp. 445–6.

26. Ibid., Ickes to the President, 17 September 1941.

27. Ibid., Pope to H.L. Ickes, 2 June 1941.

28. New York Public Library, A.U. Pope Papers, Box 4, WNM, 'Recommendations for a National Morale Service', pp. 8, 46.

29. G. Creel, 'Propaganda and morale', *American Journal of Sociology* 47, 3 (November 1941), p. 351. Creel wrote an extensive work on the CPI at the end of the war: *How We Advertized America* (New York: 1920). See also H.D. Lasswell, *Propaganda Techniques in the World War* (New York: 1927). On Creel's activities and postwar reputation, see J.R. Mock and C. Larson, *Words that Won the War: The Story of the Committee on Public Information, 1917–1919* (Princeton, NJ: 1939); S. Vaughn, *Holding Fast the Inner Lines: Democracy, Nationalism and the Committee on Public Information* (Chapel Hill, NC: 1980).

30. New York Public Library, A.U. Pope Papers, Box 4, CNM, 1941, 'A Plan for National Morale', 21 February 1941.

31. R. Benedict, 'Race problems in America', *The Annals* 216–18 (July 1941), pp. 74–5.

32. See on this subject D. Frezza, 'Informazione o propaganda: il dibattito americano tra le due guerre', in M. Vaudagna (ed.), *L'Estetica della politica* (Bari: 1989), pp. 103–28.

33. R.D. Casey, 'The press, propaganda and pressure groups', *The Annals* 219–21 (1942), p. 66.

34. Steele, 'Preparing the public for war', pp. 1642–3.

35. P.H. Odegard and A. Barth, 'Millions for defense', *Public Opinion Quarterly* 5, 3 (Fall 1941), pp. 399–411.

36. Library of Congress, Ickes Papers, Box 247, Conference on Propaganda Committee, 28 November 1940, pp. 3, 4, 11.

37. Ibid., p. 9.

38. New York Public Library, A.U. Pope Papers, Box 4, CNM, G. Harrison, War Generation no. 2, p. 7.

39. G.W. Allport, 'Liabilities and assets in civilian morale', *The Annals* 216–18 (July–November 1941), p. 89.

40. New York Public Library, A.U. Pope Papers, Box 4, CNM, 'Recommendations for a National Morale Service', p. 3.

41. Franklin D. Roosevelt Library, F. Biddle Papers, Box 1, E.A. Bernays to F. Biddle, 25 January 1940.

42. Odegard and Barth, 'Millions for defense', p. 403.

43. E.A. Purcell, jun., *The Crisis of Democratic Theory: Scientific Naturalism and the Problem of Value* (Lexington, Ken.: 1973), pp. 115–232; J.T.

Kloppenberg, *Uncertain Victory: Social Democracy and Progressivism in European and American Thought, 1870–1920* (New York: 1986); see also D. Frezza, 'Hitlerism Abracadabra: Le scienze sociali americane e la crisi della democrazia (1920–1941)', *Passato e Presente* 35 (1995), pp. 37–64.

44. M. Lerner, 'The pattern of dictatorship', in *Ideas are Weapons* (New York: 1938), p. 512.

45. L. Farago, *The Axis Grand Strategy: Blueprints for the Total War* (New York: 1942).

46. J.M. Keynes, 'Art and the state', *The Listener*, 26 August 1936, in *The Collected Writings of J.M. Keynes* (New York: 1982), vol. 28, pp. 341–9; see, on the whole subject, G.L. Mosse, 'L'autorappresentazione nazionale negli anni Trenta negli Stati Uniti e in Europa', in *L'Estetica della politica*, pp. 3–43.

47. D. Riesman, 'Government education for democracy', *Public Opinion Quarterly* 5, 2 (June 1941), pp. 195–210.

48. Library of Congress, Ickes Papers, Box 247, Conference on Propaganda Committee, 28 November 1940, pp. 7, 9.

49. Ibid., Box 379, WNM, W. Onslow, memorandum to H.L. Ickes, 21 March 1941.

50. Ibid., Box 379, WNM, memorandum about the use of National Monuments.

51. New York Public Library, A.U. Pope Papers, Box 4, CNM, 'The First Year and After', 25 August 1941.

52. R.W. Steele, 'The greatest gangster movie ever filmed: prelude to war', *Prologue* 11, 4 (Winter 1979), p. 224.

53. FDR Library, L. Mellett Papers, Off. Corr., Box 6, Mellett to the President, 25 February 1942.

54. Doherty, *Projections of War*, p. 27.

55. Ibid., p. 74.

56. Library of Congress, Ickes Papers, Box 379, WNM, Pope to H.L. Ickes, 11 February 1941.

57. G.W. Allport, 'The nature of democratic morale', in G. Watson (ed.), *Civilian Morale: Second Yearbook of the Society for the Psychological Study of Social Issues* (Boston, Mass.: 1942), p. 3.

58. See, among others W.E. Hocking, 'The nature of morale', *The American Journal of Sociology* 47, 3 (November 1941), pp. 302–20; the whole issue is dedicated to this subject-matter from different angles: H.S. Sullivan, 'Psychiatric aspects of morale', pp. 277–301; J. Ulio, 'Military morale', pp. 321–30; J.D. Landis, 'Morale and civilian defense', pp. 331–9; J.R. Angell, 'Radio and national morale', pp. 352–9; R.E. Park, 'Morale and the news', pp. 360–77; W. Wanger, 'The role of movies in morale', pp. 378–83; H. Durant, 'Morale and its measurement', pp. 406–14; L. Wirth, 'Morale and minority groups', pp. 415–33; E. Shils, 'A note of governmental research on attitudes and morale', pp. 472–80. See also D.C. Miller, 'The measurement of national morale', *American Sociological Review* 6, 1–6 (December 1941), pp. 487–98; S. Washburn, 'What makes morale?', *Public Opinion Quarterly* 5, 1–4 (Winter 1941), pp. 519–31.

59.   For a study of social psychology focused on differences between demo-
       cratic and authoritarian groups, see R.K. White and R. Lippitt, *Autocracy
       and Democracy: An Experimental Inquiry* (New York: 1939; 1954).
60.   Sullivan, 'Psychiatric aspects of morale', p. 292.
61.   Park, 'Morale and the news', p. 366.
62.   Frezza, 'Hitlerism Abracadabra', pp. 56–60.
63.   Park, 'Morale and the news', p. 377.
64.   New York Public Library, A.U. Pope Papers, Box 4, CNM, 'A Plan
       For National Morale', 21 February 1941, pp. 12–13; Explanatory Index,
       p. 2.
65.   H. Cantril, *The Invasion from Mars* (Princeton, NJ: 1940).
66.   Riezler, 'The social psychology of fear', p. 498.
67.   Watson, *Civilian Morale*, pp. 30–47.
68.   Ibid., p. 31.
69.   Sanderson, 'Sociology a means to democracy', pp. 1–9.
70.   New York Public Library, A.U. Pope Papers, Box 4, CNM, Recom-
       mendations for a National Morale Service, pp. 2, 3.
71.   C. Friedrich, 'Issues of informational strategy', *Public Opinion Quarterly*
       7, 2 (Spring 1943), p. 83.
72.   New York Public Library, A.U. Pope Papers, Box 4, CNM, 1941, 'A
       Plan for a National Morale Service', 21 February 1941, p. 13.
73.   Ibid., Citizens Center Project of the Committee for National Morale, 31
       August 1942. The setting-up of a research program at a community level
       included some interesting suggestions by Margaret Mead for psycholo-
       gical projects: ibid., 9 September 1942. She also worked in a community
       project in the Upper West Side of New York City.
74.   Ibid., L. Srole, 'First Progress Report of Research into the Total Impact
       of War upon Ameriton, U.S.A.', pp. 1, 13, 14.
75.   FDR Library, L. Mellett Papers, Off. Corr., Box 6, Mellett to E. Angell,
       4 March 1944.
76.   New York Public Library, A.U. Pope Papers, Box 4, CNM, Council for
       Democracy, First Annual Report, October 1941.
77.   Ibid., L. Srole, 'The Total Impact of War', p. 13.
78.   R.H. Bayor, *Neighbors in Conflict: The Irish German Jews and Italians of
       New York City, 1929–1941* (Baltimore, Md.: 1978). For a recent work on
       ethnic minorities in American history, see R. Takaki, *A Different Mirror.
       A History of Multicultural America* (Boston and New York: 1993).
79.   Benedict, 'Race problems in America', p. 75.
80.   Wirth, 'Morale and minority groups', p. 415.
81.   H.B. Hoskins, 'American unity and our foreign-born citizens', *The
       Annals* 219–21 (1942), p. 153.
82.   FDR Library, L. Mellet Papers, Off. Corr., Box 6, memorandum by H.
       Hoskins, Division of American Unity, 28 July 1941.
83.   Ibid., Box 6, E. Angell to General Drum, 3 June 1942; ibid., Angell to L.
       Mellett, 3 June 1942. See also ibid., F. Biddle Papers, Off. Corr., Box 1,
       'Suggested Plan for Treatments of Enemy Nationality'.
84.   Ibid., T. Mann *et al.* to President F.D. Roosevelt, 12 February 1942.
85.   Ibid., L. Mellet Papers, Off. Corr., Box 6, 'Suggested Plan', p. 2. For the

Italian experience, see C. Pavone, *Una guerra civile: Saggio storico sulla moralità della resistenza, 1943–1945* (Torino: 1991).

86. Frazier, 'Ethnic and minority groups in wartime, with special reference to the negro', pp. 375–7.

87. The American Committee had been set up by Franz Boas with the help of Ruth Benedict and other scholars at Columbia University in 1939 for the promotion of meetings on this subject. A 'Manifesto on the Freedom of Science' was signed by 1,600 scientists and scholars; publication of pamphlets and other educational material was intended to have a wide distribution in communities and educational institutions.

88. Wirth, 'Morale and minority groups', p. 421.

89. Allport, 'Liabilities and assets in civilian morale', p. 90.

90. FDR Library, L. Mellet Papers, Box 5, Off. Corr., L. Ruppel to M. Le Hand, 17 February 1941.

91. N. Lichtenstein, *Labor's War at Home: The C.I.O. in World War II* (Cambridge and New York: 1982).

92. New York Public Library, A.U. Pope Papers, Box 4, CNM, memorandum on 'Experiences in Negro Employment by the Council for Democracy', pp. 3, 5.

93. FDR Library, L. Mellet Papers, Box 10, Off. Corr., memorandum from the Council for Democracy, 1943.

94. Wirth, 'Morale and minority groups', pp. 427, 430.

95. FDR Library, L. Mellett Papers, Box 10, Off. Corr., Angell to General E. Wood.

96. 'The genetic basis for democracy: a panel discussion on race and race prejudice', pamphlet by the American Committee for Democracy and Intellectual Freedom (New York, 1939), p. 21.

97. Hoskins, 'American unity and our foreign-born citizens', p. 158.

98. FDR Library, L. Mellett Papers, Box 6, Off. Corr., memorandum by H. Hoskins, Division of American Unity, 28 July 1941, pp. 1–2.

10

The Other Side of War:
Overseas Marriages between British Women
and American GIs in World War II

Jenel Virden

He would have liked to have been married before D-Day but you had to go through your superior officer and his commanding officer was not going to let any of his men marry an English girl, period. So you just put in the application and that was it; it didn't go anywhere. You just did not have any other avenue open except to get the girl pregnant. Believe me, some of them did that deliberately.[1]

Rosa Ebsary

British war brides became immigrants to America by virtue of their marriages to American citizens. These marriages occurred, for the most part, in Great Britain during the war. However, authorities from both the United States and British governments attempted to discourage and sometimes even stop the marriages of these women and American servicemen. The issue of wartime marriages required that officials carefully balance individuals' civil liberties and governments' wartime priorities. The American military was concerned about marriage-related 'distractions' such as allotments, insurance, and domestic arrangements. The army, in particular, saw these marriages as complications. Hence, it would help a GI who wanted sex by providing condoms and medical treatment, but would hinder relational commitments; it recognized the human urge for fraternization, but not for partnership. The result of this policy often meant that British women who dated GIs were suspect and their reputations called into question. However, the couples persevered in the face of opposition; by insisting on marriage, they forced the authorities to change their policies.

Although the high incidence of overseas marriages was unique to World War II, the question of marriage between American servicemen and women of foreign nationality was not. In 1918, soon after American troops began to arrive in Europe, the American Expeditionary Force (AEF) command received requests from American servicemen for permission to marry French women. US Army officials did not approve of these unions. The War Department and the army recognized the need to safeguard the civil liberties and rights of American

197

citizens, so they did not officially deny men the right to marry. Naturally, the US military believed the main concern of army personnel
should be the conduct of the war with Germany. They did not want
soldiers to pursue personal matters.

The AEF soldiers, however, refused to comply and demanded a
clear statement of rules governing marriage. Eventually the military
decided to follow a policy whereby 'headquarters declined to give express
consent to marriage or to refuse the same'.[2] The US Army's method of
discouraging marriage was to ignore the problem. Hence, the issue of
marriage between American soldiers and French women fell to the
French government. French civil law aided the US Army's attempt to
stop marriages. The French government required couples to have
wedding banns read in the groom's home town, creating an obvious
problem for American soldiers. However, the US Army came to the
help of soldiers when the French government insisted that Americans
prove they were not already married. A statement from commanding
officers that a soldier's affidavit declaring his single status was true, to
the best of the army's knowledge, accompanied applications. This
requirement brought the US Army into the process, albeit reluctantly.

Commanding officers of the AEF in World War I had various objections to overseas marriage. One colonel of a cavalry unit noted:

> When Pvt W asked permission to marry I refused, as I did in other
> cases, on the grounds that this was no time to be undertaking new
> responsibilities and obligations; that we were over here to fight
> when the time came; and to spend the rest of the time getting ready
> for it and not to marry and raise families. If Pvt W is allowed to
> marry this girl it will lead to a number of other cases just exactly like
> this. I have been through the whole thing twice before in Cuba and
> the Philippines.[3]

The colonel's objections indicate that the army had experienced similar problems with reconciling the inhumanity of war and the urges of
human nature at least as far back as the Spanish–American War. There
is little research on the war-bride issue in any war, but the limited
information about this topic *vis-à-vis* World War I does provide a good
basis of comparison with the situation in World War II. Officers of the
AEF in the Great War voiced many of the same concerns and tried to
discourage marriages in much the same way as commanders of the US
Army of World War II. During World War I, army officials hoped that
by pointing out potential problems they could stop soldiers from developing relationships with foreign women. The officials suggested that
commanding officers let their men know that marriage did not confer
special privileges on the foreign-born wife of a serviceman and that

women of dubious character might be preying on men for the express purpose of financial gain in the form of allotments and insurance. However, the army agreed that instances of pregnancy did warrant expedition of the marriage between soldiers and the women 'in trouble', as happened in World War II. World War I army officials raised similar objections concerning women in the nurses' corps and the Red Cross, with the added stipulation that they would discharge any woman in these two services who did contract a marriage, and return them to the United States. In March 1919 the military authorities estimated that 'several thousands' of marriages had taken place between American soldiers and foreign women.[4]

The point of comparison between World War I and World War II, however, is limited where marriage is concerned. Far fewer Americans served overseas in World War I compared to World War II, and they served for a much shorter time. While marriage between young American soldiers and women overseas was not unknown before the 1940s, the global nature of the conflict in World War II – the size of the armies involved, the length of service, and the numbers of troops sent overseas – provide a better basis for an examination of war brides. A good place to begin an investigation is with the Chaplain Corps, whose mandate included the performance of all ecclesiastical duties as well as providing guidance and counseling to soldiers on a variety of personal matters. Marriage and fraternization were two of the issues that chaplains confronted in their capacity as moral arbiters. Their role in the marriage of servicemen included discussing the seriousness of the married state with the GI and prospective brides to determine their understanding of the responsibilities of marriage and, on some occasions, coming to conclusions about the desirability of permitting a particular marriage to take place.

In 1939, in anticipation of the build-up of the armed forces, the army changed its regulations regarding the duties of the Chaplain Corps. Henceforth, chaplains could no longer conduct marriages for enlisted men below grade three without specific written permission of the army. In 1940, the army extended its restrictions and insisted that it would not re-enlist men who married without obtaining written consent. At the same time, servicemen could no longer be court-martialed for failure 'to take prophylactic treatment after illicit sexual intercourse', contracting a venereal disease, or 'having thus incapacitated themselves for duty'. The army, in other words, condoned sex, but not marriage.[5] Since the moral well-being of troops fell within the range of duties for the Chaplain Corps, the chaplains shouldered much of the burden of dealing with sexual issues.

Army chaplains' work involving wartime marriage took place at bases both within the United States and overseas. The number of marriages increased within the United States in the early years of the war. Hence, chaplains at various training bases and army posts devoted much of their time to the issue of matrimony. The substantial increase in numbers of marriages worried many officials concerned about hasty courtships and the uncertainty of wartime. This concern over the moral welfare of soldiers dictated much of the work of army chaplains in World War II. The Chaplain Corps' determination to protect men from the 'evils' of pre- and/or extramarital sexual relations often pitted them against other branches of the US Army. Many chaplains voiced concern over the lack of moral standards in the army and complained of the 'Army's blind eye' policy regarding questions of sex. They noted that the army did nothing to end the practice of off-base houses of prostitution in some overseas areas. Some chaplains charged that the army, by participating in the regulation of local bordellos, contributed to the moral decline of the men. In addition, the provision of condoms to servicemen as they left bases, and the establishment of prophylactic stations for their use upon return, allegedly acted to encourage immoral behavior. In one chaplain's opinion, the profusion of dirty pictures in servicemen's publications and the display of erotic art on airplanes, as well as profane language and jokes, led to a decline in moral conduct. These issues made the chaplain's job of moral guardian more difficult.[6]

Army rules and regulations concerning marriage and fraternization also made a chaplain's job more complex. In May 1942, just four months after the arrival of the first American troops in Great Britain, a chaplain in Northern Ireland requested clarification of army policy regarding overseas marriage. The army responded by sending the chaplain a list of what it considered to be the major drawbacks. Marriage to an American citizen did not automatically give the foreign-born wife United States citizenship. This represented a change in immigration policy since World War I; US citizenship now required a three-year residence within the United States of the foreign-born wife. The army also pointed out to the chaplain that marriage did not mean that the soldier could live off-base while overseas. Echoing World War I concerns, the judge advocate noted that a soldier could be moved at any time and 'the girl who marries a soldier may reasonably expect to be "left behind" at any moment ... and it would be unwise to become dependent upon the soldier for support'.[7] The army also warned the chaplain that he should investigate carefully a soldier's current marital status to avoid the problem of bigamy, which, if it occurred, would mean the foreign wife would have no rights at all. In addition, though marriage would help the foreign-born wife in terms of emigration to the United States, actual transportation to America would be difficult at best, and she could not expect to accompany her husband on his return after the war.

The army often reiterated these points in its correspondence to chaplains relating to soldiers' marriages. As in World War I, the US Army in World War II viewed marriage in general, and overseas marriage in particular, as undesirable. The military was far more concerned with waging war and, reasonably, saw the marriages of its men as a distraction from its primary objectives. Hence, authorities continued to do as much as they could, without directly violating the soldiers' civil liberties, to discourage couples from marrying. War Department circulars and army regulations concerning marriage stressed these points. The army required any soldier contemplating marriage to obtain his commanding officer's permission. At first the army tried to impose a three-month waiting period, but later reduced this to two months. Commanding officers could waive the waiting period at their own discretion, which left some flexibility for cases of illegitimacy and pregnancy. The army stressed two additional points on the subject of overseas marriages. First, it was important for the soldier to comply with all civil requirements in the country where the marriage was to take place; failure to do so could result in an invalid marriage. Second, the army still held out against any marriage that would appear to bring discredit to the military. Although the army mentioned the last point frequently, it never really defined what it meant by discredit. The army clearly wanted to retain control over soldiers' marriage plans.[8]

Other Chaplain Corps' duties entailed dealing with the outside publicity generated by the news of overseas marriages. In 1942, Chief of Chaplains Major General William Arnold heard from a very unhappy woman in Sioux City, Iowa. She stated that she believed the best course of action for the army to take regarding overseas marriages was to ban them. Due to the length of the war and the time soldiers would spend overseas, the vast numbers of American soldiers in the service, and the anticipated high casualty rate, she reasoned that America would be short of men of marrying age at the end of the war. This problem would result in numerous instances of American girls who would lead lonely and unfulfilled lives in direct consequence of the army policy of allowing soldiers to marry foreign-born women. She pointed out that 'already thousands of American girls know they face spinsterhood and a life of loneliness and unhappiness ... To allow Americans to marry Irish, English, Australian and Icelandic girls during all the years the war may last will be tragic for American girls'.[9] She noted that recent publicity often stressed the opportunity these marriages provided for the United States and other countries to become closer allies. From her point of view, however, the moral and social ramifications, as well as the simple distress of American girls, were not worth the sacrifice. She predicted that 'a war of five years or even less will mean hundreds of thousands of such marriages'.[10]

Arnold's assistant responded to the woman's letter by suggesting that his office was 'of the opinion that relatively few American soldiers will marry foreign girls' and press reports were exaggerating the few cases that had occurred by May 1942. He assured her that her fears were 'needless since the number who will marry foreign girls ... will be practically negligible'. He also commented that since the Chaplain Corps was well represented throughout the army, the soldiers who did contemplate overseas marriage would be subject to influence from chaplains who 'will counsel and advise the soldiers accordingly'.[11] The exchange between the woman in Iowa and the Chief of Chaplains Office serves as an excellent example of civilian concern over overseas marriages and the power of the press in publicizing this phenomenon. The first marriages received attention from various news sources, including the soldiers' magazine *Yank* and newspaper *Stars and Stripes*. Opposition within the United States to overseas marriages sometimes bordered on the hysterical. United States congressmen received hundreds of letters from irate citizens concerning the practice of allowing American soldiers to marry foreign women while overseas. Press accounts when the war brides eventually arrived in the United States made a point of stressing how wrong the American public had been previously to object to the marriages. Fear that foreign women were taking advantage of GIs was the basis of most complaints.

The question of overseas marriages caused concern among the chaplains themselves. Chaplain Captain Charles Dever recorded his own reaction to the subject of wartime marriages in response to a questionnaire. He noted that in general he approved 'of the marriages in the sense that the soldiers have something more or less tangible to steady their lives and therefore make better soldiers. However, many of them are marriages that come as a result of the uniform and the stress of the times.'[12] A number of chaplains in overseas stations shared Captain Dever's concerns. Some chaplains faced the problem of trying to reconcile army policy with their own moral standards and religious functions. In 1943 a chaplain stationed in Iceland wrote to the Chief of Chaplains Office to complain about army policy forbidding American soldiers serving in Iceland to marry. He noted that while the army provided condoms and prophylactic stations for men who went out on pass, 'the man who came from America, unmarried and not engaged, and who wanted to remain decent and get married could not do so'. The chaplain was unable to offer any comfort to soldiers who came to him for help and advice. The problem was especially acute because army policy meant there were approximately two hundred illegitimate children in Iceland. The chaplain suggested that this was 'a policy encouraging bastardy'.[13] The response of the Chief of Chaplains Office was typical of army policy on these issues: the problem of overseas marriages should be left to the local army authority of each region. The Chief of Chaplains Office noted that there had even been a recent conference on the subject of overseas marriage, which had concluded that the best course of action was to counsel delay. In the specific case of illegitimate births, the army authorities advised the chaplain in Iceland to let men know that they could have allotments deducted from their pay for children they wished to acknowledge. The response from the chief of chaplains did not address the deeper moral question that the chaplain's letter had highlighted. Instead, the chaplain in Iceland was reprimanded with an admonition:

> that chaplains devote themselves to advising those under their moral and religious care to be long suffering and patient in the midst of difficulties and to work, hope and pray for a victory that will make for a world where freedom really exists and its fruits may be enjoyed. The chaplains by their good example and hopeful attitude can add a mighty stimulus toward the prosecution of the war and ultimate victory. When chaplains are short-sighted, growlers and easily discouraged, the way becomes dark indeed.[14]

Like the rest of army policy relating to moral and religious issues, this advice from the Chief of Chaplains Office offered no real solution and clearly put the conduct of the war above moral considerations as well as the physical and emotional welfare of soldiers, women and children.

To their credit, the Army and War Departments were equally reluctant to become involved in requests for firmer prohibitions of marriage or a more restrictive approach to moral issues. The previously cited examples of chaplains' complaints concerning the army attitude toward prostitution and the encouragement of prophylactic treatment are cases in point. Additionally, other chaplains took exception to the army policy of allowing marriages at all. One chaplain submitted a report to his superiors suggesting that the army should discourage wartime marriages at all costs. Of paramount importance to this chaplain was not the moral issue of men's souls but rather the more prosaic consideration of their wallets. He believed that the majority of women contracting overseas marriages were doing so for the express purpose of cheating the government out of allotments and benefits. He stated that it was outrageous that foreign women 'who have never been in the country, born its tax burden, or shared in its cross of war' could profit from marrying an American. He went on to suggest that:

> the lure of American gold, freedom, and glamor lowers the bars. Most AWOLs are tracable [sic] to sex affairs: but, American men are too galant [sic], honorable, and yet emotional in foreign lands to

make sound decisions in marriage matters. More red tape should be added to make marriage harder and harder to win.[15]

The War Department's response to this complaint was typical of the hands-off approach mentioned earlier. Policies and regulations on overseas marriages consistently followed a pattern of first attempting to discourage, and then sitting back and allowing nature to take its course. The army decision-making process during World War II on this particular issue proves that policy did not dictate actions, but rather followed events. When the American GIs first began seeking permission to marry foreign-born women, the army tried to prohibit the marriages; and when the GIs insisted on pursuing their civil liberties concerning moral questions (both marriage and sexual relations), the army policy then began to play a game of catching up with the soldier. As a result, military authorities issued circular after circular and each new regulation or policy was a belated attempt to deal with a *fait accompli*. For example, wartime marriages had been grounds to refuse re-enlistment earlier, but, when this failed to stop marriages, the regulation changed. The army then insisted on a three-month waiting period and the commanding officer's approval. The waiting period later changed to two months, with the possibility of having the period waived. The army, at one time, dismissed American soldiers of World War II for contracting a venereal disease, but later provided them with condoms and pro-stations. The military could not regulate social behavior, despite repeated attempts; it could not control GI conduct, no matter which approach they adopted.

The American Red Cross, an institution purportedly responsible for soldiers' welfare and morale, also became involved in the issue of overseas marriage. Red Cross participation included the controversial topic of marriage investigations. Early in the war, military authorities asked the Red Cross to conduct investigations into the backgrounds of potential GI brides. Red Cross representatives visited the homes of the women and subsequently submitted reports on their family circumstances. When news of these investigations spread into the public domain, a furor arose. The Red Cross was accused of conducting character investigations. As a result of this negative publicity, the American Red Cross subsequently changed its policy and removed itself from the practice of marriage investigations. From the American Red Cross's point of view, 'Those advocating Red Cross participation noted the aftermath of the last war when the hasty Franco-American marriages resulted in many tragedies and much unhappiness. If American soldiers and the French girls had been properly advised probably a great many of these domestic misfortunes would have been avoided.'[16]

The American Red Cross took a very paternalistic approach to discouraging overseas marriage, in much the same way as the US Army. In addition, the American Red Cross (like the army) believed that it was capable of determining what constituted adequate foundations for a marriage, an assumption that begs for argument. Both institutions seemed to assume that couples contracting overseas marriages were not doing so out of love, but rather for some hidden reason which, once discovered, could be brought to light, thus stopping the process. The participants in question were usually consenting adults, but the agencies involved felt it was their responsibility to pass judgment on these marriages. Even if one concedes that the army's concern for keeping all military personnel focused on the conduct of the war was legitimate, this paternalistic approach raises some interesting ethical questions.

From late 1943 onward, the American Red Cross's only responsibility was to provide information to the soldier and his bride on military regulations governing marriage. It also acted as a clearinghouse for soldiers interested in obtaining information on the legal ramifications of international marriage, and counseled servicemen and their war brides on United States government policies concerning immigration and citizenship. The American Red Cross followed its more traditional role of catering to soldiers' welfare by keeping servicemen informed of the rights of dependents to military allotments, giving monetary aid when necessary and helping soldiers to verify birth certificates and other legal documents. After marriage, the Red Cross provided counseling to war brides on the nature of American society and culture. These services were all available on a voluntary basis.[17] The American Red Cross followed the same procedures in most overseas theaters.

The attitude of numerous agencies towards overseas marriages had various effects on the women involved. Potential war brides had to confront resistance to their future plans at every turn. They were the victims of the pervasive idea that somehow they were suspect. The marriage investigations were just one procedure that threw doubt on the morals and character of any foreign woman who met and married an American soldier. A reputation for being fast and loose followed many of these women from the time they were dating the GIs until after they landed in the United States. As Joan Posthuma recalled of her experience: 'I went up to get my papers [and] I got this very snooty girl. You had to have your marriage certificate and your birth certificate and everything and I handed them in and she looked at it and she said, "What were you doing, waiting on the dock for the first Yank to get off the boat?"'[18] Ivy Hammers blamed the military: 'I resent the way the U.S. Army treated some of the girls. Some of them were treated like dirt, as if they were asking for the moon.'[19]

The women's own governments also dealt with the problems of international marriage. Since British servicemen met and married women of other nationalities while serving overseas, the British government had to address the question of overseas marriages from both sides. The Foreign Office played a major role in handling British officials' concerns about these international marriages. The Air Ministry gathered considerable information from various Allied legal staffs about the rights of British women who married foreigners. The ministry drew up an outline of the consequences of marriage of British women to numerous Allied soldiers, including those from America, Belgium, Czechoslovakia, Holland, France, Norway, and Poland. This information was for use by British officials when counseling women about marriage to foreigners. The British government was less concerned over the legal status of the considerable number of British women who married soldiers from commonwealth nations such as Canada, Australia, South Africa, and New Zealand.[20]

The most important issue in the view of the British government was the woman's nationality upon marriage. For the British war bride who married a Dutch, Czechoslovakian, Belgian, Norwegian, or Polish serviceman, marriage led to automatic citizenship in their husband's country with a consequent loss of British citizenship. The British woman who married a Frenchman could declare herself a French citizen and at the same time retain her British citizenship. Marriage to an American, as the United States military authorities had pointed out in directives on numerous occasions, did not automatically give American citizenship to the spouse. Immigrants to America could only obtain citizenship through application for naturalization after a period of residency in the United States. The United States government reduced the period of residency for war brides from five to three years. The Air Ministry's summary of rights did not mention the status of the woman's British citizenship upon marriage to an American. The British government eventually allowed dual citizenship, as long as women did not formally renounce their British citizenship. For the war brides this meant potential future access to health and pension services in Britain.[21] The ministry also provided considerable additional information on the nature of interracial marriages between British women and black American soldiers. The British government reiterated a point that the American military had frequently noted, namely 'that a marriage which is against the law of any state of domicile of either party … will be invalid everywhere'. The ministry went on to explain that interracial marriages fall within this category in parts of the United States, where 'such marriages are … regarded as odious'.[22]

A further complication pertained to the status of children born between British women and men of the Allied forces. The concern here was whether children born in Britain of British women and Allied servicemen were automatic citizens of their father's country. For each of the Allied nations on the ministry's list, children in these international marriages acquired citizenship from both the parents' countries, until adulthood.

The British government's disquiet over the legal ramifications of these marriages was understandable. If, for some reason, problems developed in areas of citizenship and validity of marriage, British women needed to understand their rights. For example, Australian women who married Americans automatically lost their citizenship upon marriage but did not receive American citizenship. Consequently, Australian war brides were stateless. The issue of citizenship became even more important as the war ended and women began the process of being reunited with their husbands.

The British government's concern about the rights of its female subjects was understandable also in the face of the attitude of American officials. The American military had made it very clear that it was not happy about the romantic liaisons that its servicemen developed in Britain during the war. The British government was equally dubious about these marriages. Whereas the American government feared the marriages were a distraction to the war effort and an attempt by British gold-diggers to get either American money or entry to the United States, the British government worried that American servicemen were deceiving part of its citizenry and taking advantage of women during unstable wartime conditions. Regardless of all these objections by United States and British authorities, wartime marriages occurred regularly.

The two United States armed forces' publications, *Yank* and *Stars and Stripes*, carried articles and letters about overseas marriages and military regulations throughout the war. In a July 1942 article in *Yank* the headline, 'Don't Promise Her Anything – Marriage Outside the U.S. Is Out', overstated the situation. The article, however, noted that marriage to a foreign woman was possible, but required a commanding officer's permission. The article also warned that 'Washington sources are inclined to doubt that commanding officers of expeditionary forces will approve marital ventures except in rare cases.' The Washington, DC authorities counseled against marriages due to the potential conflict between agencies on issues such as immigration and the 'sudden and frequent movement of troops'.[23]

Yank and *Stars and Stripes* also served as forums for GI questions about overseas marriages and subsequent problems. Several GIs wrote to ask if their wives would have to wait to gain entry to the United States as part of the immigration quota for Britain. The advice column let them know that foreign-born wives of American servicemen could

enter the United States as non-quota immigrants. Other GIs asked
how to get a furlough from Europe to go back to England to marry,
inquired whether a marriage conducted without a commanding officer's
permission was valid, and sought to learn what the citizenship status of
war brides would be. These publications also reported stories about
the first marriages in some theaters of operation, problems of GIs rotated
home who were unable to get their fiancées into the United States to
get married, and the status of dependency allotments after marriage.
The volume of stories in the pages of *Yank* and *Stars and Stripes* illus-
trates the frequency of these wartime weddings. One reporter noted
that, of the original hundred single members of a United States unit in
Northern Ireland, fifty were engaged or already married to Irish and
English women within a year of the unit's arrival.[24]

On the one hand the United States military saw these marriages
as 'a passing fad with post-war complications' and tried to discourage
them.[25] On the other side British authorities wanted the American
military to 'exercise increased caution' when granting permission for
soldiers to wed.[26] The men and women involved were caught in the
middle. One former GI, Ted Hammers, remembered hearing about 'a
lot of fellows. They wouldn't O.K. them to get married. Lots of them.
They figured it was just a fling and they would be sorry.'[27] Rosa Ebsary
recalled that families also tried to discourage marriages. Speaking of
her own case, she said that her brothers 'went and told everybody
about it. I remember one of my sister's former boyfriends saying "Et
tu, Brute?" I really must say that everybody liked Edwin but they
weren't really crazy about the idea.'[28] June Porter, a younger war bride,
recalled the resistance of her family when she:

> had a letter that asked me to marry him, he wanted to get engaged
> … My mother said 'No way.' I was then seventeen going on
> eighteen … and she had married when she was 17. Of course I was
> obviously throwing it up at her. I said, 'Well, you got married.' I
> begged for a week. My mother and father said, 'No way. You can't
> go all that way, you're too young.' At the end of the week I had
> broken them down. One week.[29]

Perhaps the worst part of this resistance was the sense of isolation it
created. It took fortitude for many brides and husbands to overcome
all the objections. The sense of frustration prompted Sybil Afdem to
reflect that:

> You had some horrendous tales from everybody. I honestly can't
> think of one person that I knew that said 'Good for you, go and get
> it.' Not one. They all knew tales of people who got over there and

they were left there with nothing or they had got over there and there was nobody to meet them and nowhere to go. They never told you of anybody who went over there and was happy ... We didn't have that much family really but everybody, all our family, all our friends, they did everything to dissuade me from coming.[30]

While British and American authorities and civilians on both sides of the Atlantic voiced anxiety over the motivations behind marriages, the GIs and British women had a wholly different opinion. Their marriages were not the result of grand designs, or dictated by any ulterior motives. Many women resented being questioned about their motives. Rosa Ebsary pointed out that she was 'twenty-one and Ed was twenty-four. This was not an overnight deal ... I hadn't gone haring and scaring around the country. Ed and I wrote every day to each other, I still have a trunk full of letters.'[31] For many women the decision to marry an American was the same as the decision to marry anyone, it was based on strong emotion. Sybil Afdem confessed that her husband was 'all I could see. He was my life, my whole life, always, even to the day he died.'[32]

Servicemen also resented the obstacles to, and innuendos about, wartime marriages. One GI in Northern Ireland, responding to comments made by a Washington, DC official against overseas marriages in the pages of *Yank*, pointed out that military regulations governing marriages were so complex and lengthy that these marriages were not hasty or ill-conceived. The GI noted that American servicemen did not need somebody suggesting that the United States government should make marriage even more difficult to conclude. There was already, in his opinion, enough red tape in place. He asked the official if 'it ever occur[red] to you, sir, that we who have married over here could be in love with our wives just as much as we would be if they were American? Or that for many of us, "the girl who married dear old dad" may have been a "foreigner" too?'[33]

To the British war brides and American GIs the issue of overseas marriage had little to do with military regulations or social issues; it was simply a case of meeting someone, falling in love and getting married. While the war and the authorities did have an impact on these relationships, it was, more importantly, a case of young couples who came together at marriageable age, when they would have been meeting people of the opposite sex, courting and getting married had they stayed at home and had there been no war. Undoubtedly the war did temporarily free up the morals of British society, but the data used to support this thesis – i.e., a rise in venereal disease and illegitimacy rates – do not translate to the issue of marriage.

The ages of the men and women when they met and married help us to understand the phenomenon of war brides. The American GIs in the 1989 survey were, on average, twenty-five when they got married; the British war brides were twenty-one. They were a uniformly young segment of society. Having met and married in large numbers in Britain during the war, once it was over the women faced the consequences of their marriages to a foreigner. The majority of British women had grown up expecting to get married and raise children, but they had not expected to marry anyone other than a fellow countryman. Many of these women had children after marriage, but before they lived with their husbands as man and wife. Their courtships had been unusual due to the war, and the war and their different nationalities also made their marriage situations unique. Once married, the couples did not quietly 'settle down'. War brides' marriages to Americans meant emigration, a prospect that few British women had entertained before meeting their GI husbands.

Notes

Editors' note: this paper, presented at the Middelburg Conference, has also been published by Jenel Virden as chapter 3 in her book: *Goodbye, Piccadilly: British War Brides in America* © 1996 by the Board of Trustees of the University of Illinois. We acknowledge the permission of the author and of the University of Illinois Press.

1. Interview with Rosa Ebsary, 29 April 1991, Seattle, Washington.
2. Lt. Col. Albert B. Kellogg, *Marriages of Soldiers* [of World War I], Army War College, Historical Section, July 1942, Box 262, Chief of Chaplains, Record Group 247, File 291.1, Marriages, National Archives, Washington, DC, p. 1.
3. Ibid., pp. 4–5.
4. George Kent, 'Brides from Overseas', *Reader's Digest* 97 (September 1945) suggests eight thousand overseas marriages in World War I.
5. War Department Circular 14, 1 February 1940, Box 197, Chief of Chaplains, Record Group 247, File 291.1, Volume I, October 1920–January 1942 Marriages, National Archives, Washington, DC.
6. Director of Intelligence of the Army Service Forces to Office of the Chief of Chaplains, 'Reports on Conditions Overseas to Chief of Chaplains', 3 March 1944, Box 195, Chief of Chaplains, Record Group 247, File 250.1, Morals and Conduct (Misc.), Volume II, January 1944–December 1945, National Archives, Washington, DC.·
7. C.E. Brand to Chaplain O'Connor, 29 May 1942, Box 197, Chief of Chaplains, Record Group 247, File 291.1, Marriages, Volume II, 24 February 1942–31 August 1942, National Archives, Washington, DC. The residency requirement before citizenship application was shorter for wives of American citizens than for regular immigrants; most immigrants had to wait five years before applying for citizenship.

8. Jenel Virden, 'British War Brides of World War II: A Passing Fad with Post-War Complications' (Master's thesis, Washington State University, 1983), pp. 17–20.
9. Letter to William Arnold, 24 May 1942, Box 197, Chief of Chaplains, Record Group 247, File 291.1, Marriages, Volume II, 24 February 1942–31 August 1943, National Archives, Washington, DC.
10. Ibid.
11. Letter, 28 May 1942, ibid.
12. Joseph O. Ensrud to Director, Public Relations, War Department, 7 January 1943, 'Request for Clearance', ibid. Presumably this related to marriages in the United States, since he signed his letter from Fort Monmouth, New Jersey.
13. Chaplain Karl L. Darkey to Chaplain George Rixey, 1 September 1943, Box 198, Chief of Chaplains, Record Group 247, File 291.1, Marriages, Volume III, 1 September 1943–31 May 1944, National Archives, Washington, DC, p. 1.
14. Frederick W. Hagan to Chaplain Darkey, 14 September 1943, ibid., p. 2.
15. William R. Arnold to Director of Military Personnel Division ASF, 17 February 1945, 'Marriages of Enlisted Personnel', Box 198, ibid., pp. 1–2.
16. Charles K. Gamble to Richard F. Allen, 12 November 1943, Box 985, American Red Cross, Record Group 200, File 618.4, War Brides Australia, National Archives, Washington, DC, p. 2.
17. Nyles I. Christensen to Colonel H.H. Baird, 29 February 1944, ibid., pp. 2–3.
18. Interview with Joan Posthuma, 9 May 1991, Seattle, Washington.
19. Interview with Ivy Hammers, 16 May 1991, Sequim, Washington.
20. J.E. Hengham Park to Foreign Office, 5 September 1944, Foreign Office, 371/42310, Public Record Office, Kew, United Kingdom.
21. Some women in the survey were unaware of these aspects of dual citizenship, while others were well informed. The retention of British citizenship may perhaps have added to the transition to American life by providing the war brides with some comfort knowing they retained certain rights as British subjects.
22. Hengham Park to Foreign Office, p. 1.
23. *Yank*, 1 July 1942, p. 2.
24. *Stars and Stripes*, 25 January 1945, p. iv. Other articles noted in text are contained in *Stars and Stripes*, 3 October 1942, p. 4; *Yank*, 7 January 1944, p. 9; ibid., 2 February 1945, p. 16; ibid., 23 February 1945, p. 18; ibid., 2 March 1945, p. 16; ibid., 15 June 1945, p. 14; ibid., 10 August 1945, p. 14; ibid., 21 April 1944, p. 16; ibid., 10 August 1945, p. 14.
25. R.P. Hartle to Lt. Gen. Andrews, 'Reference to letter from Andrews on 13 Apr', 20 April 1943, Adjutant General Files, Record Group 332, ETO G-1 Section, National Archives, Washington, DC.
26. Pfc William F. Sprague, *The Problems of Marriages in the European Theater of Operation*, April 1944, Admin File 518, Adjutant General's Files, Record Group 332, National Archives, Washington, DC, p. 12.
27. Interview with Ted Hammers, 16 May 1991, Sequim, Washington.

28.   Interview with Rosa Ebsary, 29 April 1991, Seattle, Washington.
29.   Interview with June Porter, 22 April 1991, Edmonds, Washington.
30.   Interview with Sybil Afdem, 21 December 1981, Everett, Washington.
31.   Interview with Rosa Ebsary, 29 April 1991, Seattle, Washington.
32.   Interview with Sybil Afdem, 21 December 1981, Everett, Washington.
33.   *Yank*, 21 September 1945, p. 18.

11

Guns, Butter, and Civil Rights:
The National Association for the Advancement of
Colored People and the Vietnam War, 1964–1968

Manfred Berg

In the mid-1960s, the National Association for the Advancement of
Colored People (NAACP) had reason to believe that it was close to
achieving its goals. Since its founding in 1911, America's oldest and
largest civil rights organization had fought racial discrimination in the
courts, through legislative lobbying, and by mobilizing black voters.
Although it targeted all levels of government, this struggle was based
on a firm belief that the stranglehold of segregation, disfranchisement,
and violence could only be broken by vigorous action of the federal
government.[1] Finally, after decades of tokenism and compromise with
racism, a president had come to the White House whose promises
were followed by deeds. With the Civil Rights Act of 1964 and the
Voting Rights Act of 1965, the administration of Lyndon B. Johnson
proposed, secured, and enacted the first effective civil rights legislation
since the end of Reconstruction. Moreover, under the label of the
Great Society, the President initiated the most sweeping social reforms
since the New Deal, which particularly benefitted blacks and other
disadvantaged minorities. However, while declaring his War on Poverty,
LBJ also began escalating American involvement in a much less figura-
tive war in Vietnam, which would eventually divert resources from
his domestic agenda, polarize the American people, and destroy his
presidency.[2]

The civil rights movement reacted to the Vietnam War in very
different ways. The radical wing, centered around the Student Nonviolent Coordinating Committee (SNCC), quickly positioned itself in
fundamental opposition to the war and became increasingly militant in
its protests. The leader of the Southern Christian Leadership Conference (SCLC), Martin Luther King, jun., also registered his concerns
early on, but for some time maintained hopes that the Johnson administration might come to a peaceful solution before he began campaigning
against the war. The leadership of the NAACP, in contrast, chose loyalty
to country and President, arguing that Vietnam and the struggle for
civil rights were entirely separate issues and that the War on Poverty
need not be impaired because, in its view, America could afford both
'guns and butter'. Thus, the Vietnam War became one important

element in the split of the civil rights movement during the second half of the 1960s. Surprisingly, this topic has rarely been addressed. The standard accounts of both the civil rights and the anti-war movements only mention it in passing, with the main focus remaining on the opponents of the war.[3] This article attempts to shed some light on the other side of the story by analyzing the policy and discourse of the NAACP beyond the obvious charge of opportunism. It will argue that the NAACP's reaction to the Vietnam War was shaped by concepts of loyalty and patriotism that had been part and parcel of the civil rights struggle for decades. The conviction that a moderate, integrationist civil rights organization could not afford to oppose a war waged in the name of democracy involved a good deal of moral and intellectual hypocrisy, but politically the decision to steer clear of the Vietnam issue worked much better than critics have been willing to acknowledge.

Lyndon B. Johnson and the NAACP made for an unlikely romance. Although a New Deal Democrat and certainly not a race-baiter, the Texan usually stayed within the limits of racial liberalism imposed by his fellow southerners in Congress. His voting record on civil rights, which the NAACP circulated during his presidential bid in the 1960 primaries, compared rather unfavorably to those of both John F. Kennedy and Richard M. Nixon. When LBJ joined the Democratic ticket and was elected Vice-President, civil rights advocates viewed this as a strengthening of southern influence. But as head of the Equal Employment Committee, Johnson came out as a spokesman for blacks, and when he succeeded the slain President Kennedy, he immediately declared civil rights a top priority. A week after he was sworn into office, Johnson called NAACP Executive Director Roy Wilkins to the White House, assuring him of his sincerity and asking him in return for his cooperation. Subsequently, Wilkins became a close political ally and a friend of the President, and the two men continued to hold each other in high esteem until Johnson's death in 1973. Other NAACP leaders were equally impressed by LBJ, who made a point of being available not only for Wilkins or Washington Bureau Chief Clarence Mitchell, but also for regional activists like Charles Evers and Aaron Henry of Mississippi.[4]

The passing of the Civil Rights Act in July 1964 underscored both Johnson's prowess as a political operator and his genuine commitment to civil rights. The NAACP not only heeded the President's call for a halt to demonstrations, but, to all intents and purposes, it also abandoned its long-standing policy of non-partisanship to ensure the defeat of the Republican nominee, Arizona Senator Barry Goldwater, who had voted against the Civil Rights Act and ran as a states' rights champion. In a nationwide, all-out voter registration drive, the NAACP helped bring about a record registration and turnout of black voters.

While Johnson received 61 per cent of the total popular vote, his share in predominantly black districts exceeded 90 per cent. A triumphant Roy Wilkins congratulated him: 'The People have not spoken; they have shouted.'[5]

The bonds of mutual loyalty would endure through Johnson's presidency and largely determine the NAACP position toward Vietnam. But there was more to the story than 'pay[ing] the price of silence'.[6] For over fifty years, the NAACP had maintained that African Americans were entitled to the privileges of US citizenship because, like all other Americans, they were willing to assume its duties and fight for their country. The citizen-soldier ideal, deeply embedded in the American democratic creed, had been a readily available source of discourse to legitimize the claim for black civil rights since the times of the Civil War.[7] Although the rewards were questionable at best, the middle-class, college-educated black leadership of the NAACP took patriotism and wartime loyalty for granted and marveled at black heroism. Vietnam, however, was different from previous wars the United States had engaged in. There was no declaration of war and no dramatic event – the Gulf of Tonkin incident notwithstanding – that would spark a patriotic fire within the general population. Like most Americans, the leaders of the NAACP initially looked at Vietnam not as a war, but as a foreign policy issue with no direct links to their primary concerns.

Interestingly enough, the first challenge came from within the organization. In April 1965, the executive board of the NAACP branch of Flint, Michigan, passed a resolution which urged negotiations to end 'the civil war in Viet Nam' and an 'immediate withdrawal of American forces'. The resolution, which also denounced the 'arrogated role of international policemen' taken on by the United States, triggered a prompt censure from the national office demanding its repudiation on the grounds that it did not reflect any official policy of the NAACP, which could only be determined by the national convention. This disapproval was not merely procedural. In a staff memorandum, Gloster Current, the national director of branches, called the Flint resolution an attempt of 'the left-wing ... to create problems over our country's Viet Nam policy', and, referring to the 1950 annual convention resolution against communist infiltration, he declared: 'We do not want our branches getting involved in left-wing shenanigans.'[8] When peace activists called for an 'Assembly of Unrepresented People' in Washington on 6–9 August 1965, the twentieth anniversary of the dropping of the atomic bomb, to protest racial discrimination and the war in Vietnam, Roy Wilkins forbad any official NAACP participation because, in his view, the civil rights theme was merely a pretext. This was not quite true, but the event was indeed dominated by the New Left, and the demonstrations, although a far cry from what was yet to come, turned out to be much too unruly for a respectable civil rights organization.[9]

These reactions were typical for a NAACP leadership whose anti-communist stance had become a standard since the 1930s, when the Communist Party had challenged the Association's claim for the political representation of African Americans. Old animosities and a genuine belief in the promise of American democracy were reinforced by the vicious red-baiting of white supremacists against the NAACP, which tried to avoid the taint of communist affiliations at all costs.[10] Unfortunately, though, the linkage between civil rights and the Vietnam issues was not an invention of Old or New Left infiltrators, but instead came directly from the center of the civil rights movement. In July 1965, no lesser figure than Martin Luther King declared that communism could not be defeated by bombs and that the war had to be stopped by negotiating with the Vietcong. Since the statement received nationwide media attention, Roy Wilkins felt compelled to respond. In his weekly syndicated newspaper column, he acknowledged King's 'personal devotion to peace and non-violence', but called the proposal to merge the civil rights and peace movements – which King denied having made – 'a tactical error' and 'a costly dissipation of energies and resources'. For the millions of African Americans struggling for equality and opportunity, Selma, Alabama, was closer than Saigon.[11]

Wilkins failed to see, however, that Vietnam was hitting home quickly. Young African-American men, like the GI from Georgia whose wife was arrested when trying to register to vote, would soon have to ask themselves why they should fight in Indochina. In McComb, Mississippi, members of the Mississippi Freedom Democratic Party (MFDP), an organization created by SNCC to challenge the state's racist regular Democrats, gave the most radical answer at that time, when a former civil rights activist was killed in Vietnam. Their July 1965 statement urged blacks to resist the draft or stage hunger strikes to be discharged, so they would not be looked upon as traitors 'by all the colored people of the world'. MFDP spokespersons hastened to state that the widely publicized and criticized declaration did not represent official policy, but added: 'It is easy to understand why Negro citizens of McComb, themselves the victims of bombings, Klan-inspired terrorism, and harassment arrests, should resent the death of a citizen of McComb while fighting in Viet Nam for "freedom" not enjoyed by the Negro community of McComb.'[12]

With the congressional struggle for the Voting Rights Act in its final stage, the call for draft resistance appeared 'child-like and mischievous in the extreme' to NAACP leader Wilkins. In addition to Gloster Current's exacting a fervently patriotic declaration from the Mississippi NAACP, he lashed out in his weekly column at the MFDP for 'tinker[ing] with patriotism at a time when their country is engaged in an armed conflict', and lectured on black heroes from the War of Independence to Pearl Harbor who had done infinitely more for their race than the 'young squirts' down in Mississippi. Although Wilkins was inevitably correct that the MFDP statement would be exploited by the foes of civil rights, alienate white liberal supporters, and hurt its challenge of the state's segregationist congressional delegation, his patronizing history lesson on what one critic has labeled the 'prove yourselves worthy' approach would ring increasingly hollow.[13] In essence, he was demanding that young black men fight and die in Vietnam, so that civil rights leaders could put their 'loyalty, heroic service and sacrifice ... on the bargaining table' to negotiate rights guaranteed by the US Constitution. The message from McComb to fight for freedom in Mississippi thus put on its head Wilkins's argument that the civil rights movement had no concern with the Vietnam War because Selma was closer than Saigon.

Although the debate on the movement's position toward the Vietnam War had begun during the summer of 1965, no civil rights group had, so far, formally declared its opposition. The resolutions of the NAACP annual convention did not address the issue, and the SCLC board took a position that was in fact closer to Roy Wilkins than to Martin Luther King. Even the SNCC, while stating its opposition to 'organized war wherever it occurs', reaffirmed that its 'major commitment' was 'interracial democracy in the South' and that it had no plans for becoming involved in anti-war protests as an organization.[14] But, with the number of US troops in Vietnam increasing tenfold during 1965, to a staggering 200,000, the issue became ever more pressing. To many of the young civil rights activists, especially those affected by the draft, it was not a matter of pragmatic priorities, as Wilkins chose to see it, but a deep moral and personal concern.

In January 1966, the SNCC crossed the line to open protest after one of its registration workers was murdered in Tuskegee, Alabama, for trying to use a 'whites only' restroom. In an angry statement, it accused the US government of hypocrisy and deceit in its professed concern for the freedom of both the Vietnamese people and African Americans, equating the violence in Alabama to that in Vietnam: 'Sammy Younge was murdered because United States law is not being enforced. Vietnamese are being murdered because the United States is pursuing an aggressive policy in violation of international law.' The SNCC declared its support for draft resisters unwilling 'to contribute their lives to United States aggression'.[15] Opposition to the draft and to the war in Vietnam had become an integral part of the SNCC's radicalizing racial perspective, which led to the coining of the 'black power' slogan by its leader Stokely Carmichael in June 1966 and to the

subsequent exclusion of white members – a course that the NAACP
condemned as 'black racism'. Radical critics did not stop urging blacks
not to fight 'yellow people' for the benefit of white racism; they also
saw Vietnam as an all-out attempt to destroy the civil rights movement
and, ultimately, as leading to racial genocide against African Americans. Draft resistance, a SNCC position paper of August 1966 stated,
was a 'necessity', because 'the best way to break up the organization
would be to draft all the young men who are of draft age and send them
to Vietnam and have them shot', setting the stage 'for our destruction
as a race in this country'.[16]

Not surprisingly, NAACP leaders considered not the draft, but the
call for draft resistance the greater danger to the civil rights movement. The NAACP had immediately distanced itself from the January
1966 SNCC paper, and Roy Wilkins lamented that the public identified 'any action by any group … as action by "the civil rights
movement"'. In a private meeting with Vice-President Humphrey,
Wilkins, Mitchell, and National Urban League (NUL) leader, Whitney
Young, protested that the administration seemed to 'treat all of the
civil rights leaders alike when the SNCC outfit engages in the most
outrageous attacks on the President and the Administration'.[17] The
complaint referred to a presidential pet project, the White House
Conference on Civil Rights, which was scheduled for the coming
spring and designed to reaffirm support for Johnson's Great Society.
The list of the more than 2,000 participants, although heavily dominated by moderates, included the SNCC and a few other militant
groups. The preparations for the conference provided a splendid opportunity for NAACP leaders to demonstrate their loyalty and usefulness
to the administration. In late March, a strategy meeting of representatives of all major civil rights organizations, except the SNCC, widely
reflected the NAACP's position on Vietnam. Although it was conceded
that civil rights leaders, as citizens and individuals, had 'a perfect right
to express their concern', the discussion only highlighted the potentially adverse effects of such statements, such as loss of revenue and
support, the dilution of energies, and the confusion of friends, 'including
the Administration', as the minutes of the meeting tellingly added in
brackets. Urging restraint on dissenters, the following consensus was
reached:

> It was felt that there can be only one position of unity on Vietnam –
> and that is not on the issues of the war itself, but on those issues only
> as they effect the Great Society program. Concern should be rather
> for matters such as minimum wage, guaranteed income, massive re-
> training programs, etc., in order that Negro boys returning from
> Vietnam will return to better working conditions here at home.[18]

The strategy to limit dissent from the administration's war policy to 'express[ing] concern for any attempt to divert needed domestic funds to the Vietnam effort' was effectively carried out during the White House Conference on Civil Rights in June 1966. With the SNCC's refusal to participate – among other reasons, because it could not 'in good conscience meet with the chief policy maker of the Vietnam war to discuss human rights in this country when he flagrantly violates the human rights of colored people in Vietnam' – it was the delegates of the Congress of Racial Equality (CORE) who tried to raise the issue.[19] Similar to the SCLC, CORE leaders had individually spoken out against the war for some time, but the organization had adopted no formal position. In fact, the resolution that it tried to pass through several conference committees strictly took the approach agreed upon in March by limiting criticism to the squandering of resources and the need for domestic reforms. Since America had not yet 'demonstrated its ability and willingness to afford both "guns and butter"', the resolution demanded that it made 'equal opportunity for its minority citizens the number one priority ... and cease its involvement in Vietnam'. The latter was, of course, completely unacceptable at a conference sponsored by the White House to build consensus. It was safely voted down or tabled in all committees and replaced by a formula that urged the President 'to continue and intensify his efforts to bring the war in Vietnam to an early and honorable end so that the same and even a much greater level of Federal funds and Federal leadership can be focused to fulfill these rights today'.[20]

The NAACP's stand on Vietnam was certainly welcomed by the administration, but it did not go without criticism from members and supporters. Although few in number, the protests following the repudiation of the SNCC's anti-war declaration of January 1966 are remarkable for their bluntness and their exposure of the inconsistencies and blind spots of the NAACP's official policy. A member from Kentucky, for instance, resigned the membership of his entire family because the NAACP had become 'the leading Uncle Tom of the civil rights movement' and Wilkins himself 'an Administration houseboy'. He found it intolerable that the NAACP leader condemned the riots in American inner cities, but remained silent about US violence in Vietnam, where black GIs, whose real enemies were at home, were killed at a much higher proportion than white soldiers.[21] Wilkins countered such attacks with the standard line that the civil rights struggle, on which 'people of good will' could not disagree, had to be evaluated separately from the issues involved in the Vietnam conflict, 'concerning which men of genuine good will can and do disagree'. One critic sardonically enquired how there could possibly be disagreement over the brutality of the warfare against civilians, or over the destructive impact of the war on the hopes of impoverished African Americans for a better life in the United States: 'Is it so difficult for the NAACP to take a position on Vietnam?', he asked. 'It is not required that a timetable or blueprint be provided for our government to follow. However, all men of good will can and should agree that we have a right and duty to insist that our government stop committing the evils mentioned above and start doing good.'[22] This was hardly a radical demand, nor could it be denied that civic involvement to correct mis-guided governmental policies represented the very tradition on which the NAACP was built. Still, Wilkins insisted that the NAACP as a civil rights organization had no right to commit its members to a stand on the war, just as these members did not expect the organization to speak out on wildlife conservation – a rather unfortunate analogy to the carnage in Vietnam. In a virtual twist of logic, he added that the plight of the Vietnamese was 'a reason of substance for action by a civil rights organization in opposition to the war'.[23] Was the suffering inflicted by the war only relevant to those who had already joined the ranks of the anti-war forces?

If Wilkins's 'separate issues' doctrine, as it will be called here, was an indication of his own naivety, his argument that the NAACP leader-ship had no mandate on Vietnam was less than honest. At the same time that he rebuked the SNCC declaration, he sent a telegram to Johnson, congratulating him on his January 1966 State of the Union address in which the President had boasted that America was strong enough 'to pursue our goals in the rest of the world while still building a Great Society at home'. Clearly speaking as the NAACP executive director, Wilkins wired: 'Your call for carrying on domestic crusade for the Great Society projects including all aspects of anti-poverty pro-gram along with fulfilling our nation's commitment in Vietnam is the right call and is a challenge to every American.'[24] This was not only a supportive statement on the President's Vietnam policy, it also made the connection between domestic and foreign politics by implying that the NAACP's stand on Vietnam might be predicated on the adminis-tration's continued commitment to civil rights and social reform. Whereas this looked like the familiar loyalty game, it accepted at least one realm of legitimate criticism, namely the 'guns and butter' rationale, which increasingly gained credibility while the American war effort unfolded. In his congressional message, Johnson himself had conceded that '[b]ecause of Vietnam we cannot do all that we should ...', and had announced that the Vietnam expenditures for the coming fiscal year would increase by $5.8 billion, whereas the increase in all other budget items would total only $0.6 billion combined.[25]

This did not mean, however, that the NAACP would shift its posi-tion, nor did the intensifying disputes over the war prompt its leaders to speak out in public. Quite to the contrary, the dogged congressional battle for a new civil rights bill to ban racial discrimination in housing provided every incentive to maintain cooperation with the administration and to steer clear of an issue as divisive as Vietnam, especially at a time when black urban unrest fueled a backlash against the civil rights movement. Unlike all previous twentieth-century wars with US involvement, when the NAACP had vigorously monitored and protested racial discrimination in the armed forces, there was no systematic investigation of conditions in Vietnam. An African-American sergeant who had inquired about this issue was told that the NAACP had received no complaints from black soldiers and that '[w]hatever discomforts they have to endure and whatever sacrifices they are called on to make appear to be the same as those which confront all American servicemen in the area'.[26] The patriotic image of blacks and whites fighting side by side nicely espoused the NAACP's success in ending racial segregation in the military, but it eclipsed the sordid fact that African Americans were paying a high price for integration. Facing almost exclusively white selective service boards, they were twice as likely to be drafted than their white peers, disproportionately assigned to combat units, and suffered a casualty rate vastly in excess of their overall proportion in the US troops in Vietnam. The high death toll and the inequities of the draft had become a major concern far beyond radical circles. But, in the spring of 1966, when the NAACP New Jersey state conference asked the national office to determine an official position 'in light of ... the high mortality rate of our Negro fighting men', Wilkins shunned the issue by repeating that theirs was not a peace organization and that in matters such as these members were free to express themselves through other groups.[27]

The ostrich posture seemed to work. Except for the few critical voices mentioned above, there is no evidence of widespread discontent among the NAACP membership, let alone of organized opposition, to the leadership's Vietnam policy between the summer of 1966 and the spring of 1967. Although Gloster Current, always wary of communist subversion, feared that the 'left wing' would make Vietnam 'the biggest problem' of the forthcoming 1966 convention, only a single branch submitted a pertinent resolution. The Greenwich Village, New York, branch – a hotbed of radicalism, according to Current – mildly criticized the undermining of the Great Society and the disproportionate draft of blacks, but asked for nothing more than 'that this convention acknowledge the fact of detrimental effects that the defense and military activities have upon the Civil Rights Movement. And furthermore that the local branches be encouraged to consider and debate these issues'. This resolution was, nevertheless, safely rejected.[28]

Without serious pressure from its members, the NAACP leaders could simply remain silent unless directly challenged from within the civil rights movement. Ironically, the radicalization of the SNCC and, somewhat less, of CORE made their task easier. While, in early 1966, the SNCC had still defended its opposition to the war in moderate civil rights discourse, in August Stokely Carmichael defied the mainstream leaders by announcing the SNCC's participation in an anti-war protest during the wedding of LBJ's daughter Luci. An appeal to good taste and political shrewdness by Wilkins, King, Whitney Young, and labor leader A. Philip Randolph was rebuffed in language replete with contempt and moral righteousness, accusing them of being more concerned about the happiness of Luci Johnson than about the plight of black and Vietnamese people, and dismissing them as the President's dupes.[29] Such provocative symbolism might have boosted the 'egos of the demonstrators', as the appeal alleged, but it is doubtful whether it accomplished much for the cause of peace.

Although the SNCC remained vocal in its criticism, it could hardly claim to be the representative voice of the African-American community at large. In addition, its conceptualization of the war as waged by whites against blacks and Asians did not help build an integrated anti-war movement.[30] Martin Luther King, in contrast, was quite a different challenge to the politics of acquiescence pursued by the NAACP, the NUL, and other established black groups. By the mid-1960s, the SCLC leader had become America's best-known and most respected civil rights spokesman, whose 1964 Nobel Peace Prize and impeccable commitment to non-violence lent moral authority to his opposition to the Vietnam War. Relations between King and the NAACP had been characterized by cooperation and rivalry over the years, not least motivated by a considerable personal jealousy on Roy Wilkins's part.[31] Although the NAACP leader, born in 1901, was almost thirty years King's senior, he could hardly patronize him in the same way as he could the 'SNCC kids'.

King's word carried weight. When the SCLC board, on King's initiative, adopted an anti-war resolution in April 1966, NAACP leaders were seriously worried that this might increase pressure on the Association.[32] But while speaking about the brutalities, the waste, and the questionable morality of the war, King had avoided breaking openly with the Johnson administration, nor did he advocate the merging of the civil rights and anti-war movements. In early 1967, however, his moral concerns had become so compelling that he committed himself to full-scale opposition, entirely aware that this would destroy his influence with the White House and hurt the SCLC financially. On 4 April, Martin Luther King delivered a sermon before an audience of about 3,000 clergy and laypersons at New York City's Riverside Church which was widely publicized and immediately became the subject of national controversy. The speech was not only his first direct attack on both the Johnson administration and the old guard civil rights leaders, but, perhaps, was also one of the most forceful political and moral indictments ever made of US Vietnam policy.[33] Silence, King contended, was betrayal, and those who criticized him for mixing peace and civil rights did not know the nature of his calling nor did they know 'the world in which they live'. Insisting that he did not wish to make Hanoi or the National Liberation Front (NLF) 'paragons of virtue', he relentlessly exposed the broken promises of the Great Society, the atrocities against Vietnamese civilians, the corruption of the American-backed Saigon regime, and the paranoid fear of communism that led America to deny the legitimate claim to self-determination. Vietnam was 'but a symptom of a far deeper malady in the American spirit', and to overcome this malady King called for a 'radical revolution of values' that would do away with poverty, racism, and militarism and lead to a 'world-wide fellowship'. Interwoven with humanistic and religious discourse was a fairly realist appraisal of the origins of the Indochina conflict and the inconsistencies of American involvement. King's political demands included putting an end to all bombing, a unilateral cease-fire, the enactment of safeguards against the spreading of the war to neighboring countries, the acknowledge-ment of the NLF as a negotiating partner, and the setting of a date for the withdrawal of all foreign troops. Such steps certainly abandoned the goal of victory, but they also did not necessarily mean immediate withdrawal and the acceptance of defeat. Any nuances of the speech, however, were lost in the outrage provoked by King's indictment of the US government as 'the greatest purveyor of violence in the world today', and by his equation of the use of napalm and defoliants to the medical crimes committed in Nazi death camps.

Predictably, the reaction among liberal supporters of the Johnson administration was overwhelmingly negative. In the White House, the speech was taken as final proof that King had come under communist influence. The NAACP felt compelled to act in order to avert damage from the civil rights movement. On 10 April 1967 the board of directors met to determine, for the first time, an official NAACP position on the Vietnam War. The resolution, which was introduced by the black UN diplomat and Nobel Peace Prize recipient Ralph Bunche, basically reiterated well-known phrases like the conflation of civil rights and peace being 'a serious tactical mistake', and vowed that the NAACP would 'st[i]ck to the job for which it was organized'.[34] The executive secretary was less restrained. In his weekly column, Wilkins insisted that King could only speak for himself and that the over-whelming majority of black Americans, although wary of the war's detrimental effects, wanted continued priority given to the civil rights and anti-poverty struggles. In a thinly veiled exercise in red-baiting, Wilkins reminded his readers of communist attempts during World War II to subordinate the civil rights struggle to their party goals. Nevertheless, African Americans had been loyal to their country and received the abolition of segregation in the military as their 'prize dividends'.[35] He did not say, though, which 'prize' they could expect this time around.

After more than two years of large-scale US involvement in Vietnam, the NAACP had finally been forced to take an official position. Although its language was evasive and did not even mention Martin Luther King by name, the resolution of the national board of directors was clearly meant to repudiate his Riverside speech. The SCLC leader was somewhat surprised by the criticism his sermon had drawn from large quarters of the liberal camp and moderate civil rights groups, but he did not back down and participated in a huge anti-war rally in New York on 15 April alongside CORE's Floyd McKissick, Stokely Carmichael, whose followers were flying Vietcong flags, and many other black and white peace activists. For Gloster Current, the event marked 'a resurgence of the left such as we have not had since World War II', and he warned against massive infiltrations of NAACP branches to get them aboard the peace movement.[36]

Many rank-and-file members of the NAACP, however, worried more about the unity and integrity of the civil rights movement than about organizational and ideological rivalries, and were deeply troubled by the national leadership's open denunciation of Martin Luther King. The protest letters sent by members and supporters ranged from mere dismay over the attacks on King to angry resignations of membership and withdrawal of financial support. What angered critics most was the unwavering insistence on the 'separate issues' doctrine, despite the high casualties among blacks in Vietnam and the mounting racial turmoil at home. Protests outnumbered supportive statements by two to one, but the number of letters found in the files of the NAACP is too small to determine the sentiments of the 440,000-strong membership at large. Perhaps a member of the NAACP branch in Kent, Ohio, was not far off the mark when he described the branch as evenly split between the national board of directors and King. In any case, enough members and branches were disenchanted with the 'hands off' policy on the Vietnam War, as a San Francisco branch called it, to force the issue onto the agenda of the annual convention in Boston in July 1967.[37]

In reaffirming and fully quoting the 10 April declaration, the resolution adopted by the annual convention proved that the leadership was safely in control. It urged the Johnson administration 'to pursue with vigor all avenues which will lead to a just and honorable peace' and complained about 'the disproportionate number of Negroes fighting

... in Vietnam', but made it clear that for the NAACP the key issue was 'guns and butter':

> The NAACP expresses its concern with those who support the proposition that this nation must choose between 'guns and butter'. We feel that many who are opposed to domestic spending for social welfare programs find it too easy to hide their reactionary sentiments behind this slogan ... The NAACP recognizes the vast wealth and resources available in this nation and cannot accept the 'either/or' proposition. We insist that even if 'guns' must regrettably enter into the national picture, our society can and must devote the massive resources needed to meet essential and pressing domestic needs.[38]

In sending the message that the Association would not interfere with Vietnam as long as the administration kept its commitment to the War on Poverty, the resolution aligned the NAACP as closely with Johnson's Vietnam policy as the principle of non-partisanship and its official 'separate issues' doctrine allowed. With painful losses for the Democrats in the 1966 congressional elections, soaring racial unrest, and Martin Luther King in open opposition, the administration was indeed eager to include the NAACP, the Urban League and other 'moderate' black groups into a 'guns and butter' coalition, which could hold the center against both rightist hawks who tried to use Vietnam to curb the Great Society, and the anti-war movement, which undermined the credibility of the American war effort and the liberal consensus at home. In confidential memoranda sent to Wilkins, the director of the Office of Economic Opportunity (OEO) – the principal War on Poverty agency – and his civil rights adviser had bitterly criticized King for splitting the civil rights movement, encouraging North Vietnamese defiance, and playing into the hands of congressional conservatives.[39] Denying that, if it were not for Vietnam, Congress would appropriate more funds for the War on Poverty, the OEO reaffirmed the administration's belief in the strength of the American economy to sustain both 'wars' at one time and advocated a 'green power' coalition – defined as 'economic and dollar power' – that would unite all organizations willing to concentrate on economic opportunity for blacks.

Money, of course, seemed to be of central importance. Proponents of the 'guns and butter' approach could point to impressive growth rates in the GNP and personal income, to declining unemployment and poverty levels, and to multiplying federal expenditures for social and educational programs. In his memoirs, LBJ proudly cited his 'statistics of progress' and professed that he would pursue the same 'guns and butter' policy if he had to do it all over again.[40] Critics, in contrast, charged that all of this fell far short of eradicating poverty, and that Vietnam had vastly surpassed the War on Poverty on the administration's list of priorities. No one could overlook that by 1967 the United States was spending over $2 billion per month on the war in Vietnam, more than the entire annual budget of the OEO.[41] Whether Vietnam actually destroyed the financial foundations of the War on Poverty is, however, difficult to determine and perhaps less important than it may appear. Undoubtedly, the total of direct war costs amounted to $140 billion, but it is by no means certain that these funds would have been spent on social programs. It is equally questionable whether anti-war protest, black or white, could have been silenced by more generous spending on the Great Society. The major domestic problem with the American Vietnam policy was not a lack of funds or resources, but a lack of consensus over its military purpose and its moral and political justification.

Hence, the guns, butter, and civil rights discourse of the NAACP had much less to do with economics than with preserving consensus. It offered a compromise formula to gloss over the blind spots of its Vietnam position, appease internal dissent, and maintain working relations with both the administration and moderate war critics. As an operative policy, however, it was all but useless. Unlike World War II, when civil rights leaders had deliberately tried to use loyalty and sacrifice to press for a 'double victory' of democracy abroad and at home, an elusive and limited war like Vietnam offered little political opportunity to capitalize on the black contribution to the war effort.[42] Openly playing the loyalty game would have required an unqualified pro-war stand, and would have seriously discredited the NAACP's own 'separate issues' doctrine among its membership and the civil rights movement at large. Significantly, NAACP leaders were very hesitant to make the link between civil rights and African Americans fighting in Vietnam. Only after the Open Housing Act had stalled in Congress for over two years would Roy Wilkins remind the Republican leadership: 'Negro servicemen are not fighting in Vietnam for fun and glory ... They have had equality in the jungle, in hospital beds and in coffins. They want it now in housing on any street in their country where they can afford to buy or rent.' Ironically, the act was passed in the wake of the assassination of the most articulate African-American war critic, Martin Luther King.[43]

Wilkins's statement of April 1968 remained the only explicit reference to Vietnam in his weekly press columns throughout that year, the time in which LBJ's war policy and his presidency finally unraveled. Politically, the 'guns and butter' approach had utterly failed. The Vietcong's Tet Offensive of January 1968 had highlighted the fact that even formidable US military power was unable to win a decisive and meaningful victory, and led to a dramatic loss of public confidence in the war effort. The vision of a Great Society perished in the wake of violent racial conflict and political polarization. On 31 March 1968, President Johnson announced that he would not seek re-election, allowing him to be free to concentrate fully on bringing about an honorable peace. In May negotiations began in Paris.[44]

Of course, the war was far from over. The Nixon administration would expand the conflict into Laos and Cambodia and escalate the bombing in North Vietnam; the last American combat troops were withdrawn in 1973. For the NAACP, however, Johnson's retreat rendered both personal loyalties and the guns, butter, and civil rights rationale obsolete. Still, there were few political options to change course at once. Having maintained for three years that the war and civil rights were separate issues, the Association could hardly jump onto the peace bandwagon immediately thereafter. Despite all the turmoil that Vietnam had brought upon America, the issue was not decisive in the 1968 election campaign. The platforms of both Democrats and Republicans gave the impression that the liquidation of US involvement by negotiation and 'Vietnamization' was close at hand.[45] With the elections much more a referendum about 'law and order' than about the war, the NAACP could concentrate on the registration of black voters to fend off the third-party campaign of former Alabama Governor George Wallace, whose racism and chauvinism found considerable support among white, blue-collar workers in the North. Since Richard Nixon catered to the white southern vote and presented himself as a 'law and order' candidate, black voters and the NAACP had nowhere else to turn than to the Humphrey campaign. Perhaps Robert Kennedy might have been able to build a broad anti-war and anti-poverty coalition had his presidential bid not been cut short in June 1968 by an assassin's bullet.[46]

Nixon's election seemed 'bad luck' for the NAACP. Although the new administration did not set out to dismantle the social programs and civil rights achievements of the 1960s, its 'go slow' approach on school integration and the nomination of conservative southerners to the Supreme Court led to various clashes. And despite the fact that Nixon had asked the NAACP executive secretary to serve on his Commission on an All-Volunteer Armed Force, explaining that both the end of the draft and the substantial reduction of expenditures on Vietnam were required by national interest, the expansion of the war in Indochina only reinvigorated protests.[47] With opposition against the war becoming more and more mainstream, the NAACP gradually went on record with anti-war statements. When four students were killed in May 1970 by rampant national guards at Kent State University, Ohio, Roy Wilkins placed the dead on the same level as victims of the black civil rights struggle, applauding the outrage over both the killings and the

escalation of the war. A few months later a joint statement by the
NAACP and the Urban League demanded the immediate termination
of the war. In 1972, Wilkins would even make the claim that 'an end
to U.S. involvement in the Indochina war' had 'long been integral to
NAACP policies and programs'.[48]

This was, of course, a bold assertion. Even after it had been freed
from the shackles of loyalty to Johnson, and faced an administration
that it cordially disliked, the NAACP never came out as a strong anti-
war voice. There was little reason to do so, because the challenges
from within the civil rights movement had virtually ceased: Martin
Luther King was dead; the SNCC and CORE had all but disintegrated; militants like the Black Panther party, which celebrated the
Vietnam War as a revolutionary war of colored people against white
imperialism, did not consider themselves a part of the civil rights
movement and had no mass following. When Panther leader Huey
Newton offered the Vietcong 'an undetermined number' of black volunteers 'to assist you in your fight against American imperialism', an offer
politely turned down, Roy Wilkins only mildly scoffed at how a guy 'as
smart and articulate as Huey Newton' could be so out of touch with
the needs and sentiments of black Americans.[49] In 1973, the NAACP
official even co-chaired a commission that investigated police brutality
against the Black Panthers. The report by Wilkins and Ramsey Clark,
a former attorney-general in the Johnson administration, contained
the following passage:

> There is a common thread that runs through the violence of B-52
> raids in Indochina, police shooting students at Jackson State
> College in Mississippi, and the slaughter of prisoners and guards at
> Attica State Penitentiary in New York ... The Vietnamese, the black
> students, the convicts and their guards are expendable. Until we
> understand that ... [the] faceless victims of Jackson State and on all
> sides in the Indochina war, are human beings equal in every way to
> our children and ourselves, we will see no wrong in using violence
> to control and destroy them.

This was language highly reminiscent and no less 'radical' than that of
the 'young squirts' whom Wilkins had castigated in 1965.[50] The NAACP
leader had certainly come a long way.

For more than half a century, the quintessential goal of the NAACP
had been the full inclusion of African Americans in the mainstream
of American life. It is, therefore, hardly surprising that the attitude of
the Association toward the war in Vietnam did indeed largely reflect
mainstream society. Its traditional concepts of loyalty and patriotism
left it unprepared for the elusive character of the war and its agonizing

moral issues. Like the majority of Americans, the NAACP leaders and its rank and file were unenthusiastic about the war, but they accepted that the United States as a world leader had to honor its military commitments and could not admit defeat. In the end, they also just wanted to get out and forget about the mess.

Invoking a long-term historical perspective, the NAACP leadership was unable to see black opposition to an American war other than as outright stupidity and a disservice to the race. Like W.E.B. Du Bois during World War I, Roy Wilkins was convinced that to 'close ranks' in wartime was the only viable option for African Americans if the cause of civil rights was to be advanced and damage averted.[51] In addition, the racist stereotype that black soldiers were inferior and unreliable lingered on in the minds of leaders whose lives had been dedicated to promoting black self-respect and gaining recognition from the society at large. Their role models were men like the African-American army captain, who combined commitment to civil rights and patriotism by serving in Vietnam and being an active NAACP member in civilian life, and who, when interviewed by the NBC television network in 1967, professed that the enemies of the United States were his enemies and the enemies of the black people.[52] Dissent was only condonable in the form of individual commitment to non-violence that did not challenge the moral position of those who were not paci-fists. From Wilkins's perspective, the conflict between the NAACP and Martin Luther King was one of ethical purism versus experienced pragmatism, with the former ignoring the 'realities' of America's 'position as the leader of the Western world'.[53]

To dismiss war critics as youthful idealists ignorant of world politics and history was convenient, but hardly warranted. There were black authors who came up with quite realistic analyses of US involvement in Indochina, and careful pondering of black self-interest and the options for the civil rights movement. Students, such as those in the SCLC's Atlanta-based Peace Education Project, were eager to explore both the origins of the Indochina conflict and historical analogies, such as the interwar appeasement policy. Some radicals were even too pessimistic in their 'realist' appraisal of US military power, like the SNCC worker and author Julius Lester, who wrote in 1968 that, after three years of bombing, North Vietnam was desperate for peace, and that an end of the war with Vietnam unified under communist leadership was unfortunately a 'beautiful fantasy'.[54] If militants often indulged in flamboyant and presumptuous rhetoric, the pragmatic 'realism' of the NAACP leadership, as embodied by its 'separate issues' and 'guns and butter' doctrines, took on a lot of hypocrisy. It more or less deliberately ignored the drain of resources for domestic reform, the disproportionate number of black draftees and casualties, and the racist undertones of the war itself. Realism also meant that the Association shied away from supporting blacks who had lost their jobs for protesting the war. Moreover, when in 1966 the Georgia legislature refused to seat the SNCC member and Representative-elect Julian Bond because of the Committee's anti-war declaration, the NAACP limited its activity to a mildly worded cable requesting the seating of Bond, while distancing itself from the SNCC's position on Vietnam. The NAACP Legal and Defense Fund refused to represent Bond in court because, allegedly, his was not a case of racial discrimination. What the 'separate issues' doctrine graciously overlooked was that, as one critic wrote, 'the most fervent supporters of the war in Vietnam are men and organizations whose names read like a Who's Who of racism in America'.[55]

But, for all its inconsistencies, the NAACP policy on Vietnam seems to have been good politics, not just because it kept the Association's influence with the Johnson administration. After all, the civil rights groups that became radicalized over Vietnam and the black power issue all disintegrated, whereas the NAACP endured. Moderation clearly payed off. The NAACP, the Urban League, and the Legal and Defense Fund all dramatically increased their outside income, while contributions to CORE, the SNCC, and the SCLC plummeted. Pleasing white liberal supporters, however, did not necessarily alienate the NAACP's black base. It remained the largest membership organization of the civil rights movement and the number of its members actually grew by more than 20,000 between 1965 and 1969.[56] As described above, there was sharp criticism of the Association's official position on Vietnam among its members and supporters, but this did not mean that these critics would also leave the organization. Nor was Vietnam necessarily the most important concern to dissenters. A 1968 challenge by a group of self-declared 'Young Turks', which attacked the leadership for bureaucratic paralysis and aloofness from the black masses, did not even mention the Vietnam issue. No resolution concerning the war was introduced at the 1968 annual convention in Atlantic City.[57]

This was hardly an accident. For all the racial inequities that were involved in the conduct of the war, the African-American community at large seems not to have differed significantly from white Americans in their attitude towards the war, let alone subscribed to Black Panther ideology that their freedom depended on 'a strong Vietnam which is not the puppet of international white supremacy'. In retrospect, radicals grudgingly conceded that the majority of blacks went along with the war policy, blaming it, as usual, on manipulation and false consciousness. The appeal to racial brotherhood remained very limited; for most African Americans, the Chinese Communist Premier Chou En-lai was 'no close relative', as Roy Wilkins had once scoffed. Even the morally forceful anti-war protest of Martin Luther King was fully approved by only a quarter of blacks, according to polls taken after his Riverside speech.[58] Obviously, the assessment of the NAACP leadership that Vietnam was not the foremost issue on the minds of African Americans proved basically correct.

Although remarkably successful, the NAACP's dodging of the Vietnam War as a concern for the civil rights movement still appears hypocritical and opportunistic. In the final analysis, however, its opportunism was due to a firm and genuine belief in American democracy. For half a century the NAACP had struggled to make the system work, and now that it obviously had begun to work, its leaders simply would not consider the possibility that a foreign war might destroy their hopes. They adopted a strategy of denial and chose to ignore the problem unless directly challenged from within the civil rights movement. As far as the 'separate issues' doctrine meant acquiescence to Johnson's war policies, it was justified in the discourse of political realism. With Congress passing legislation for civil rights and equal opportunity, with the courts increasingly sympathetic to minority rights, and with a friendly president in the White House, it seemed sheer madness to offend the majority of the society by voicing opposition to the Vietnam War, at least as long as dissent was even more unpopular than the war itself. But, even after the politics of liberal consensus had unraveled, Vietnam would not loom large in the NAACP's assessment of a time that it considered, above all else, as the historical watershed of the civil rights struggle; a time during which, as Lyndon Johnson, upon leaving the White House, assured Roy Wilkins, together they had made 'America a better place for all its people'.[59]

NAACP leaders could not have agreed more, and resolved that they would not let Vietnam taint the record of their hero who, according to Clarence Mitchell, 'made a greater contribution to giving a dignified and hopeful status to Negroes in the United States than any other President, including Lincoln, Roosevelt, and Kennedy'. The war, of course, was to be blamed on bad counsel. When Johnson died in January 1973, Roy Wilkins's eulogy would not even mention the ominous word and merely stated: 'The goal of peace was in his heart though he was held to a course by advisers he trusted.'[60] In the end, LBJ, who had always wanted to be remembered for his domestic reforms and was distraught by the notion that his name would be forever linked with Vietnam, could still count on his old friends from the NAACP.

Notes

1. There is no scholarly history of the NAACP and its strategies available at this time. The two most recent books are inadequate in both sources and interpretation and are hardly useful even as an introduction, see

Minnie Finch, *The NAACP: Its Fight for Justice* (Metuchen, NJ: 1981); Jacqueline L. Harris, *History and Achievement of the NAACP: The African American Experience* (New York: 1992); Langston Hughes, *Fight for Freedom: The Story of the NAACP* (New York: 1962), is completely outdated. The best studies dealing with specific NAACP policies are Robert L. Zangrando, *The NAACP Crusade against Lynching, 1909–1950* (Philadelphia, Pa.: 1980); Mark V. Tushnet, *The NAACP's Legal Strategy against Segregated Education, 1925–1950* (Chapel Hill, NC: 1987). I am currently working on a study of the NAACP's struggle for African-American voting rights from its founding to the present, entitled 'The Ticket to Freedom'.

2.   On Johnson's civil rights policy, see Mark Stern, *Calculating Visions. Kennedy, Johnson, and Civil Rights: Perspectives on the Sixties* (New Brunswick, NJ: 1992), pp. 160–230; Johnson's declaration of 'unconditional war on poverty', in his State of the Union Message of 8 January 1964, *The Public Papers of the Presidents: Lyndon B. Johnson* (Washington, DC: 1963/4), vol. 1, pp. 112–18, especially p. 114. On Johnson's escalation of the war, see George C. Herring, *America's Longest War. The United States in Vietnam, 1950–1975. America in Crisis* (2nd edn; New York: 1986), pp. 108–43.

3.   For the literature of the anti-war movement, see Tom Wells, *The War Within: America's Battle over Vietnam* (Berkeley and Los Angeles, Calif.: 1994), pp. 116–17, 129–31; Charles DeBenedetti, *An American Ordeal: The Antiwar Movement of the Vietnam Era* (Syracuse, NY: 1990), pp. 158–9, 172–5; Nancy Zaroulis and Gerald Sullivan, *Who Spoke Up? American Protest against the War in Vietnam, 1963–1975* (Garden City, NY: 1984), pp. 69–70, 108–10; Melvin Small and William D. Hoover (eds), *Give Peace a Chance: Exploring the Vietnam Antiwar Movement. Essays from the Charles DeBenedetti Memorial Conference* (Syracuse, NY: 1992), does not specifically address blacks or the civil rights movement. Thomas Powers, *Vietnam: The War at Home. Vietnam and the American People 1964–1968* (New York: 1973), pp. 138–63, only deals with the civil rights movement in general. For the literature on the civil rights movement, see Manning Marable, *Race, Reform, and Rebellion: The Second Reconstruction in Black America, 1945–1990* (2nd edn; Jackson, Miss., and London: 1991), pp. 99–101; Harvard Sitkoff, *The Struggle for Black Equality, 1954–1992* (2nd edn; New York: 1992), pp. 204–6. Clayborne Carson, *In Struggle: SNCC and the Black Awakening of the 1960s* (2nd edn; Cambridge, Mass.: 1995), pp. 183–9; and August Meier and Elliot Rudwick, *CORE: A Study in the Civil Rights Movement, 1942–1968* (Urbana, Ill.: 1975), pp. 414–15; Clyde Taylor (ed.), *Vietnam and Black America: An Anthology of Protest and Resistance* (Garden City, NY: 1973) is a useful source which, however, only contains material on the radical critics; Robert W. Mullen, *Blacks and Vietnam* (Washington, DC: 1981), also deals predominantly with the militants. Herbert Shapiro, 'The Vietnam War and the American civil rights movement', *Journal of Ethnic Studies* 16 (Winter, 1989), pp. 117–41, is basically a chronological account of Martin Luther King's attitude toward the war.

4.   For the congressional voting records of the respective candidates, see the

synopsis of 10 June 1960 in: Records of the National Association for the Advancement of Colored People, Library of Congress, Manuscript Division, Washington, DC (hereafter NAACP), Group III, Series A, Box 72. On the meeting with Wilkins, see the NAACP press release of 2 December 1963, NAACP III, A, 68; Roy Wilkins with Tom Mathews, *Standing Fast: The Autobiography of Roy Wilkins* (1st paperback edn; New York: 1994), pp. 295–6 and, on their subsequent relationship, 295–307. For Evers, Henry, and Mitchell, see their testimonies in 'Civil Rights During the Johnson Administration, 1963–1969', a collection from the holdings of The Lyndon Baynes Johnson Library, Austin, Texas, Library of Congress, Manuscript Division (hereafter CRLBJ), Part III: Oral Histories, Reel 1, Frames 950–79; Reel 2, Frames 168–228; Reel 3, Frames 110–83.

5. For the NAACP strategy during the 1964 campaign and the election results, see, instead of numerous archival references, Henry Lee Moon, 'How we voted and why', *The Crisis* 72 (January, 1965), pp. 27–31; Wilkins's telegram of 5 November 1964, NAACP III, A, 175.

6. Steven F. Lawson, *In Pursuit of Power: Southern Blacks and Electoral Politics, 1962–1982*, Contemporary American History Series (New York: 1985), p. 9.

7. I have dealt with the citizen-soldier ideal and its effects on voting rights in my own 'Soldiers and Citizens: War and Voting Rights in American History', in David K. Adams and Cornelis A. van Minnen (eds), *Reflections on American Exceptionalism*, vol. 1 of European Papers in American History (Keele: 1994), pp. 188–225.

8. See Current's memorandum of 22 April 1965, NAACP III, A, 328, which contains the text of the resolution, John Morsell's censure, and his own comments.

9. For the call for the assembly and Wilkins's memorandum of 30 July 1965 to branches, see NAACP III, A, 328. For the background of the assembly, see DeBenedetti, *Ordeal*, pp. 120–1; Zaroulis, *Who Spoke Up?*, pp. 69–70.

10. On the conflicts of the 1930s, see Wilkins, *Standing Fast*, pp. 158–61; for the late 1940s and the 1950s, see ibid., pp. 209–11; Herbert Hill, 'Communist Party – Enemy of Negro Equality', *The Crisis* 58 (June/July 1951), pp. 365–71, 421–4; Alfred Baker Lewis, 'The Problem of Communist Infiltration', ibid. 61, pp. 585–8. Also see the Roy Wilkins Column of 2 May 1965, 'The Comrades', Roy Wilkins Papers, Library of Congress, Manuscript Division (hereafter Wilkins Papers), Box 39. The weekly Wilkins Column was featured by more than thirty newspapers nationwide.

11. For King's statement, see David J. Garrow, *Bearing the Cross: Martin Luther King, JR, and the Southern Christian Leadership Conference* (New York: 1986), pp. 429–30; Wilkins's reaction in his column of 18 July 1965, 'Sidetrack', Wilkins Papers, Box 39.

12. For the GI from Georgia, see the released statement by SCLC Community Education Director, Hosea Williams, of 23 July 1965, Papers of the Southern Christian Leadership Conference, Martin Luther King Center for Nonviolent Social Change, Atlanta, Georgia (hereafter SCLC),

Box 169. For the statement of the McComb MFDP, see the *New York Times*, 31 July 1965, copy in NAACP III, 232. For the MFDP declaration of 31 July 1965, see Papers of the Student Nonviolent Coordinating Committee, Martin Luther Center for Nonviolent Social Change, Atlanta, Georgia (hereafter SNCC), Box 169.

13.   For the declaration of the Mississippi NAACP of 13 July 1965, see Current's memorandum of 3 August 1965, NAACP III, A, 232; Wilkins Column, 29 August 1965, 'Negroes and the Draft', Wilkins Papers, Box 39; on the adverse reaction among the precious few white supporters in Mississippi, see John Dittmer, *Local People: The Struggle for Civil Rights in Mississippi. Blacks in the New World* (Urbana and Chicago, Ill.: 1994), pp. 349–51; Clyde Taylor, 'Black Consciousness in the Vietnam Years', in *Vietnam and Black America*, pp. 7–20.

14.   'Resolutions of the 1965 Annual Convention', NAACP III, A, 20; for the SCLC board, see Garrow, *Bearing the Cross*, pp. 437–9; SNCC declaration of 9 August 1965, by John Lewis, SNCC, Box 165.

15.   Declaration of 6 January 1966, printed in Taylor, *Vietnam and Black America*, pp. 258–60.

16.   On the genesis of the black power slogan and the SNCC's radicalization, see Carson, *In Struggle*, pp. 206–11, 215–28, 236–42; Wilkins Column, 4 June 1966, 'SNCC's New Road', Wilkins Papers, Box 39. The 'black power' theme became a major controversy within the civil rights movement which cannot be dealt with here. For the SNCC draft resistance paper, see SNCC, Box 165.

17.   Wilkins Column, 16 January 1966, 'SNCC's Foreign Policy', Wilkins Papers, Box 39. The column was brought to the attention of the White House before publication, typed copy in CRLBJ, Part I: The White House Central Files, Reel 2, Frames 769–70. Humphrey's memorandum of 22 January 1966, for Joe Califano, ibid., Frame 774.

18.   On the background of the White House Conference, see Lawson, *Pursuit*, pp. 44–8; minutes of the 23 March 1966 meeting in Wilkins Papers, Box 7.

19.   The SNCC's decline to participate was released on 23 May 1966; copy in NAACP IV, 50. CORE National Director James Farmer had criticized US involvement in Vietnam as early as 1964, but blocked a formal resolution: Meier and Rudwick, *CORE*, p. 404.

20.   For the deliberations on the Vietnam resolution, see CRLBJ, Part IV: Records of the White House Conference on Civil Rights, 1965–6, Reel 9, Frames 476–8, 511–13; Reel 13, Frame 353; Reel 14, Frames 741–72; CORE resolution. Reel 12, Frame 402; resolution adopted: Reel 15, Frame 8.

21.   Henry Wallace to Roy Wilkins, 13 January 1966, NAACP IV, A, 86.

22.   Roy Wilkins to Joseph Stern, 4 March 1966, and Stern's reply of 14 March 1966, NAACP IV, A, 86.

23.   Wilkins to Joseph Stern, 17 March 1966, NAACP IV, A, 86.

24.   Johnson's message to Congress, 12 January 1966, in *The Public Papers of the Presidents: Lyndon B. Johnson* (1966) vol. 1, pp. 3–10. Wilkins's telegram, 13 January 1966, NAACP IV, A, 35.

25.   *The Public Papers of the Presidents*, vol. 1, pp. 4, 8.

26. On the fight against discrimination in the military, see Harris, *History and Achievement*, pp. 85–102. Archival material on the topic can be found in NAACP I, C, 374–80, and NAACP II, G: Veterans Affairs File, 1940–50. See letter of 9 June 1966 by Sgt. Robert L. Hollis to NAACP and Wilkins's reply of 1 July 1966, NAACP IV, A, 86.

27. On the draft and the casualty rates of blacks in Vietnam, see Jack D. Foner, *Blacks and the Military in American History* (New York: 1974), pp. 202–6; telegram of 14 March 1966 by Irene Smith, president of the New Jersey state conference of NAACP branches, to Wilkins, and Wilkins's response of 20 May 1966, NAACP IV, A, 86. Also see the letter of 18 January 1966, by C.R. Roquemore, Kansas, president of NAACP state conference, to Kansas Governor William H. Avery protesting that not a single black served on a draft board in the state, NAACP IV, A, 19.

28. Memorandum of 14 April 1966 by Gloster Current to Wilkins and other national NAACP officers. Memorandum of 5 May 1966 by Current, with the Greenwich branch resolution attached, NAACP IV, A, 87; resolutions of the 1966 convention in Los Angeles, NAACP IV, A, 3.

29. See the undated circular letter by Marion Barry to the membership organizations of the Leadership Conference on Civil Rights, which stressed the imbalance in pursuing freedom abroad and at home, the inequities of the draft, and the organizational danger for the SNCC, NAACP IV, A, 87. For the exchange of telegrams on the Luci Johnson wedding, see the NAACP press release, 4 August 1966, ibid.; Wilkins, *Standing Fast*, pp. 320–1. The 1966 CORE convention embraced both the black power slogan and pledged support for draft resisters: Meier and Rudwick, *CORE*, pp. 414–15.

30. DeBenedetti, *Ordeal*, p. 158.

31. The conflicts between the NAACP and other civil rights groups cannot be dealt with here at length, but will receive careful attention in my 'Ticket to Freedom'. The Wilkins Papers contain FBI memoranda, obtained by Wilkins under the Freedom of Information Act, on 1964 talks between Wilkins and bureau representatives, according to which Wilkins denounced King as a 'liar', a 'sexual degenerate', 'dumb', sympathetic to communism, and more. See memorandum of 27 November 1964, by C.D. DeLoach to Mohr, FBI File 62-78270-16, and memorandum of 16 March 1965, by A. Jones to C.D. DeLoach, FBI File B, 1958–74, Wilkins Papers, Box 24. Since there is no independent corroboration of these talks, they must be taken with extreme care. There can be no doubt, however, that Wilkins resented the publicity and praise that King received for his role in the civil rights movement.

32. On the SCLC board resolution, see Garrow, *Bearing the Cross*, pp. 469–70; memorandum of 14 April 1966 by Gloster Current to Roy Wilkins *et al.*, NAACP IV, A, 87.

33. For the evolution of King's position on Vietnam, see Garrow, *Bearing the Cross*, pp. 540–74 and *passim*. The Riverside Church speech is printed in James Melvin Washington (ed.), *A Testament of Hope: The Essential Writings and Speeches of Martin Luther King, Jr.* (San Francisco, Calif.: 1991), pp. 231–44.

34. For the reaction to King's speech, see Garrow, *Bearing the Cross*, pp. 553–4. For the minutes of the 10 April 1967 meeting of the NAACP National Board of Directors and the text of the resolution, see NAACP IV, A, 10.

35. See Wilkins Column, 15 April 1967, 'Dr King's New Role', Wilkins Papers, Box 39.

36. For the spring mobilization, see Garrow, *Bearing the Cross*, pp. 556–7; DeBenedetti, *Ordeal*, pp. 174–7; Zaroulis, Sullivan, *Who Spoke Up?*, pp. 110–14. The rally attracted at least 125,000 marchers. There were similar demonstrations all over the country; memorandum of 16 April 1967, by Gloster Current to Roy Wilkins *et al.*, NAACP IV, A, 87.

37. The folder 'Vietnam: Correspondence, 1967', NAACP IV, A, 86, contains about 70 letters altogether. See letter of 20 April 1967 by Sidney Jackson to *LIFE Magazine*, NAACP IV, A, 87. Statement of the San Francisco Central City branch is contained in a memorandum of 18 May 1967, by Gloster Current to Roy Wilkins *et al.*, NAACP IV, A, 79. Also see the common declaration of the Astoria, Long Island City, and the Greenwich Village branches of May 1967, NAACP IV, C, 55.

38. 'Resolutions Adopted by the Fifty-Eighth Annual Convention of the NAACP at Boston, Massachusetts', 10–15 July 1967, NAACP IV, A, 5, pp. 25–6.

39. Memoranda of 3 April 1967, by Sargent Shriver and Maurice A. Dawkins; undated memorandum of late April/early May 1967 by Dawkins, copies in NAACP IV, A, 50.

40. Lyndon Baynes Johnson, *The Vantage Point: Perspectives of the Presidency 1963–1969* (New York: 1971), pp. 342–3.

41. Herring, *America's Longest War*, p. 145; James T. Patterson, *America's Struggle Against Poverty, 1900–1985* (2nd enlarged edn; Cambridge, Mass.: 1986), p. 147; on the war costs, see Claudia Goldin, 'War', in Glenn Porter (ed.), *Encyclopedia of American Economic History: Studies of the Principal Movement and Ideas*, 3 vols (New York: 1980), vol. 3, pp. 935–57, especially p. 938, table 1.

42. I have explored the concept of war as a political opportunity at length in Manfred Berg, 'Soldiers and Citizens', p. 189 and *passim*, especially pp. 206–11, for its significance during World War II.

43. Wilkins Column, 6 April 1968, Wilkins Papers, Box 44. On the passing of the Open Housing Act, see Hugh Davis Graham, *Civil Rights and the Presidency: Race and Gender in American Politics 1960–1972* (New York: 1992), pp. 127–9.

44. On the swing of the public mood after Tet, see DeBenedetti, *Ordeal*, pp. 208–15. In his memoirs LBJ, not very convincingly, maintains that he never had a second presidential term in mind, *Vantage Point*, pp. 425–37.

45. Cf. Arthur M. Schlesinger, jun. (ed.), *History of American Presidential Elections* (New York: 1985), vol. 9, pp. 3763–4, 3792–3.

46. For the voter registration during the 1968 presidential campaign, see the staff memorandum of September 1968 by W.C. Patton and his report for November and December 1968, NAACP IV, A, 63. Wallace still carried all states of the deep South and collected more than 13 per cent

of the popular vote: Schlesinger, *History of American Presidential Elections*, vol. 9, p. 3865. Robert Kennedy had widespread appeal among black voters but, due to clashes during his tenure as attorney-general, his relations with NAACP leaders were not too cordial: Wilkins, *Standing Fast*, pp. 330–1.

47. On the clashes between the NAACP and the Nixon administration, which culminated during the 1972 annual convention, see 'Civil Rights during the Nixon Administration, 1969–1974', Library of Congress, Manuscript Division, Part I: The White House Files, Reel 4, Frames 215–46; Wilkins, *Standing Fast*, pp. 332–4. For the general topic, see John Robert Greene, *The Limits of Power: The Nixon and Ford Administrations. America since World War II* (Bloomington and Indianapolis, Ind.: 1992), pp. 38–51; letter of 28 March 1969 by Richard Nixon to Roy Wilkins, Wilkins Papers, Box 8.

48. See Wilkins Column, 16 May 1970, 'Death is White', Wilkins Papers, Box 40. Wilkins bitterly criticized, however, the fact that the American public was much less outraged when the victims were black students, DeBenedetti, *Ordeal*, p. 286; letter of 3 May 1972 by Roy Wilkins to black representative Charles Diggs, jun. (D-MI), Wilkins Papers, Box 9.

49. Letter of 29 August 1970, by Huey P. Newton to the National Liberation Front of South Vietnam and reply of 31 October 1970, by Nguyen Thi Dinh, printed in Taylor, *Vietnam and Black America*, pp. 290–5; Roy Wilkins Column, 15 August 1970, 'Huey's Plan', Wilkins Papers, Box 40. On the Black Panthers and Vietnam in general, see Mullen, *Blacks and Vietnam*, pp. 13–17, 39–47.

50. Printed in Clayborne Carson *et al.* (eds), *Eyes on the Prize: Documents, Speeches, and Firsthand Accounts from the Black Freedom Struggle, 1954–1990* (New York: 1991), pp. 517–28. See especially p. 519, footnote 13.

51. See Du Bois's famous editorial 'Close Ranks', *The Crisis* 16 (July 1918), p. 111. The controversy over the origins, intent, and background of Du Bois's editorial has recently been renewed. See William Jordan, '"The damnable dilemma": African-American Accommodation and Protest during World War I', *Journal of American History* 81, 4 (1995), pp. 1562–83; Mark Ellis, 'W.E.B. Du Bois and the Formation of Black Opinion in World War I: A Commentary on the "damnable dilemma"', ibid., pp. 1584–90. Tempting as it may be, the parallels in the debates over black accommodation and protest during the First World War and the Vietnam War cannot be explored here.

52. Quoted in Addison Gayle, jun., '"Hell No, Black Men Won't Go"', in Taylor, *Vietnam and Black America*, pp. 44–54, especially p. 45.

53. See letter of 1 June 1967, by Wilkins to Senator Ernest Gruening (D-Alas.), NAACP IV, A, 27.

54. For an informed and sober analysis of the Vietnam War and its impact on black Americans, see for example Robert S. Browne, 'The Freedom Movement and the War in Vietnam', in Taylor, *Vietnam and Black America*, pp. 61–78. Browne was a black intellectual who had lived for several years in Vietnam and spoke Vietnamese. For the SCLC's Peace Education Project in 1966–7, see SCLC, pp. 175–6; Julius Lester, 'On

Vietnam', undated reprint from the *Guardian Newsletter*, SNCC, Box 59.

55. See the letter of 19 April 1966, by John Morsell to the Mamaroneck, New York branch, concerning the case of a schoolteacher whose tenure had been terminated because of his anti-war activities, NAACP IV, A, 86; telegram of 10 January 1966 by Roy Wilkins to the Georgia House of Representatives, NAACP IV, A, 50. On the NAACP Legal and Defense Fund, which had been established as an independent organization for tax reasons, see the history written by its long-time director, Jack Greenberg, *Crusaders in the Court: How a Dedicated Band of Lawyers Fought for the Civil Rights Revolution* (New York: 1994), p. 409. Greenberg tells that he was against the war, but also did not wish to involve the LDF in the anti-war movement. See Gayle, '"Hell No, Black Men Won't Go"', p. 52.

56. For the development of funding, see Herbert H. Haines, 'Black Radicalization and the Funding of Civil Rights: 1957–1970', *Social Problems* 32 (1984), pp. 31–43, especially tables 1 and 2. In 1967 NAACP outside income grew by 116.7 per cent, while SCLC's stagnated and CORE and SNCC lost more than 30 per cent of their 1966 outside income. For the membership figures, see Martin N. Marger, 'Social Movement Organizations and the Response to Environmental Change: The NAACP, 1960–1973', *Social Problems* 32 (1984), pp. 16–31, especially table 1. In 1965, the NAACP had about 440,000 members and in 1969, 462,000. The following year membership plummeted to 360,000, but this was clearly due to a doubling of membership fees.

57. See the 'Young Turk' manifesto in NAACP IV, A, 80. The memorandum of 3 July 1968 by Gloster Current on the strategy of the 'Young Turks' for the upcoming annual convention also does not mention Vietnam, NAACP IV, C, 55. For the resolutions introduced at the 1968 convention, see the memorandum of 6 June 1968 by Gloster Current to NAACP units, NAACP IV, A, 7. The 1968 convention of the Urban League, however, did demand the prompt withdrawal. See Guichard Parris and Lester Brooks, *Blacks in the City: A History of the National Urban League* (Boston, Mass. and Toronto: 1970), p. 447.

58. See Eldrige Cleaver, 'The Black Man's Stake in Vietnam', in Taylor, *Vietnam and Black America*, pp. 273–9, especially p. 276. For the charge of manipulation, see Taylor's introduction, ibid., pp. xxi–xxii; Wilkins Column, 18 July 1965, 'Sidetracks', Wilkins Papers, Box 39; Garrow, *Bearing the Cross*, p. 562. Almost half of the black respondents thought King was wrong.

59. Letter of 23 January 1969 by LBJ to Roy Wilkins, Wilkins Papers, Box 8. In his address to the 1968 NAACP annual convention, LBJ had told Wilkins that they were wearing scars of honor from both the left and right, letter of 22 June 1968, CRLBJ, Part I, Reel 5, Frames 151–3.

60. For the Mitchell quote, see CRLBJ, Part III, Reel 3, Frame 181. For similar statements, see Charles Evers, ibid., Reel 1, Frame 955; Aaron Henry, ibid., Reel 2, Frame 228; Thurgood Marshall, ibid., Reel 3, Frame 65; Roy Wilkins, ibid., Reel 3, Frame 985; Wilkins Column, 24 January 1973, Wilkins Papers, Box 47.

12

The Long Shadow:
The Third Indochina War, 1975–1995

Stanley I. Kutler

It would seem that time and distance erode memory. We adjust, we lose the intensity ... For many of us, years later, Vietnam is seen with a certain tempered nostalgia. A half-remembered adventure, we feel, many of us, proud of having 'been there,' forgetting the terror, straining out the bad stuff, focusing on the afterimage ... We have forgotten, or lost the energy to recall, the terribly complex and ambiguous issues of the Vietnam War ... What to fight for? When, if ever, to use armed forces, as instruments of foreign policy? What regimes to support, and how, and under what conditions? To what extent and by what means do we, as a nation, try to make good on our beliefs and principles – opposing tyranny, preserving freedoms, resisting aggressions?

Tim O'Brien, quoted in *To Heal a Nation* (1985).

As the last shots of the Second Indochina War echoed in Saigon in April 1975, the Academy Awards presentations unleashed the first shots of the Third Indochina War, one that largely rekindled and extended 'the war at home'. Accepting an award for the best documentary film, the producers of *Hearts and Minds*, a blatantly anti-war film, read a letter from a Vietcong official thanking 'our friends in America' who had worked for the cause of peace for both America and Vietnam. The statement unleashed a flood of protest calls to the network. Network officials frantically lobbied the Academy, which, towards the end of the evening, wheeled out its heavy artillery. Frank Sinatra, a national icon, read a prepared statement from apologetic Academy officials: 'We are not responsible for any political references made ... tonight'; Sinatra then expressed regret that they had been made.[1]

The incident was a warning that the anti-war movement, unbridled and largely unfettered for nearly a decade, would operate with a different writ and less appeal in postwar America. Although American participation in the war had seemingly been discredited, enemies of the anti-war movement ironically felt freer and less constrained to counter-attack against those whom they regarded as political and cultural dissidents, if not revolutionaries. Moreover, they wasted little time in targeting the anti-war movement as responsible for the fall of Vietnam. The new battlegrounds ranged from politics to the conduct of foreign and military policy, to culture and to history – even to what James William Gibson has called 'Warrior Dreams', which have fantasized the war's most violent moments. Vietnam magnified a political and cultural bifurcation in American life that has left a deep fault-line among a myriad of issues.

After helicopters had evacuated the last Americans from Saigon in April 1975, President Gerald Ford looked to an end of the debate over Vietnam: 'America can regain the sense of pride that existed before Vietnam. But it cannot be achieved by refighting a war that is finished as far as America is concerned.' But the nation has continued to fight and re-fight that war endlessly, whether over a decision to intervene in the Persian Gulf or in Bosnia, over the Vietnam War draft status of a presidential candidate, or how to memorialize the war's dead.

Waves of euphoria and self-congratulation usually sweep a nation in the wake of war: the Civil War, the Spanish–American War, and World Wars I and II come readily to mind. After the Korean conflict, Americans were simply relieved that it was over, readily forgot it, and went on with their lives. The Vietnam War, however, was another matter. Everything was open to reconsideration: political decisions involving the war; military tactics and strategy; the fate of POWs and MIAs; the future course of foreign policy; the motives of those who opposed the war; the treatment of veterans; and how (and even, if) the nation would memorialize the war – these were only some of the issues that seemed to spill as much ink as the war had spilled blood. The upshot has been that Vietnam left the USA terribly divided, with a legacy of bitterness and a civil war unique in intensity and length in American history. Since 1973 Vietnam has cast a long shadow over American life, whether it involves foreign and defense policies, military doctrine, or the nature of patriotism. It resonates for the United States as the Algerian War has done for France – for nearly forty years. Former President Ronald Reagan described the war as a great 'noble cause' which failed only because of a failure of national will. For others, Vietnam contradicted both the most principled ideals of the nation's foreign policy as well as those of its very being. One thing is certain: Vietnam – together with the civil rights revolution and Watergate – was a transforming event, one that scarred generations of Americans at the time and to come, in a fashion similar to that of the Great Depression of the 1930s. The Vietnam intervention fractured a two-decade-long foreign policy consensus in the United States. It provoked an unprecedented wave of protest and dissent, in and out of the government, which left the administration virtually paralyzed in its conduct of the war, and the populace at odds and in disarray.

The 'lesson' of World War II was that the United States had to be 'involved' in the world; the western hemisphere could no longer afford splendid isolation. Americans were told that they had a special responsibility for defending principles of liberty and democracy, and particularly to use their power on behalf of the weak and threatened. In a more practical way, Americans also accepted the notion that they had 'vital interests' – geopolitical and economic – to protect against those who threatened the 'American Way of Life'. But for many Americans after 1965 the Vietnam conflict involved neither vital American interests nor defense of democratic principles. The upshot was a 'war at home' which dissolved the foreign policy consensus and left society deeply divided. The viability and workability of American institutions were at stake; the credibility of government and leaders, the military, and educational institutions was challenged and shaken, leaving them all severely scarred.

The end of American involvement in Vietnam in 1973 generated another war, one that has lasted for more than two decades. Both sides invoke the 'lessons' of Vietnam as an injunction against subsequent interventions or as an argument for more firepower and more effort to win. Americans continue to fight over imagined POWs, the MIAs, and the veterans – fights that spill over into squabbles over the design of war memorials or over the military bona fides of political candidates. The skirmish lines of the battles over this war have lingered, bitterly dividing Americans over political and cultural issues, and over the rendering of history itself.

Vietnam was a non-issue in the 1976 presidential campaign. Perhaps the war was too recent; perhaps America just preferred to forget. Gerald Ford certainly wanted to put it behind him; Jimmy Carter had other issues. In 1950 Republicans had wasted little time in raising the question 'Who lost China?', but a quarter of a century later the nation's preoccupation with domestic issues, particularly Watergate and the question of morality in political life, made Vietnam seem remote. All that changed dramatically in the next election. In 1980 Ronald Reagan made much of restoring American power and prestige, both of which had been badly damaged by the Vietnam War. He thought it was time to recognize 'that ours was, in truth, a noble cause'. He readily justified the war as part of the continuing struggle against the Soviet Union: 'Let us tell those who fought in that war that we will never again ask young men to fight and possibly die in a war our government is afraid to let them win.' Thus Reagan had it all his way. He honored the memory of those who fought and died, and he played the usual conservative theme that more firepower, more commitment of men and *matériel*, would have carried the day. The failure to do so, he warned, had created the 'Vietnam Syndrome', which had made Americans reluctant and apologetic in their opposition to aggression. Five months into his presidency, Reagan declared that the 'Vietnam Syndrome', which he now defined as a domestic disrespect for the military, had been dispelled.[2] The occasion, fittingly enough, was a commencement speech at the US Military Academy. Most of all, Reagan gave legitimacy to what had been only a *sub silentio* theme: the United States could have won the war if it had not been betrayed at home.

Curiously, the 'noble cause' line was only a minor part of Reagan's speech, in which he accepted the Veterans for Foreign Wars' endorsement; he played on familiar themes of peace through strength, the need to withstand Soviet aggression, and to remember veterans and their entitlements. But the media quickly jumped on the 'noble cause' line, depicting Reagan as foolish and out of touch. On the contrary, his remarks touched deep wells of sentiment in the nation. He had said in 1976 that America had intervened in Vietnam to 'counter the master plan of the communists for world conquest'. He was never alone in that judgment.[3]

Although Reagan refused to take part in the dedication of the Vietnam Memorial in 1982, he spoke repeatedly about POWs in Vietnam and his determination to rescue them. Perhaps one might justify the latter as necessary to appease his natural constituency; but was it similarly necessary to refuse to dedicate the memorial? After all, here was his opportunity to say to the more than 50,000 combat dead, that 'in truth', yours was a 'noble cause'. Instead of visiting the memorial wall, Reagan did his best to involve the United States in a Central American adventure, both in El Salavador and in Nicaragua. Here, he might have exorcized the ghost of Vietnam; instead, he had to rely upon the pathetic, inept, almost comic-opera, doings of Colonel Oliver North. Public opinion and a suspicious Democratic Congress, however, proved virile enough to thwart even this most popular of presidents.

When George Bush took his oath of office in January 1989, he put his finger on Vietnam as the issue responsible for so much bickering and contentiousness in American life. The words were eloquent; the new President was a man with unmistakable credentials for patriotism.

> We need compromise; we've had dissension. We need harmony; we've had a chorus of discordant voices … There's grown a certain divisiveness. We've seen the hard looks and heard the statements in which not each other's ideas are challenged, but each other's motives … It's been this way since Vietnam. That war cleaves us still. But, friends, that war began in earnest a quarter of a century ago; and surely the statute of limitations has been reached. The final lesson of Vietnam is that no great nation can long afford to be sundered by a memory.

Eloquent and true; but did the new President bury the issue?

Bush himself resurrected the 'lessons' of Vietnam as he prepared the nation for intervention in the Persian Gulf crisis from August 1990 until March 1991. That mobilization must be understood against the backdrop of Vietnam. The War Powers Resolution of 1973 required congressional approval for dispatching American troops. The Resolution, however, had been conveniently ignored for nearly two decades, as presidents regularly insisted on their commander-in-chief prerogatives to order military action without congressional approval. In a previous Persian Gulf crisis with Iran, President Reagan finally agreed to 'consult' with the congressional leadership, thus giving them more or less what they wanted. But the 1990–1 crisis clearly seemed different. Substantial numbers of American troops would be committed and Saddam Hussein's stockpiles of chemical weapons and missiles for some promised a dangerous war, if not a protracted one. Bush and the Democratic congressional leadership engaged in a stylized waltz. On the one hand, the President feared congressional repudiation of his policy; on the other hand, Democrats had their own doubts about a vote, fearing to be seen as 'soft on Saddam'.

When the President formally asked Congress to approve a resolution authorizing 'all necessary means' of expelling Saddam from Kuwait, he chided Congress for its failure to support him – a not-so-subtle reminder of the Nixon–Ford–Kissinger thesis, which argued that Congress had undermined the effort in Vietnam. George Mitchell, the Senate majority leader, retorted that the President wanted a resolution passed overwhelmingly, and without much debate. The Democratic leadership favored maintaining economic sanctions. Nevertheless, the resolution passed both the Senate (52–47) and the House (250–183). The Senate came within three votes of defeating Bush's request, reflecting the national division. Most of all, it reflected the bitter, divided memory of Vietnam. All sides used Vietnam to serve their own purposes. For the interventionists, the lesson of Vietnam dictated that the nation should never engage in a war that it did not intend to win; the opponents remembered the pain and suffering of a divided nation, and were determined never to enter war without popular support.[4] (Incidentally, the principle of having overwhelming public support as being a cardinal feature of American foreign and military policy since Vietnam is somewhat ironic. If congressional votes are any indication, America went into Vietnam with enormous public support, as evidenced by the Tonkin Gulf Resolution. For the Persian Gulf War, however, the Senate was nearly equally divided.)

With congressional approval in hand, Bush frantically, even desperately, raised the specter of Vietnam. But quiet, eloquent appeals would not work; only another war, with a decisive military result, could exorcize the ghost forever, Bush believed. From December 1990 onward, he consistently promised 'no more Vietnams', that he would give the military enough force to win, and that he would put no limits on its ability to fight. In a January 1991 speech to the Reserve Officers Association he pledged that 'this will not be another Vietnam'. He completely subscribed to the military's demands for overwhelming force: 'Never again will our armed forces be sent out to do a job with one hand tied behind their back.' It would be the perfect political war: prevail quickly and with as few casualties as possible. In a 6 February speech to the Economic Club of New York, Bush promised that 'this is not and will not be another Vietnam, ... with an ill-defined ending'. After the cease-fire, but hardly with the decisive victory he promised, Bush nevertheless declared all of his aims achieved: 'It's a proud day for Americans and by God, we've kicked the Vietnam syndrome once and for all.' The 'victory' over Iraq had 'reestablished credibility' for the United States, ensuring, he said with some curious logic, that this would now require less US intervention abroad.[5]

Bush was not the first – and undoubtedly will not be the last – to declare a requiem for the Vietnam syndrome. Yet presidential rhetoric simply will not loosen the Vietnam War's grip on the United States, nor will it change the dramatic events and impact of that event. Ironically, Bush himself continued to exploit it in the 1992 campaign, questioning Clinton's patriotism for having opposed the war. Gone now was Bush's lament that Vietnam 'cleaved us still'; no 'statute of limitations' operated against demagoguery. In what appeared to be an act of desperation, Bush took his stand with those who saw Vietnam as a 'noble cause', despite a political policy, coupled with the work of the protestors, that had handicapped the American effort. He complained that certain factions had tied one hand behind the back of its military and had prevented them from prevailing. Later, Bush criticized anti-war protestors who objected to the war's immorality. It was their action, he charged, that was immoral, for it restrained the military and deprived them of victory.

The Persian Gulf War is an anomaly in modern times – a classic set-piece, resembling a 'war games sandtable'. It was not Vietnam, which had been 'a low-intensity ground war, fought guerrilla-style by fanatical ethnic factions, in a complex physical environment', where smart weapons had proved to be of minimal use, and where astronomical losses had been suffered, in treasure and blood.[6] The proposed intervention and police work in Haiti in 1994 raised the meaning of Vietnam anew. Americans learned how elastic the so-called 'lessons' could be, as the 'war hawks' of 1991 suddenly found them to be a restraining force, and not merely a bad precedent to overcome with strong medicine. The Republicans, though not in command in Congress, dominated the institution, in great part as a result of the perceived unpopularity and undoubted political weakness of President Clinton. Opponents of both Clinton and the idea of intervening in Haiti conveniently raised the Vietnam War's 'lessons' and their emotional symbolism in a bitter congressional debate. The assault on the President bordered on the vicious. Joel Hefley (R–CO) called Clinton's move 'unadulterated insanity'. Contending that the President was positioning the nation to do battle, he remarked: 'Well, I say it's never too late for Bill Clinton to get a little combat experience.' With equal bitterness, Hefley expressed his contempt for Haiti. On a slightly higher level, Curt Weldon (R–PA) attacked the Haiti mission as nation-building, akin to what had developed in Somalia. Memories of that recent disaster, and the loss of American lives, clearly shaped Weldon's remarks. But curiously, the intervention in South Vietnam, which may have been America's most ambitious nation-building program, is rarely mentioned in the same critical way as Somalia or the potential task in Haiti. Thomas Ewing (R–IL) was a rare exception when he noted that 'we should have learned a lesson in Vietnam'.

Richard Durbin (D–IL) chided the Republicans for their silence at the time of Grenada and Panama, incidents that he regarded as similar to that proposed for Haiti. Durbin, who opposed all such interventions, also properly noted that Republican enthusiasm for a Persian Gulf War style of congressional debate ignored, first, their own hostility to a debate at the time and their willingness to grant the President *carte blanche*, and, second, that the Bush administration never enthusiastically supported the 'very clear edicts' of the Constitution on a congressional voice in war. Senator John McCain (R–AZ), a former prisoner of war, noted that the nation disagreed on what exactly were the lessons of the Vietnam War. But he thought that all agreed that the nation would not embark on any military venture without popular support. Although McCain believed the President did not have to secure congressional approval, he thought it imperative that he marshal political support.[7]

The 1992 presidential campaign witnessed a new turn in the long retaliatory war against the Vietnam protesters, resulting in Bill Clinton becoming another casualty of the war. Republican congressmen, dominating the televised, evening sessions – known as 'Special Orders' – of the House of Representatives, regularly denounced Clinton as a 'useful idiot' of the Soviets who deserved to be 'tried as a traitor or even shot'.[8] Yet polls as late as October 1992 consistently showed that at least three-quarters of respondents said that allegations of Clinton's manipulation of his draft status would have no effect on how they voted. On 18 September, a Gallup Poll similarly showed three-quarters saying that the charges would not make them doubt his ability to serve as commander-in-chief. The controversy nevertheless raised an unshakable character issue which Clinton could not escape: a significant number of Americans believed he had lied about his dealings on the draft. Most striking of all was Clinton's defensiveness about his personal opposition to the war.

Clinton was the first President in nearly fifty years who had not served in the military, but he was the first to appear at the Vietnam Memorial – on Memorial Day in 1993. Certainly, it was one of his more eloquent moments: 'Can any American be out of place [here]?', he asked. 'And can any Commander in Chief be in any other place but here on this day? I think not.' Clinton understood that the veterans were the proper medium for American reconciliation on the issue of the war: 'No one has come here today to disagree about the heroism of those whom we honor.' The President was greeted with enthusiastic applause, but the media centered on the catcalls of 'Draft Dodger!', 'Liar!', and 'Shut up, coward!', which flowed from the perimeter. Television commentators naturally focused on that drama, but strangely they missed the significance of the prevalent youth of the protestors, most of whom were probably not even alive when the war ended. Some media sources reported that many of the veterans present were delighted that the President appeared.[9]

The protest was not without its own irony. Of the half a million men in Vietnam during the height of the war, less than 10 per cent served in combat – and the record is clear: most opposed it. They deserted in record numbers, mutinied on several occasions, and even 'fragged' their own leaders. In 1968, nearly 200 GIs were court-martialed for attacking their officers. And what about the soldiers at Fort Hood who refused to serve? what about the race riots at China Beach? or the veterans' march on the 1972 Republican convention? All this seemed forgotten as media attention focused on one young man's not-so-uncommon and ambiguous record of dealing with his draft board.

By the time Clinton faced conscription, some 15.5 million men had been deferred or disqualified from the draft. Some simply played the deferment game; others, like the writer James Fallows and his Harvard classmates, resorted to various subterfuges such as deliberately losing weight in order to escape.[10] More than half the eligible males found various means to avoid service. In 1971, 15,000 veterans threw away their medals on the Capitol steps. Did Congressman Robert Dornan (R–CA), especially notorious for his questioning of the President's loyalty and manliness, ask that these men be shot?

Clinton has said that he feels an 'extra obligation' to make overtures to the military: 'I want to make sure that these good people who make up our military don't feel unnecessarily estranged just because they don't know me and they're not sure we shared enough common experience'.[11] The President's critics would readily point to such remarks to explain what they regard as his craven attitude towards the military on such issues as tolerance of homosexuals, women in combat, and the commitment of troops. Undoubtedly, the President's vagueness on his draft record weakened him on the character issue, and it has been magnified so as to leave him marginalized, even occasionally paralyzed, on questions of foreign and military policy.

Since 1971 public opinion polls have shown a steadily increasing belief that the war was a mistake. In that year 61 per cent of Americans agreed with such a position, while 28 per cent did not. The figures did not change much through the rest of the 1970s and 1980s, but in 1990 74 per cent thought the United States had made a mistake, while the number of supporters dropped to 22 per cent. Similarly, the war's corrosive effects had become more apparent by 1991. As a result of the Vietnam War, 38 per cent strongly agreed that they had less trust in their leaders, while another 33 per cent agreed with that position to a certain extent. On the issue of whether the United States should be more cautious about military involvement abroad, 42 per cent agreed strongly and 33 per cent agreed with some reservations. The loss of faith was readily apparent. In 1988, 36 per cent strongly agreed that leaders could not be trusted to give reliable information to the public, and another 34 per cent more or less agreed.

Yet the curious thing is that, however disenchanted Americans became with the war, a significant majority believed that the United States and South Vietnam could have won had the nation made a stronger military effort. In a 1990 poll, 53 per cent responded affirmatively to that position, while 37 per cent rejected it. A year later, 69 per cent responded that they believed that American soldiers were still being held in Southeast Asia (and another 11 per cent were not sure). This was nearly twenty years after the American withdrawal, and involved servicemen who had been reported as missing long beyond that. But what is one to believe? The same 1990 poll that reported a belief that the United States could have won the war found that only 67 per cent of the respondents knew that Americans had fought with the South Vietnamese against the North! In any event, such a contradiction throws light on the confusion, anger, and even violence of the responses towards the war. And all this has been fueled, I would argue, by a cynical manipulation of the culture, whereby political leaders and cultural profiteers eagerly complement one another for ideological and material gain. It is a process that ruthlessly exploits such innocents as MIA families, the uninformed young, and well-meaning people, deeply committed to their brand of patriotism. Simple-minded revisionism is a much easier lesson to absorb than memories of painful times and events.

Even as Ford appealed to Americans not to refight the war, he gave comfort to those who believed that America could have won. '[I]f we had made available for the next three years reasonable sums of military aid and economic assistance', he was certain that South Vietnam would have been viable, able to withstand any economic or military challenges. Wittingly or unwittingly, Ford confirmed the historical revisionism that Richard Nixon had already launched.

Choosing history as another battleground in the new Vietnam War carried with it a classic stab-in-the-back thesis. America lost, it has been argued, because of a policy limited to 'gradual escalation', laid down by civilians with no understanding of war, and who refused to delegate proper authority to the military who would have pushed for a decisive use of power. A corollary from this is the notion that the war was lost by Congress, because of its timidity and fear of anti-war agitators. Once the Paris Peace Accords were signed, Congress balked at any further aid to South Vietnam. Furthermore, the Watergate affair emboldened Congress to assault President Nixon's authority even further: the USA, it claimed, had won the war; General Philip Davidson, General William Westmoreland's aide, argued that America had never been defeated on the battlefield. Ford blamed Congress, and both Richard Nixon and Henry Kissinger, in their various memoirs, have blatantly charged Congress with giving up on the war.[12] They want it both ways: having secured 'peace with honor', they argued, Congress then defeated them where the North Vietnamese could not. In short, they continued, the USA could have won if only there had been more will and more firepower. And all of this conveniently overlooks Admiral Elmo Zumwalt's devastating dismissal of the Paris agreement, which allowed Hanoi to maintain its troops in the South. Two words, he said, did *not* characterize the document: peace and honor.

Richard Nixon, the inveterate revisionist, best reflected the backlash against those who widened the war and those who opposed it in his 1985 book, *No More Vietnams*. Ever fearful of being the 'first president to lose a war', Nixon insisted that he 'won' it by 1973, but was denied victory by 'a spasm of congressional irresponsibility', anti-war and liberal activists who hoped for a communist triumph, and, of course, the media. 'It was misreported then, and it is misremembered now', he charged.

Nixon conveniently ignored the sober assessment of the war he had made in his earlier memoir. 'The real problem', he wrote regarding Vietnamization, was 'that the enemy is willing to sacrifice in order to win, while the South Vietnamese simply aren't willing to pay that much of a price in order to avoid losing.' In that book, too, he admitted that his peace agreement allowed Hanoi to keep an estimated 120,000 troops in the South. In *No More Vietnams*, Nixon insisted that Vietnamization was a great success, that the Paris agreements 'tacitly required' the North's withdrawal, and Hanoi 'had pledged to stop the infiltration of men into South Vietnam'. In fact, the agreement allowed North

Vietnamese troops in the South to replace 'armaments, munitions and war material' after the cease-fire. Eight years later, as the Bush administration prepared to assume office, Nixon made it clear that he had intended to continue the conflict when he announced his opposition to lifting the trade embargo. He cited Hanoi's failure to provide full information on POWs and MIAs and that it had failed to comply with the Paris Accords.[13]

The politicization of the POW/MIA issue thrived in the cultural chasm of post-Vietnam America. There are no American prisoners of war in Southeast Asia – not now, and not since Operation Homecoming in early 1973. And none has known this better than the political leaders who shamelessly exploited the issue for ulterior reasons, and the host of charlatans who cruelly deceived families and government officials. Simply put, the issue became one of trust in the word of the American government. The conviction that Vietnam had retained POWs and refused to cooperate on the MIA issue stemmed from a refusal to believe the statements of governmental officials. Presidents Reagan and Bush, among others, fostered and encouraged this belief in order to further their own policies toward Vietnam. This is more than a myth, as recent books have suggested;[14] from the start the affair has been a cruel hoax, foisted on the American public by those who wanted, first, to extend and rationalize the Vietnam War, and then to justify twenty years of vengeful policies against Vietnam.

Nixon first raised the POW issue in 1969 in order to sustain popular support for the war. He insisted that North Vietnam release prisoners and account for MIAs before the United States would agree to withdrawal. The Vietnamese rejected that ploy, and the war continued for another four years. Throughout Nixon's first term, POWs were mere pawns. But as the United States prepared to receive them in early 1973, the Nixon administration listed 2,231 POWs and MIAs presumed to be in enemy hands. Here the government inflicted another casualty on the truth, knowing that more than half the men listed were dead. During hostilities, American air force and navy pilots readily reported fallen comrades as missing rather than dead, in order to provide ongoing benefits for surviving families. The practice was widespread and left the government in the unenviable, virtually impossible position of having to provide evidence to negate the reports of its own combatants. Furthermore, the government padded the list by including known deserters and defectors among the missing. And it knew full well that the horrors of combat coupled with the rugged terrain made it likely that few of those killed would ever be recovered.

The government's deception cost the nation dearly for the next two decades. The implication that the Vietnamese held American captives provided a rationale for the diplomatic and commercial isolation of

Vietnam until 1994. But the saddest losses came to aggrieved, innocent families, who, encouraged by politicians and ideological activists, understandably believed that the Vietnamese held their loved ones hostage. The official position that the Vietnamese had failed to account for missing Americans also justified withholding the economic aid that Nixon had promised both in the Paris Peace Accords in 1973 and in a private letter to the North Vietnamese Premier Phang Van Dong. Nixon had neither the capability (it was the season of Watergate) nor the desire to extend what the Vietnamese called 'reparations'. When the United States reneged, the Vietnamese refused to share archival information that might have shed light on the fate of MIAs. The result was a vicious, ugly circle which victimized everyone, but which conveniently served the mythic machismo images and political needs of the Vietnamese, as well as those of Nixon, Reagan, Bush, Clinton, and Ross Perot.

Make no mistake: the politicization of the Vietnam War POW/MIA issue was unprecedented; never before had the recovery of MIAs or their remains been raised in such a public manner. World War II MIAs amounted to nearly 20 per cent of those killed in combat; for Vietnam, those unaccounted for constituted less than 4 per cent of those killed. The surprising thing is the low figure of Vietnam War MIAs – approximately 2,000, compared to 78,000 for World War II and 8,100 for the Korea conflict. American control of the battlefield and efficient search and rescue operations account for the difference. Yet the hysteria and concern surrounding the Vietnam War MIAs are unique.

The POW/MIA issue fostered another two decades of conflict with Vietnam. But it also unnecessarily contributed to the 'War at Home', a division created by the Vietnam intervention and one that has persisted as we confront the history and meaning of the Vietnam adventure. 'All our POWs are on their way home', Nixon announced in early 1973. But the government's inflated lists of prisoners and MIAs undermined the President's credibility – which, it will be remembered, eroded as the Watergate affair unfolded. Family members, veterans' groups, and opportunistic politicians steadily created a litany suggesting that the Vietnamese retained American hostages, either because of their unique cruelty or to barter them for economic aid. In 1975, a not-unsympathetic congressional committee, headed by conservative veterans' activist G. V. 'Sonny' Montgomery (D–MS), found no evidence of prisoners. That conclusion only enraged the believers, aided by the Watergate climate of cynicism and distrust of government. As late as 1991, a poll revealed that more than 70 per cent of Americans believed that POWs were alive in Vietnam – and of that number, three-quarters did not believe the government was doing what was necessary to get them out. No wonder, then, that Rambo notions had such a powerful appeal. George Bush often played the POW/MIA card – not as blatantly or cleverly as Reagan, and in a manner less satisfying to the vast number of Americans who believed that Vietnam and the US government were not entirely forthcoming on the issue. And even President Clinton, when he ended the embargo on trade with Vietnam, said he believed his action would gain 'the fullest possible accounting for our prisoners of war and our missing in action'.

Despite overwhelming evidence that the POW/MIA issue was a fraud, fighting and re-fighting the Vietnam War persists in the battle of symbolic politics. When Clinton moved to end the embargo in February 1994, 38 senators voted against a non-binding resolution to do so. The President justified his action as a means of forcing the Vietnamese to divulge further information on POWs and MIAs, thus artfully neither admitting nor denying the possibility that some might still be alive. The decision to lift the embargo reflected practicality rather than any conclusive assessment of the MIA issue. American firms were poised to do business in Vietnam, desperate to compete against foreign rivals. For Vietnamese communists, now anointed as 'Red Capitalists', it must have been an ironic and amusing moment. Meanwhile, the American Chamber of Commerce, having already planted its flag on a Hanoi beachhead, might itself have reflected on the irony that Clinton, and not Reagan or Bush, had given them what they wanted. After all, no President since Franklin D. Roosevelt has been so despised and hated by business élites. And now, in the mid-1990s, just when it seemed that there was an ideological consensus agreeing that the POW/MIA issue has been settled, the new Republican chairman of the House International Relations Committee has attacked Clinton for having 'broken trust' with the American people, as he agreed to the exchange of low-level envoys. Political cynicism does not necessarily change with new players.

The Rambo films have brought enormous treasure to their makers, and at the same time gave Americans an opportunity to write history as they believed it should have turned out. The central theme is quickly apparent. John Rambo is recruited for a mission to return to Vietnam – where he said he had died many years ago – and he is asked if he has any questions: 'Just one, sir', Rambo says, his face a map of painful memories. 'Do we get to win this time?' Rambo fights on two fronts: against cruel Vietnamese, and against those insidious forces of government that 'wouldn't let us win'. His mission is to right that wrong and ultimately to defeat America's enemies as the military should have – and could have – done during the Vietnam War. The government's self-imposed restraint during the war inevitably allowed the enemy to win and resulted in the 'New War', largely based on a conservative cultural counter-assault. The Vietnam Veterans of America criticized Rambomania, saying of one of the movies: 'The war is long over; it can somehow be re-fought and "won" on the issue of alleged POWs. That only happens in Hollywood.'[15]

The culture wars that have rent the United States in the past two decades flow directly from the conflicts at home over the Vietnam War. The memory of long-haired protestors, assaulting their government's action, seemed to many to be an assault on the very values of America itself. No wonder, then, that those who reacted with scorn and contempt for the war's opponents have chosen issues such as religion, abortion, and education to strike back on behalf of some norm of values. Films, books, the debate over how to teach the Vietnam War, are all cultural battlegrounds.

Perhaps the most striking battleground in these culture wars occurred in the controversy over how to memorialize the more than 50,000 Americans who had died in Vietnam. A jury selected a design by Maya Ying Lin, a twenty-one-year old Yale architectural student, and a second-generation Chinese-American. The subtle design consisted of a sloping wall, nearly 500-feet long, rising to 10 feet at the center, and bending at a 125-degree angle. The polished black granite wall, engraved with the names of those who had died, was to be slashed into the mall's gentle green, like an open wound. The criticism of the design seemingly followed traditional conflicts between professional versus popular taste, of modernity versus tradition. But Lin's Asiatic background and what seemed to many a protest against the war, fueled the controversy. Ross Perot, who had contributed handsomely to the memorial fund, led the assault. A veteran, wearing two Purple Hearts and a three-piece suit, testified to the Fine Arts Commission in 1981 that the proposed memorial was 'a black gash of shame and sorrow ... It forms the antiwar "V" peace sign.' Nothing had changed. The soldiers in death remained the pawns of Washington politics, as conservatives made the cause their own. Surprisingly, General William Westmoreland weighed in on the side of Lin's design and then a last-minute 'backroom deal' provided for a traditional monument and a flag. Lin at first threatened to sue, but the irony of the situation was not lost to her subtle mind: 'What is memorialized', she said, 'is that people still cannot resolve that war, nor can they separate the issues, the politics, from it.'[16]

Lin proved to be more in accord with public opinion than her critics. However wounded by the racist, sexist, and political slurs that surrounded her design, she eventually saw her view – and the public's – triumph. The Vietnam Memorial Wall is the most visited monument in the nation, a statistic that eloquently refutes Lin's critics. In its first decade, between 25 to 30 million people viewed the wall and prayed, cried, or left photos or flowers.[17]

For over a decade, beginning in the early 1960s, a series of profound shocks rocked the United States. The quiet wars that rage just beneath the veneer of pluralistic peace erupted with the civil rights movement in the 1960s. The black minority challenged both the legalized and *de facto* apartheid that bounded their lives. The American intervention in the Vietnamese civil war sparked massive opposition to that policy and, for the first time, the nation divided over the role it had assumed in international affairs since 1945. Finally, the momentum for questioning the status quo, both in domestic and foreign policies, led to an assault on President Nixon, eventually resulting in his unprecedented resignation. Those upheavals and their aftermath suddenly and dramatically altered the political and social arrangements that had served the nation for some time. The civil rights revolution exposed the hypocrisy of authority; the Vietnam War undermined the respect and standing for authority and leadership; Watergate advanced those losses and gave us the resulting politics of cynicism, which, like the Vietnam War, continues to corrode American society.

In post-Vietnam America, the anti-war forces found their ranks reduced and their causes, past and present, everywhere on the defensive. It appeared as if the supporters of the war, particularly those who insisted that not enough had been done to further the American effort, had 'won' on all fronts: in politics, culture, and history. During the Persian Gulf War debate, both sides agreed on the 'lessons' of Vietnam. Any foreign intervention required, first, overwhelming popular support and, second, the United States to bring to bear overwhelming military force. In other words, Americans must fight to win, which, it was claimed, they did *not* do in Vietnam; had they done so, according to the lesson, they *could* have won.

Historians and others often toy with the past, using it promiscuously in order to further a cause, as any twentieth-century totalitarian exponent of the 'Big Lie' technique. There is a notion that the internal war that was waged over the Vietnam war resulted from the need to erase the pain of defeat. Let me suggest that the idea of a defeat stems from the right, from the very *provocateurs* of our recent battles. They have succeeded in discrediting the anti-war movement, belittling the war's opponents as liberals and counter-cultural 'McGoverniks', as Newt Gingrich has described them. It is nothing less than the revenge of the right. Meanwhile, the war's critics have lost their voice, which is a pity.

But the communist triumph was not necessarily a defeat for the United States. Americans did their best, but then finally and wisely decided that they had been fighting the wrong war in the wrong place, and that their efforts never approximated the lofty ideals that the nation had set for itself as a world power. Nearly three decades later, Secretary of Defense Robert McNamara, that most certain of warriors, admitted that the war was a mistake and that American security never was at stake – small comfort, of course, to those who served and died in Vietnam.

Think of the paradox: Americans grew to dislike and reject the Vietnam War; nevertheless, the lingering focus of their hatred and rejection
has been reflected in their distrust of government and the liberal élites
that both brought about and repudiated the war. The formal and
informal historical revisionism that became full-blown in the 1980s,
whether the history purveyed by political opportunists or cultural mani-
pulators, inescapably must be linked to the conservative resurgence
of the decade. Its strength and durability flourished in the context of
Reaganism and the assault on liberalism. History is indeed a pack of tricks
that the living play on the dead.

Notes

Editors' note: this essay is adapted from Stanley Kutler's forthcoming book
American Civil Wars: The Rights Revolution, Vietnam, and Watergate.

1. Emanuel Levy, *And the Winner Is ... The History and Politics of the Oscar
   Awards* (New York: 1987), p. 84.
2. *New York Times*, 18 August 1980; *Washington Post*, 19 August 1980;
   Chicago Tribune, 19 August 1980; *New York Times*, 31 May 1981.
3. NBC News featured Reagan's remark at the beginning of the nightly
   news and used it to cast doubt on his fitness and perhaps his sanity. Tom
   Shales, in the *Washington Post*, excoriated NBC in the context of what he
   called the 'new Unholy Trinity, the three-scoop threat of TV campaign
   coverage: a mock-analytical mania on the part of herd-instinct reporters
   who feel they cannot go home at night until they've knocked over a
   totem pole; rigid stereotyping that composes a candidate's tune and then
   allows few variations on it to creep into coverage; and the tendency to
   judge candidates only by television standards – by how they perform,
   and how they look and whether they fluff their lines', *Washington Post*, 31
   October 1980.
4. *Washington Post*, 8 January 1991; *New York Times*, 10 January 1991; *Boston
   Globe*, 10 January 1991; *Los Angeles Times*, 13 January 1991.
5. *New York Times*, 1 December 1990, 6 and 17 January 1991; *Washington
   Post*, 2 March 1991. The Persian Gulf fostered a number of myths about
   military freedom. First, there were restrictions on bombing of certain
   targets. Second, political-civilian Pentagon principals established an
   acceptable casualty rate of about 9,000, or three companies per coalition
   brigade. Department of Defense, *Conduct of the Persian Gulf War: Final
   Report*, quoted in John Mueller, *Policy and Opinion in the Gulf War* (Chicago,
   Ill.: 1994), p. 346, note 11.
6. Michael C.C. Adams, Book Review, *Reviews in American History* 21 (March
   1993), p. 160.
7. Congressional Record, 103 Cong., 2nd Sess., HR (13 September 1994),
   H9097; H9089; H9099; H9099–100; Senate 12753–54.
8. *New York Times*, 9 October 1992.

9.   The contrast between the telecast on CNN and C-Span was striking. The latter operated with one fixed camera, focused exclusively on the stage of ceremonies. CNN, looking for more sensationalism, carried the President, but with an inset showing the relatively few voices of protest. Under such circumstances, how could any viewer concentrate on the President's *words*?

10. James Fallows, 'What did you do in the war, Daddy?', *Washington Monthly* (October 1975), pp. 6–7.

11. *Chicago Tribune*, 31 May 1993.

12. See Philip Davidson, *Vietnam at War* (New York: 1991). Also see memoirs of Nixon, Kissinger, and Ford. Kissinger's comment was made at the Hofstra Conference on the Nixon Presidency in 1988.

13. Richard Nixon, *RN: The Memoirs of Richard Nixon* (New York: 1978); Richard Nixon, *No More Vietnams* (New York: 1985); *Los Angeles Times*, 9 January 1993.

14. Susan Katz Keating, *Prisoners of Hope: Exploiting the POW/MIA Myth in America* (New York: 1994); Malcom McConnell, with research by Theodore G. Schweitzer, *Inside Hanoi's Secret Archives: Solving the MIA Mystery* (New York: 1995). Both books represent some moderation of views from the 'right'; in fact, however, the POW hoax was exposed by H. Bruce Franklin, *M.I.A. or Mythmaking in America* (Westport, Conn.: 1992).

15. The writings of James William Gibson throw fascinating light on the cultural aspects of the 'New War', see *Warrior Dreams: Violence and Manhood in Post-Vietnam America* (New York: 1994); *VVA Veteran* (July 1985). It might be noted that Sylvester Stallone, the hero of the 'Rambo' series, according to his spokesman, 'had various draft statuses ... including medical and student deferments'. He served as girls' athletic coach at a Swiss school from 1965 to 1967. He received deferments while attending the University of Miami in the late 1960s. He had dropped out of school in 1960 and the next year he failed an army physical, *USA TODAY*, 18 July 1991.

16. Jan C. Scruggs and Joel L. Swerdlow, *To Heal a Nation: The Vietnam Veterans Memorial* (New York: 1985), pp. 82–4, 87, 101, 133. A bronze, traditional statue by Frederick Hart, entitled 'Three Men Fighting', portraying different ethnic groups, was added on Veterans Day in 1984, along with a flag. A decade later, the insertion of a statue of a woman was a metaphor for contemporary political demands for inclusiveness – but one that carried both the reality and practicality of that often divisive concept.

17. *Time*, 6 November 1989; *USA TODAY*, 6 November 1992.